PENGUIN BOOKS
THE PENGUIN BOOK OF NORSE MYTHS

Kevin Crossley-Holland is an author who specializes in the early literature of north-west Europe. In addition to *The Norse Myths*, his retellings and translations include *British Folk Tales* and an anthology, *The Anglo-Saxon World*, which contains his well-known versions of many of the shorter Old English poems as well as *Beowulf*. He has also translated *The Exeter Book Riddles*.

As a children's author, Crossley-Holland has been awarded the Carnegie Medal and the *Guardian* Fiction Prize, and his most celebrated books include *Storm,* the *Arthur* trilogy (translated into twenty-four languages) and *Gatty's Tale*.

Most recently, he has written the children's book *Bracelet of Bones*, in which a Viking girl follows her father from Norway to Constantinople; his new and selected poems, *The Mountains of Norfolk*; and a memoir of his childhood, *The Hidden Roads*.

Kevin Crossley-Holland was Gregory Fellow at the University of Leeds and held the Endowed Chair in the Humanities and Fine Arts at the University of St Thomas in Minnesota. He has collaborated with many composers, including Sir Arthur Bliss, William Mathias, Nicola LeFanu, Giles Swayne, Bob Chilcott and Bernard Hughes. He is an Honorary Fellow of St Edmund Hall, Oxford, patron of the Society for Storytelling and a Fellow of the Royal Society of Literature.

The Penguin Book of

Norse Myths

Gods of the Vikings

Introduced and retold by
Kevin Crossley-Holland

PENGUIN BOOKS

PENGUIN BOOKS

Published by the Penguin Group
Penguin Books Ltd, 80 Strand, London WC2R ORL, England
Penguin Group (USA) Inc., 375 Hudson Street, New York, New York 10014, USA
Penguin Group (Canada), 90 Eglinton Avenue East, Suite 700, Toronto, Ontario, Canada M4P 2Y3
(a division of Pearson Penguin Canada Inc.)
Penguin Ireland, 25 St Stephen's Green, Dublin 2, Ireland
(a division of Penguin Books Ltd)
Penguin Group (Australia), 250 Camberwell Road, Camberwell, Victoria 3124,
Australia (a division of Pearson Australia Group Pty Ltd)
Penguin Books India Pvt Ltd, 11 Community Centre,
Panchsheel Park, New Delhi – 110 017, India
Penguin Group (NZ), 67 Apollo Drive, Rosedale, Auckland 0632, New Zealand
(a division of Pearson New Zealand Ltd)
Penguin Books (South Africa) (Pty) Ltd, 24 Sturdee Avenue,
Rosebank, Johannesburg 2196, South Africa

Penguin Books Ltd, Registered Offices: 80 Strand, London WC2R ORL, England

www.penguin.com

First published by André Deutsch Ltd 1980
Published in Penguin Books as *The Norse Myths* 1982
Reprinted under the present title 1993
Reissued in this edition with a revised Bibliography 2011
1

Printed in Great Britain by Clays Ltd, St Ives plc

A CIP catalogue record for this book is available from the British Library

ISBN: 978-0-241-95321-1

www.greenpenguin.co.uk

for my mother

Contents

Fearlessness is better than a faint-heart for any
man who puts his nose out of doors. The length of
my life and the day of my death were fated long ago.

Anonymous lines from *For Scirnis*

They say miracles are past, and we have our
philosophical persons, to make modern and familiar,
things supernatural and causeless. Hence is it, that we
make trifles of terrors, ensconcing ourselves into
seeming knowledge, when we should submit ourselves
to an unknown fear.

William Shakespeare,
All's Well That Ends Well, II, iii, 1–6

I think Scandinavian Paganism, to us here, is
more interesting than any other. It is, for one
thing, the latest; it continued in these regions of
Europe till the eleventh century; 800 years ago the
Norwegians were still worshippers of Odin. It is
interesting also as the creed of our fathers; the
men whose blood still runs in our veins, whom
doubtless we still resemble in so many ways.

Thomas Carlyle

Acknowledgments

W HAT WE WRITE is partly chosen for us, partly of our own choosing; and however rapidly it may be committed to paper, a book may be a very long time in the making. My interest in myth, legend and folktale was first whetted by the stream of stories that I heard, night after night, from my parents, and then by the way in which they encouraged an awareness of religious beliefs past and present. I began to be specifically interested in Germanic tradition after my father played and recorded the first reconstruction of the Sutton Hoo harp, and after inheriting an Anglo-Saxon burial urn from my grandfather. Later, at Oxford, I started to translate Old English poetry and in this was given great encouragement and assistance by my tutor at St Edmund Hall, and later my collaborator, Bruce Mitchell. Anglo-Saxon studies lead naturally to a curiosity about the whole jigsaw of contemporary North West European culture, and the invitation of Phyllis Hunt at Faber and Faber to edit *The Faber Book of Northern Legends* stimulated me to read all the more widely in the three great bodies of early Germanic literature – Norse myths, Icelandic sagas and Germanic heroic poems. These seem to be the stepping stones that led to the writing of this book and, in making acknowledgments, it seems right to begin by offering my thanks to the people associated with them.

During the last three years I have received a great deal of literary, scholarly, practical and personal help. First, I must renew my thanks to my father for working through almost all the typescript with minute attention and making a substantial number of valuable critical suggestions. This was not the work of one morning and I am fortunate that my sternest and best critic is also so generous with his time. I must also thank Valerie and Adrian Kwaan for their most useful and supportive comments on early versions of the myths, and for helping me over the hurdle of finding a distinctive tone for my retellings. My two sons, Kieran and Dominic, have also read most of the myths; I have made use of their written and spoken commentaries and want them to know, too, that their unusual patience and understanding when I preferred work to play was a real contribution to the writing of this book.

Hermann Pálsson was kind enough to provide me with a copy of *Sorla Thattr* (Myth 13) when I had difficulty in tracking it down. Alan and Anne-Marie Caiger-Smith and Susan Stern drew my attention to, and lent me, pertinent material. Peter Redgrove and Penelope Shuttle, authors of *The Wise Wound*, went to considerable lengths to elucidate a feature of Myth 24; I am most grateful to them for permission to quote from their personal letter to me. Susanne Kurz generously helped me with the translation of a passage by Georges Dumézil. Barbara Leonie Picard did her utmost to track down the origin of the story 'How Loki Outwitted a Giant' that forms part of her *Tales of the Norse Gods and Heroes* (pp. 120–5), written nearly thirty years ago; neither she nor I have had any luck and I will be indebted to any reader who can let me know the source of this myth.

It would have been impossible to write the introduction and notes without drawing on some of the ideas and words of others far more deeply-versed in the Norse world than I, and I have made specific acknowledgments within the text. I have used copyright material from the following books and am most grateful to the authors and publishers in question: *The Poetic Edda* translated by Henry Adams Bellows (The American–Scandinavian Foundation); *The Vikings* by Johannes Brøndsted, translated by Kalle Skov (Penguin Books); *Mythes et Dieux des Germains* by Georges Dumézil (Librairie Ernest Leroux); *Myth and Reality* by Mircea Eliade (Allen and Unwin); *Gods and Myths of Northern Europe* by H. R. Ellis Davidson (Penguin Books); *The Skalds* by Lee M. Hollander (University of Michigan Press); *A History of the Vikings* by Gwyn Jones (Oxford University Press); H. Mattingly's translation of *Tacitus on Britain and Germany* (Penguin Books); Hermann Pálsson's translation of the *Eyrbyggja Saga* (Southside Publishers); E. O. G. Turville-Petre's *Myth and Religion of the North* (Weidenfeld and Nicolson); Dorothy Whitelock's translation (with David C. Douglas and Susie I. Tucker) of *The Anglo-Saxon Chronicle* (Eyre and Spottiswoode); and *The Prose Edda* of Snorri Sturluson, translated by Jean I. Young (University of California Press). I have lifted a few lines from my short history of the Anglo-Saxons, *Green Blades Rising* (André Deutsch); I have also quoted from my own translation of *Beowulf* (D. S. Brewer). I have had constant recourse to the translations of the *Elder Edda* and *Prose Edda* listed in the bibliography and, in writing my retellings, may have unconsciously lifted a phrase from them here and there.

The Arts Council of Great Britain have generously supported the writing of this book with grants in 1976 and 1978; I am especially grateful to Charles Osborne, Jacqueline Falk and Alan Brownjohn in this connexion. I have also received financial assistance from Icelandair and from Regent Holidays, where I must thank Mr H. Sigurdsson and Mr J. Noel Cairns respectively for their good offices; between them, they helped to make it possible for me, in the company of my two sons, to have a long look at the island where most of the myths were finally recorded, and I must also thank my mother for giving such a generous contribution of money, time and energy to this cause. In Deborah Rogers in London and Betty Anne Clarke in New York, I have two agents outstanding in their warmth and professionalism; I am grateful to them both for their judicious mixture of care, chivvying and confidence! I am indebted to my two sympathetic English editors, Diana Athill and Esther Whitby, for offering both the clearest understanding of my aims (and hopes!) and the most meticulous attention to detail. I should also like to thank the staffs of the British Library and the London Library for their knowledgeable and patient help. The preparation of the typescript involved a considerable amount of work; I am most grateful to Rosemary Crossley-Holland for accomplishing it all with such accuracy, speed and good humour, and trust that our association has strengthened rather than strained a family link.

That leaves me with two people to whom I owe a special debt. My American editor, Wendy Wolf, has gone far beyond the call of duty in furbishing me with detailed criticism of the draft of the typescript. Her wide-ranging knowledge of the subject, sensitivity in mixing criticism and praise and, not least, speed, are what any author should hope for and – writing as an ex-publisher – I am aware how lucky I am to have found them.

Since our first meeting in Iceland some two years ago, Hildegund Kübler has offered me immeasurable support. We have regularly discussed this book's structure and style and, above all, the meaning of the myths. Her personal understanding and practical help enabled me to press on when it would otherwise have been impossible; I am sincerely grateful to her.

Introduction

THE DRAMATIC ENTRY in *The Anglo-Saxon Chronicle* for 793 reads:

> In this year dire portents appeared over Northumbria and sorely frightened the people. They consisted of immense whirlwinds and flashes of lightning, and fiery dragons were seen flying in the air. A great famine immediately followed those signs, and a little after that in the same year, on 8 June, the ravages of heathen men miserably destroyed God's church on Lindisfarne, with plunder and slaughter.

These heathen men were Vikings, and with the destruction of the great monastery at Lindisfarne – an act which shook Christendom – they made their first substantial impact on the occident. For almost the next three hundred years, the Vikings were the most exciting and influential force in Europe and beyond; wherever they went, they took their beliefs in the old gods and it was their poets who forged the myths in the earliest versions that have come down to us.

The word Viking, meaning 'bay-men' or 'fighting men' or 'settling men', refers collectively to the Danes, Norwegians and Swedes, and the 'Viking Age' describes the period 780–1070 during which the Norsemen made a remarkable three-prong thrust south, east and west. There were two major reasons for this expansion: Scandinavia was overpopulated and the system of primogeniture forced younger sons into trying their fortunes overseas; and expanding trade routes (for example the development of Frisian trade and the increasing use of the Rhine) attracted Viking merchants and pirates. But one feels that the natural disposition of the Vikings, adventurous and aggressive and scornful of death, must have given added momentum to the impulse to raid and trade, conquer and colonise.

Sea power was crucial to the success of Viking enterprise. The Vikings depended on navigational skills and superb ships – ships which were one of the great practical and artistic achievements of pre-Conquest Europe. Clinker-built (with iron rivets linking the overlapping planks) on a keel plank that swept up into a stem at either end, they were both beautiful in line and very pliable in rough waters. They were propelled by oarsmen, perhaps fifteen or sixteen on either side in a fighting ship sitting in an enclosed deck, and by a square sail. The elaborately carved prows were decorated with a figurehead, more often than not a dragon's head, and the warriors' coloured shields hung in a row over the railings.

Sailing south, the Vikings raided and then colonised Scotland, Ireland and half of England where they had the misfortune to run into one of the most remarkable men in world history and the only king whom the English have called Great, Alfred of Wessex. They overran and settled Friesland and France as far south as the Loire; they attacked and captured Lisbon, Cadiz and Seville; for a while they commandeered the Camargue and, moving east, left their mark on the north of Italy and sacked Pisa; and some Vikings, previously settled in Normandy, pushed on to Sicily where there are still a number of men and women with the fair skin and fair reddish hair of the Norsemen.

Heading east from the Baltic, the Vikings sailed up the River Volkhov to Novgorod. From there they humped their boats overland on pine rollers to the source of the Dnieper and so made their way to Kiev, the Black Sea and Constantinople, where the Emperor's own guard consisted entirely of Vikings. Others worked their way from Novgorod to the Volga and sailed south to the Caspian Sea and Baghdad, carrying with them, in the words of Mohammed Mugaddosi, an Arab geographer writing in about 985, 'sables, squirrel, ermine, black and white foxes, marten, beaver, arrows and swords, wax and birch bark, fish teeth and fish lime, amber, honey, goat skins and horse hides, hawks, acorns, hazel nuts, cattle and Slavonic slaves'. An Arab diplomat and diarist, Ibn Fadlan, described the Vikings he encountered on the Volga in 922:

> I saw the Rus when they arrived on their trading mission and anchored at the River Atul [Volga]. Never had I seen people of more perfect physique; they are tall as date-palms, and reddish in colour. They wear neither coat nor mantle, but each man carries a cape which covers one half of his body, leaving one hand free ... Each woman carries on her bosom a container made of iron, silver, copper or gold – its size and substance depending on her man's wealth.

The 'Rus' or Swedish Vikings to whom Ibn Fadlan refers gave their name to Russia.

Sailing west, the Vikings (mainly west Norwegians) colonised Iceland in the late ninth and early tenth centuries. The manner in which a Viking decided where to settle is described on p. xxxv. From Iceland, the Vikings pushed west to Greenland which was only called 'Green' by its discoverer, Eric the Red, who founded a colony at Brattahlid, in order to entice others to follow him. And from there, they intrepidly sailed still further west. That Leif Ericsson reached Newfoundland and New England in the United States, and found 'fields of wild wheat growing there, and vines', and that his discovery quickly led to further exploration and short-lived colonisation, is not a matter of mere speculation. The Vinland Sagas and archaeological discoveries (notably at L'Anse aux Meadows in Newfoundland) have conclusively established the existence of Norse settlements there around the year 1000 – some five centuries before Columbus set sail from Portugal and 'discovered' America.

The Norsemen cut such a dash as gangers and, indeed, gangsters that it would be easy to get them out of focus. The truth is that most of them lived peaceful lives, hunting, fishing, and above all farming, for most of the time. Both in Scandinavia and wherever they settled, their society was based on a very clear social structure with three strata: earls or warriors, peasants, and serfs. 'The Song of Rig' (Myth 5) tells how Heimdall created the races of men and provides a good deal of information about their respective life styles.

As the eddaic poem *Rigsthula* shows, the serfs had a bad time of it. They were manual labourers and they were never free. Thrall and his wife Thir and their nineteen children would have lived in a single stinking hut, made with timber or with turf and clay, shared with such animals as they possessed – cattle certainly, perhaps sheep or goats or pigs, and maybe a cat or a dog. No patron god guarded the lives of these most luckless members of the community.

The great majority of the Norsemen, however, undoubtedly belonged to the peasant class whose patron was Thor. They were smallholders and freemen. Archaeological evidence shows that, at least towards the end of the Viking period, they lived in two or more buildings – a pair of parallel long-houses sometimes supplemented by a barn or two, making a three- or even four-sided complex with a courtyard in the middle.

The picture in *Rigsthula* of the peasant's staple diet can be supplemented from references in the sagas and archaeological discoveries. Johannes Brøndsted has written:

It is fair to surmise that the Vikings' daily diet included wholemeal bread made of rye; oat and barley porridge; fish (especially herrings); the meat of sheep, lamb, goat, horse, ox, calf, and pig; cheese, butter, and cream; and for drink, beer, mead, and (among the wealthy) wine. Whale meat, seal meat, and the meat of the polar bear were important foods particularly in

Norway and Iceland. Boiled meat seems to have been preferred to roasted ... Broths made from the various meats must have been a familiar dish; and the Vikings were also practised in the methods of drying meat and fish. Gamebirds, too, were an extra item in the Viking diet. The most common vegetables were cabbages and onions; and apples, berries, and hazelnuts were abundant. Honey was much in use, largely as the basis for the manufacture of sweet fermented mead ... In those countries remote from the sea but well forested, much of the Viking sustenance came from hunting elk, deer, wild boar, and bear. Hares, geese, and chickens were other popular items on the menu and, in the far north, reindeer and bison.

Food was preserved for winter consumption with ice, with whey, and with salt either taken from saltpans or extracted from kelp.

Rigsthula gives an elaborate picture of the fine halls, refined lives and sophisticated activities of the aristocratic third class, the earls or warriors whose patron was Odin. They are above all distinguished by their wealth, expressed in terms of followers, treasure, ships, and estates that passed from eldest son to eldest son. Like their inferiors in the social system, the warriors were as a rule devoted and responsible family men and customarily spent the long winters at home; the attention paid in the myths to feasting in Valhalla doubtless reflects the time given over to feasting in the halls of warriors. But it was these same men who, in the summer, assembled crews bent on exploration, trade or piracy, and they who were celebrated by the scaldic poets. The immense significance of the poet, the carrier of tradition, in an oral culture, is discussed in Note 6 and elsewhere.

When the Germanic tribesmen first migrated to Europe and north into Scandinavia, they chose their leaders, according to Tacitus, for their valour and noble birth. The man who could claim divine descent made a powerful contender, and it is this kind of power struggle that underlies 'Hyndla's Poem' (Myth 18) in which the goddess Freyja assists her human lover, Ottar, to establish his lineage. It was only as the monarchy accrued greater power and significance that it became hereditary (though Iceland spurned kingship altogether and was ruled from the first by a union of chieftains); 'The Lay of Grimnir' (Myth 12) exemplifies this more orderly tradition.

We glimpse in the myths, as in the sagas, the isolated, physically demanding lives experienced by most Norsemen. One farm was often a hard day's ride from the next, as suggested by 'The Theft of Idun's Apples', 'Thor's Journey to Utgard' and 'Otter's Ransom'; a traveller was less likely to meet other humans than some of the birds and animals that abound in the myths – a deer, an otter, a wild boar, a wolf, or at least a squirrel, an eagle, a raven. Conditions on the road were frequently demanding, taking the traveller over fells, round a glacier, or across a wilderness – journeys made all the more hazardous by the chance of prolonged violent snowstorms in the mountains and dust storms in the desert; for half the year, moreover, the light only lasted for a few hours each day.

Such cloistered circumstances strengthened the importance of the family unit. A family needed to be self-reliant and its members rallied to one another's support in times of trouble. If a man was slighted or, worse, injured or killed, the offender (as the sagas so graphically describe) could not hope to get away with it. Tacitus attributed very similar principles to Germanic tribesmen in the first century:

> A man is bound to take up the feuds as well as the friendships of father or kinsmen. But feuds do not continue unreconciled. Even homicide can be atoned for by a fixed number of cattle or sheep, and the satisfaction is received by the whole family. This is much to the advantage of the community, for private feuds are peculiarly dangerous side by side with liberty.

If, however, feuding families could not settle a dispute between themselves, it was brought before a court. An ordeal might be used to determine guilt and punishment consisted either of compensatory payment or, in the case of very substantial crime, outlawry or death.

Tacitus's reference to friendship is pertinent too. A judicious Norse family cultivated friendships both for their own sake and because a large group of people loyal to one another was less vulnerable than a small one. One special relationship existed within the family itself: a maternal uncle was especially responsible for the welfare of his nephew. This bond is discussed in Note 4 and may explain why Odin learned the nine magic songs that enabled him to secure the divine mead of poetry from his uncle, the son of Bolthor.

Both within the family and in the eyes of the law, a man and a woman had equal rights, and the outspoken woman, rather more determined than the menfolk surrounding her, is a striking and familiar character in the sagas. The woman is also prominent as *volva* or shamaness, able to go into a trance, send her spirit on a journey to obtain hidden knowledge, and answer the practical questions about social welfare and marriage prospects of the community gathered to listen to her. Freyja in her role as shamaness, going from hall to hall teaching witchcraft to the Aesir (Myth and Note 2), clearly reflects these practices.

This superstitious, family-oriented existence is the background to 'The Lay of Loddfafnir' and the whole of *Havamal* (Myth and Note 25). This great compendium of aphorisms and advice on right conduct offers a commonsensical and sober (though sometimes witty) picture of the day to day life of the Norsemen, and it is a far cry from the heady image of Vikings on the rampage. Value life itself; censure naïveté; cherish and celebrate friendships; beware of treachery; practise moderation; be hospitable (but not too hospitable); try to win the fame and good name that will outlive you: these are the leitmotifs of *Havamal.*

One stanza in that poem reads: 'Cattle die, kinsmen die, I myself shall die, but there is one thing I know never dies: the reputation we leave behind at our death.' A desire for fame, limited though it may be, was of crucial importance to the Norseman. In the absence of beliefs about a timeless afterlife, it represented his only hope of immortality. No Viking believed he could change his destiny, ordained as it was by the Norns who wove the fates of gods and men alike (Note 4) but, for all that, the way in which he lived his life was up to him. This sentiment is perfectly expressed by Skirnir in 'Skirnir's Journey': 'Fearlessness is better than a faint heart for any man who puts his nose out of doors. The length of my life and the day of my death were fated long ago.'

Since men who become embittered never win respect or admiration, those who sought fame did not rail at the undoubted hardship of their lives and the inevitability of death. Rather, they endured it or, even better, laughed at it. This accounts for the ironic tone in the fabric of the myths and explains, for example, the reaction of the gods when Tyr sacrificed his hand (Myth 7) in the interests of binding the wolf Fenrir. Men and women expected their share of trouble and the best of them attempted to use it, to rise above it and carve out a name for themselves through bravery and loyalty and generosity.

This fatalism, so fundamental to the Norsemen, is reflected in the myths. It was in the power of Odin and the Valkyries, not of men, to decide which slain warriors would be taken to Valhalla; the gold that Loki extracts from Andvari carries a curse with it; Odin knows that Balder's death is fated and can do nothing to avert it; and Ragnarok itself, 'the Destruction of the Powers', is inescapable. The time must come when all creation will be destroyed by fire and flood.

Yet, in H. R. Ellis Davidson's wise words:

In spite of this awareness of fate, or perhaps because of it, the picture of man's qualities which emerges from the myths is a noble one. The gods are heroic figures, men writ large, who led dangerous, individualistic lives, yet at the same time were part of a closely-knit small group, with a firm sense of values and certain intense loyalties. They would give up their lives rather than surrender these values, but they would fight on as long as they could, since life was well worth while. Men knew that the gods whom they served could not give them freedom from danger and calamity, and they did not demand that they should. We find in the myths no sense of bitterness at the harshness and unfairness of life, but rather a spirit of heroic resignation: humanity is born to trouble, but courage, adventure, and the wonders of life are matters for thankfulness, to be enjoyed while life is still granted to us. The great gifts of the gods were readiness to face the world as it was, the luck that sustains men in tight places, and the opportunity to win that glory which alone can outlive death.

Reading the myths, we can identify the Norseman's spirit and confidence, his boundless curiosity, extreme bravery, clannish loyalty, generosity and discipline; we can also detect his arrogance and lack of compassion, his cunning if not treachery (amply reflected in the figure of Loki), his ruthlessness and his cruelty.

COSMOLOGY

The elaborate and intricately structured Norse cosmology starts with the very moment of creation. Ice from Niflheim in the north and fire from Muspellheim in the south meet in the vast chasm of Ginnungagap, and their fusion engenders life. The first two beings are a frost giant, Ymir, and a cow, Audumla. The cow licks a man out of the ice and his three grandsons are the gods Odin, Vili and Ve. As the first myth in the cycle tells, these three brothers kill the giant Ymir and from his body create nine worlds.

The Norsemen visualised the universe as a tricentric structure – like three plates set one above another with a space between each. On the top level was Asgard, the realm of the Aesir or warrior gods. This is where the gods and goddesses had their halls, situated within a mighty citadel the walls of which were built by a giant mason as part of a wager (Myth 3). This, too, is where Valhalla was situated, the huge hall that housed all the Einherjar, the dead warriors who fought each day and feasted each evening, awaiting Ragnarok, the battle at the end of time between gods and men, giants and monsters; and this was the site of that all-consuming battle, a vast plain called Vigrid that stretched one hundred and twenty leagues in every direction. But the Aesir were not the only inhabitants of this highest realm. On this level also lay Vanaheim, where the Vanir or fertility gods lived until they fought and then united with the Aesir (Myth 2); and Alfheim, the land of the light elves, was here too.

The second level was Midgard, the middle world inhabited by men. It was surrounded by an ocean so vast that, as our most important source, the thirteenth-century Icelander Snorri Sturluson says, 'to cross it would strike most men as impossible'. Jormungand, the terrifying world serpent, lay in this ocean; he was so long that he encircled Midgard and bit on his own tail. The world of the giants, Jotunheim, lay either within Midgard (in the mountainous eastern part along the coast) as indicated on the map (see page xxi), or across the ocean; sources do not agree on this point. The giants' citadel was called Utgard, the outer world. This is where Thor and his companions were taken for a ride by the magical and evil giant king, Utgard-Loki (Myth 16).

At this level, too, in the north of Midgard, there were dwarfs; they lived in Nidavellir (Dark Home) in caves and potholes, while somewhere below was Svartalfheim (Land of the Dark Elves). No valid distinction though can be drawn between the dwarfs and dark elves; they appear to have been interchangeable.

Asgard and Midgard were connected by a flaming rainbow bridge called Bifrost (Trembling Roadway). Snorri Sturluson wrote in 'Gylfaginning', which is a part of the *Prose Edda*: 'You will have seen it but maybe you call it the rainbow. It has three colours and is very strong, and made with more skill and cunning than other structures.' We know from the eddaic poem *Vafthrudnismal* that the River Iving, which never iced over, constituted the boundary between Asgard, the world of the gods and Jotunheim, the world of the giants; in a number of myths, moreover, gods and giants made an overland journey direct from Asgard to Jotunheim without passing through Midgard. How can they have done so? It would seem physically impossible unless we tilt the Asgard- and Midgard-levels so that, at one point, they actually touch each other! This kind of problem demonstrates the limitations of logic in trying to define precisely where the worlds stood in relation to one another. It is best simply to bear in mind that the structure of the universe was basically tricentric and assume that the Norsemen themselves were rather vague and unconcerned about more exact geography.

On the third level lay Niflheim, the world of the dead, nine days' ride northwards and downwards from Midgard. Niflheim was a place of bitter cold and unending night; its citadel was Hel, a place with towering walls and forbidding gates presided over by the hideous female monster, half white and half black, of the same name. She is described in detail by Snorri Sturluson (see Myth 7 and passim). The Norsemen may have distinguished between the worlds of Hel and Niflheim; in *Vafthrudnismal*, it seems that evil men passed through Hel to die again

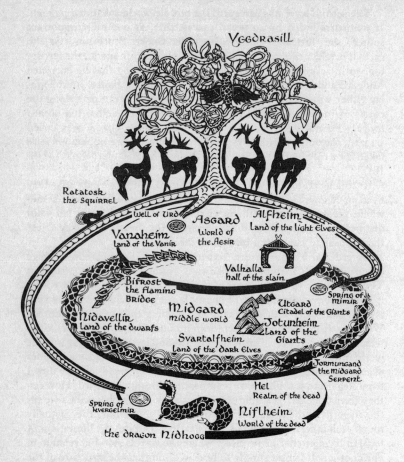

in the world of Niflhel or Niflheim (Misty Hel).

The nine worlds were, then, Asgard, Vanaheim and Alfheim; Midgard, Jotunheim, Nidavellir and Svartalfheim; and Hel and Niflheim. If Hel and Niflheim comprised one world, however, the ninth world may have been Muspellheim, the land of fire. This region had no place in the tricentric structure of the universe and we can do no better than quote Snorri Sturluson:

> The first world to exist, however, was Muspell in the southern hemisphere; it is light and hot and that region flames and burns so that those who do not

belong to it and whose native land it is not, cannot endure it. The one who sits there at land's end to guard it is called Surt; he has a flaming sword, and at the end of the world he will come and harry and will vanquish all the gods and burn the whole world with fire.

At Ragnarok, Surt is accompanied by the sons of Muspell; Snorri says that they 'will form a host in themselves and that a very bright one'; but we do not hear about these fiery inhabitants of Muspellheim on any other occasion.

The axis of the three levels and nine worlds was the mighty ash tree, Yggdrasill (the meaning of the name is discussed in Note 4). This timeless tree, which seems to have had no known origin and which will survive Ragnarok, is so vast that, as Snorri says, 'its branches spread out over the whole world and reach up over heaven'. Yggdrasill had three roots. One sunk into Asgard; under this root was the Well of Urd (Fate) guarded by the three Norns or goddesses of destiny, and this is where the gods gathered each day in council. The second root delved into Jotunheim; under this root was the Spring of Mimir (see Note 2), and its waters were a source of wisdom. Odin sacrificed one eye to drink from it and Heimdall, watchman of the gods, is said to have left his horn there until he needed it at Ragnarok. The third root plunged into Niflheim; under this root was the Spring of Hvergelmir. This was the source of eleven rivers and, near by, the dragon Nidhogg and other unnamed serpents gnawed at the root of the ash Yggdrasill.

Usually known as a Guardian Tree, Yggdrasill nourishes, and suffers from, the animals that inhabit it, feed on it and attack it. While the dragon Nidhogg gnaws the roots, deer and goats leap along the branches and tear off the new shoots; and a squirrel runs up and down the trunk, carrying insults from Nidhogg to an eagle who sits in the topmost branches, with a hawk perched between its eyes. The tree, moreover, drips dew so sweet that bees use it for the making of honey.

Yggdrasill does not only sustain animals. A stanza in the eddaic poem *Svipdagsmal* (Myth 23) mentions that the cooked fruit of Yggdrasill ensures safe childbirth. When Ragnarok draws near, it is said the ash tree will tremble and a man and a woman who hide within it, Lif and Lifthrasir, will survive the ensuing holocaust and flood. They stand alone at the end of one cycle and the beginning of another in the world of time and men.

But the tree that suffers, that cares for all living creatures and ensures continuity, is in turn sustained by the Norns, Urd (Fate), Skuld (Being) and Verdandi (Necessity). In a sense, therefore, the life not only of man but also of the guardian of men lies within their hands. Snorri Sturluson wrote:

> It is said further that the Norns who live near the spring of Urd draw water from the spring every day, and along with it the clay that lies round about the spring, and they besprinkle the ash so that its branches shall not wither or decay.

The continuing tradition of the Guardian Tree is further discussed in Note 1.

A great many mythologies have a tree or column or mountain at the centre of the world. More specifically, the symbol of three cosmic regions connected by a tree that we find in Norse mythology also appears in Vedic Indian and Chinese mythologies. H. R. Ellis Davidson has written of Yggdrasill that

> the fact that it formed a link between the gods, mankind, the giants, and the dead meant that it was visualised as a kind of ladder stretching up to heaven and downwards to the underworld. This conception of a road between the worlds is one which is familiar in the beliefs of the shamanistic religions.

The use of Yggdrasill for a shamanistic journey is the subject of Myth 4, in which Odin voluntarily hangs on the tree for nine nights, his side pierced with a spear, in order to learn the wisdom of the dead. And, indeed, the squirrel Ratatosk's carrying of insults between the eagle and the serpent can be seen to represent both the division and the unity of heaven and hell.

Nine worlds encompassed by the tree (which so becomes a symbol of universality known to mythologists as the World Tree); nine nights hanging on the tree: the number nine recurs again and again in Norse mythology. Odin learns nine magic songs from a giant that enable him to win the mead of poetry for the gods; Heimdall has nine mothers; Hermod, Odin's son, journeys for nine nights in his attempt to win back the god Balder from Hel; the great religious ceremonies at the temple of Uppsala lasted for nine days in every ninth year, and required the sacrifice of nine human beings and nine animals of every kind. Why nine was the most significant number in Norse mythology has not been satisfactorily explained, but belief in the magical properties of the number is not restricted to Scandinavia. In *The Golden Bough*, J. G. Frazer records ceremonies involving the number nine in countries as widely separated as Wales, Lithuania, Siam and the island of Nias in the Mentawai chain. Nine is, of course, the end of the series of single numbers, and this may be the reason why it symbolises death and rebirth in a number of mythologies; hence it also stands for the whole.

This section offers a guide only to the most notable features of the Norse mythical universe – the nine worlds that undoubtedly owe many of their characteristics to the volcanically active, often hostile island of Iceland in which they were finally shaped and recorded (see Notes 1 and 32). The individual myths describe that universe in much more detail – especially Numbers 1, 12, 15, 27 and 32. The way in which the giant Ymir's body is divided so that everything, even his eyebrows, were used in the creation of the world; the four dwarfs who hold up the sky; the wolves that chase the sun and moon; the giant's eyes that are tossed up into heaven and turned into stars: these and a host of other particulars become narrative elements within the cycle. It is time now to turn to the Norse pantheon.

THE PANTHEON

Snorri Sturluson, writing in Iceland in the thirteenth century, says that, excluding Odin and his wife Frigg, 'The divine gods are twelve in number ... The goddesses [who number thirteen] are no less sacred and no less powerful.' This section introduces the four principal deities, Odin, Thor, Freyr and Freyja, in some detail, and points to the principal attributes of the others; they, and other protagonists, are discussed further in the notes where appropriate.

Odin is often called Allfather: this means he was not only the actual father of many of the gods and (with his two brothers) created the first man and woman, but that he was also foremost of the gods. Snorri Sturluson is quite clear on this point:

> Odin is the highest and oldest of the gods. He rules all things and, no matter how mighty the other gods may be, they all serve him as children do their father ... He lives for ever and ever, and rules over the whole of his kingdom and governs all things great and small. He created heaven and earth and sky and all that in them is.

Germanic pre-Christian Europe was fraught with conflict between family and family, tribe and tribe, country and country. A culture finds the gods it needs and the Norse world needed a god to justify the violence that is one of its hallmarks. Odin appears to have inherited the characteristics of the earliest Germanic war gods, Wodan and Tîwaz, and is seen above all as the God of Battle. Terrible, arrogant and capricious, he inspired victory and determined defeat; in his hall, Valhalla, he entertained slain warriors, chosen and conducted there by the Valkyries, who were to fight with him at Ragnarok; and he required propitiation with human and animal sacrifice.

The same inspiration that enabled one man to win a battle enabled another to compose poetry. Thus Odin, the God of War, travelled to Jotunheim to win the mead of poetry for the gods (Myth 6), and one reason why he is so prominent in the eddaic poems may be that he was the patron of the poets who composed them!

Odin was not only the God of Battle and the God of Poetry; he could also act as a seer. Like a shaman, he could send out his spirit, sometimes riding on his eight-legged steed Sleipnir, sometimes in another shape, on journeys between worlds; like a shaman, he could win wisdom from the dead. In the eddaic poem *Voluspa*, and in his voluntary sacrifice on the world ash Yggdrasill (Myth 4), we see him as the God of the Dead.

Odin is a formidable presence. He has only one eye and wears a wide-brimmed hat to escape instant recognition; he always wears a blue cloak and carries the magic spear Gungnir; on his shoulders sit the ravens Huginn (Thought) and Muninn (Memory), birds of battle symbolic also of flights in search of wisdom; and from the high seat of Hlidskjalf, in his hall Valaskjalf, he could survey all that happened in the nine worlds. He is a terrifying god: maybe a god to be respected, but not a god to be loved.

Thor, son of Odin and Earth, was second in the pantheon and it is clear from the terms in which he is described by the eddaic poets, Snorri Sturluson and the saga writers, and from the large number of place names embodying his name, that he was the most loved and respected of the gods. While Odin stood for violence and war, Thor represented order. With his hammer Mjollnir, he kept the giants at bay and was physically strong enough to grapple with the world serpent, Jormungand. Men invoked him in the name of law and stability.

Odin championed the nobly born – kings, warriors, poets; Thor championed the farming freemen (Myth 22) who constituted the majority of the population. His physical image fits this role well; he was huge, red-bearded, possessed of a vast appetite, quick to lose his temper and quick to regain it, a bit slow in the uptake, but immensely strong and dependable. The eddaic poets (and Snorri Sturluson in their wake) may have exaggerated Odin's significance; according to the eleventh-century historian Adam of Bremen, Thor was the greatest of the Norse gods and, in the great temple as Uppsala, his statue occupied the central position between Odin and Freyr.

The second myth in this collection which forms a complete cycle, beginning with the creation and ending with the destruction of the nine worlds, describes a war between the warrior gods, the Aesir, and the fertility gods, the Vanir. This conflict appears to embody the memory of a time when two cults struggled for the possession of men's minds and, as invariably happens when one religion replaces another, were ultimately fused. Thor thus took on characteristics associated with fertility and made them his own. The hammer Mjollnir, for instance, was not only an instrument of aggression but also of fertility (see Note 10). Likewise, Thor was the cause of thunder (the noise made by the wheels of his chariot) and lightning (fragments of a whetstone were lodged in his head) and, in the words of Adam of Bremen, Thor was held to control 'the winds and showers, the fair weather and fruits of the earth'.

The most important of the fertility gods, however, was Freyr, God of Plenty. Freyr appears to have been a descendant (who somehow changed sex) of Nerthus, the Earth Mother whom Tacitus described as having been worshipped in Denmark in the first century AD. And Snorri Sturluson writes: 'Freyr is an exceedingly famous god; he decides when the sun shall shine or the rain come down, and along with that the fruitfulness of the earth, and he is good to invoke for peace and plenty. He also brings about the prosperity of men.' The idol of Freyr at Uppsala had a gigantic phallus and Freyr was clearly invoked not only for the increase of the earth but also for human increase. Freyr's principal possessions, the ship Skidbladnir and the boar Gullinbursti, are both ancient fertility symbols, and the one surviving myth directly concerned with him (Myth 11) is a celebration of all that he stands for.

Freyr's father was Njord and his sister was Freyja (see page xxx for discussion of goddesses) and all three were involved in the exchange of leaders when the Aesir and Vanir made a truce (Myth 2). Njord, the senior god of the Vanir, governed the sea and the winds and guarded ships and seafarers. His hall was called Noatun or shipyard. Njord married the frost giantess Skadi and his son the frost giantess Gerd in myths which both symbolise the union of opposites (see Notes 9 and 11).

There are a bewildering number of theories about another of the leading gods, Heimdall, but he, too, was probably originally one of the Vanir. He was associated with the sea and was the son of nine maidens (perhaps nine waves). According to Snorri, 'He needs less sleep than a bird, and can see a hundred leagues in front of him as well by night as by day. He can hear the grass growing on the earth and the wool on sheep, and everything that makes more noise.' His stamina and acutely developed senses made Heimdall the ideal watchman for the gods. His hall Himinbjorg (Cliffs of Heaven) stood near the rainbow Bifrost, and he owned the horn Gjall whose blast could be heard throughout the nine worlds. Heimdall is also identified in the prose preface to the *Rigsthula* as the progenitor of the races of men (Myth 5); we do not know enough about his origins to be sure why he and not Odin (who, with his brothers, actually created the first man and woman) appears in this context.

Another leading god, Tyr, was a son of Odin, although one source (Myth 17) makes him the son of the giant Hymir. Like Odin, he inherited characteristics from earlier Germanic gods of battle, and his origins are discussed in Note 7. He is the bravest of the Aesir and only he is prepared to sacrifice a hand so that the wolf Fenrir can be bound (Myth 7), thereby ensuring the safety of the gods until Ragnarok.

Ragnarok is precipitated by the death of Balder, the gentle and beloved son of Odin and Frigg, who is felled by a mistletoe dart thrown by his own brother Hod, a blind god whose aim is guided by the evil Loki. Balder's character is discussed in detail in Note 29; in the inimitable words of Snorri Sturluson:

> There is nothing but good to be told of him. He is the best of them and everyone sings his praises. He is so fair of face and bright that a splendour radiates from him, and there is one flower so white that it is likened to Balder's brow; it is the whitest of all flowers. From that you can tell how beautiful his body is, and how bright his hair. He is the wisest of the gods, and the sweetest-spoken, and the most merciful, but it is a characteristic of his that once he has pronounced a judgement it can never be altered.

None of the remainder of the twelve 'leading' gods feature significantly in the surviving myths. Forseti, the son of Balder and Nanna, was god of justice; Bragi, son of Odin, was god of poetry and eloquence; Ull was particularly concerned with archery and skiing, and was invoked in duels; Vali, son of Odin and his mistress Rind, who avenged Balder's death by killing his unwitting murderer, and Vidar, son of Odin and the giantess Grid, who will avenge Odin's death, both survive Ragnarok.

Apart from the twelve principal gods three other male inhabitants of Asgard must be mentioned. Honir (Myths 2, 8 and 26) was involved in the exchange of leaders between the Aesir and Vanir. His most pronounced characteristic appears to have been his indecisiveness and he was associated with Odin and Loki on several occasions. It seems that after Ragnarok he will be Odin's successor as first among the gods. Secondly, Hermod, a son of Odin, makes one significant appearance: his name implies resolve and it is he who journeys to the underworld of Hel in an attempt to recover his dead brother Balder. And, finally, there is Loki.

The son of two giants and yet the foster-brother of Odin, Loki embodies the ambiguous and darkening relationship between the gods and the giants. He is dynamic and unpredictable and because of that he is both the catalyst in many of the myths and the most fascinating character in the entire mythology. Without the exciting, unstable, flawed figure of Loki, there could be no change in the fixed order of things, no quickening pulse, and no Ragnarok.

Snorri Sturluson says that Loki

> is handsome and fair of face, but has an evil disposition and is very changeable of mood. He excelled all men in the art of cunning, and he always cheats. He was continually involving the Aesir in great difficulties and he often helped them out again by guile.

This is a very fair description of the Loki of the earlier myths: he is responsible for a wager with a giant which imperils Freyja (Myth 3) but by changing both shape and sex, characteristics he has in common with Odin, he bails out Freyja and the gods; his shearing of Sif's hair is more mischievous than evil, and he makes handsome amends in the end (Myth 10); and although his deceit leads to the loss of the golden apples of youth (Myth 8), he retrieves them again.

Loki's origins are particularly complex and he has been compared to a number of figures in European and other mythologies; it is now generally accepted, though, that he was no late invention of the Norse poets but an ancient figure, and one descended from a common Indo-European prototype. Noting this turn and turnabout quality in Loki's make-up, H.R. Ellis Davidson has also tellingly compared him to the Trickster of American Indian mythology:

> The trickster is greedy, selfish, and treacherous; he takes on animal form; he appears in comic and often disgusting situations, and yet he may be regarded as a kind of culture hero, who provides mankind with benefits like sunlight and fire. At times he even appears as a creator. He can take on both male and female form, and can give birth to children. He is, in fact, a kind of semi-comic shaman, half way between god and hero, yet with a strong dash of the jester element, foreign to both, thrown in.

But, as time goes on, the playful Loki gives way to the cruel predator, hostile to the gods. He not only guides the mistletoe dart that kills

Balder but stands in the way of Balder's return from Hel; his accusations against the gods at Aegir's feast (Myth 30) are vicious and unbridled; even when fettered, he remains an agent of destruction, causer of earthquakes. And when he breaks loose at Ragnarok, Loki reveals his true colours: he is no less evil than his three appalling children, the serpent Jormungand, the wolf Fenrir and the half-alive, half-dead Hel (Myth 7), and he leads the giants and monsters into battle against the gods and heroes.

We hear far less about the goddesses in the myths; and since Snorri Sturluson asserts their equality with the gods, we can only assume a disproportionate number of stories concerning them have been lost. Freyja is the only 'divine' goddess to have survived as a fully rounded and commanding figure. With her father Njord and brother Freyr she came to represent the Vanir when they exchanged leaders with the Aesir. Her husband was called Od (sometimes equated with Odin) and Freyja is often described weeping for this shadowy figure who had for some reason left her. Freyja was invoked by pre-Christian Scandinavians as goddess of love, and is portrayed in the myths as sexually attractive and free with her favours: on two occasions, giants lusted after her; she sold herself to four dwarfs (Myth 13) in exchange for the Necklace of the Brisings – the most striking symbol of her fertility; and the giantess Hyndla roundly censured her for riding on her human lover Ottar (Myth 18) and for leaping around at night like a nanny goat.

Freyja was also associated with war. She rode to battle in a chariot drawn by two cats and the eddaic poem *Grimnismal* says that she divided the slain with Odin; half went to Valhalla and half to her hall, Sessrumnir, on Folkvang (Field of Folk). The end of Myth 13 displays this warlike face of Freyja, while it is noteworthy that in Myth 17 the alias of Freyja's lover Ottar is Hildisvini, which means 'battle-boar'.

War and death stand shoulder to shoulder and, like Odin, Freyja had connexions with the world of the dead. She was said to have been mistress of magic and witchcraft (Myth 2) and owned a falcon skin which enabled her spirit to take the form of a bird, travel to the underworld, and come back with prophecies and knowledge of destinies. But although a great deal about the practice of shamanism in pre-Christian Scandinavia (and Freyja's association with it) can be adduced from contemporary sources, no myth survives that displays Freyja as seer or *volva*.

Of the other twelve 'divine' goddesses, Gefion was also counted among the Vanir, and the story of how she tricked Gylfi, the King of Sweden (Myth 21), establishes her connexion with agriculture in general and ploughing in particular. Eir was goddess of healing; Sjofn and Lofn were concerned with firing human love and bringing together those 'for whom marriage was forbidden or banned', while Var heard the marriage oath and punished those who strayed from it; Vor was a goddess from whom nothing could be hidden and watchful Syn was invoked by defendants at trials; Snotra was wise and gentle and knew the value of self-discipline; Saga was distinguished only for drinking each day with Odin in her hall Sokkvabekk; and Lin, Fulla and Gna appear to have been no more than handmaidens to Odin's wife, Frigg.

It is a pity that we do not know more about Frigg herself, who shared with Odin a knowledge of men's destinies. Like Freyr, she must have had her origin in the image of the Earth Mother: she was the daughter of Fjorgyn, the Goddess of Earth; she was invoked by women in labour; and her maternal qualities are evident in her mourning for the loss of her son Balder. H. R. Ellis Davidson has written of the likely connexion between Freyja and Frigg:

> The two main goddesses of Asgard indeed suggest two aspects of the same divinity, and this is paralleled by the twofold aspect of the fertility goddess in the Near East, appearing as mother and as lover. Sometimes both roles may be combined in the person of one goddess, but it is more usual for the different aspects to be personified under different names. It is even possible to recognise a triad of goddesses, such as Asherah, Astarte, and Anat of Syria, or Hera, Aphrodite, and Artemis of Greece. Here the three main aspects of womanhood appear side by side as wife and mother, lover and mistress, chaste and beautiful virgin. Frigg and Freyja in northern mythology could figure as the first two of such a trio, while the dim figure of Skadi the huntress might once have occupied the vacant place.

We know rather more about other female inhabitants of Asgard than about some of the 'divine' goddesses. Idun, the wife of Bragi, was custodian of the apples of youth, and the myth of how she was tricked by Loki into leaving Asgard and then kidnapped by the giant Thiazi is one of the most haunting in the cycle (Myth and Note 8). Like Idun, Sif, the wife of Thor, must have been a fertility goddess; she had incomparable golden hair and its loss is the starting point for Myth 10. Nanna was Balder's loyal wife; her heart broke at the sight of him lying dead on the ship Ringhorn and she was cremated with him and accompanied him to Hel. And Sigyn was no less loyal to her husband Loki; when he was bound by the gods, she stood beside him and with a bowl caught the deadly venom that dripped from a snake's fangs on to his face.

The gods and goddesses symbolise specific beliefs and many of them have highly distinctive personalities. Giants and dwarfs, on the other hand, appear as a genera. There is little to choose between one giant and another, one dwarf and the next. The giants largely represent the forces of chaos, attempting through physical force, trickery and magic to upset the order of the universe. They range from the blunt and brutal Geirrod and Hrungnir, both disposed of by Thor, to the wily and evil Utgard-Loki, who sees Thor off the premises. But the distinction between gods and giants is far from absolute. Some gods have bad qualities, some giants have good; and the gods and giants do not only fight one another, but form friendships and embark on love relationships. Perhaps it is legitimate, indeed, to see the gods and giants not as polarised opposites but rather as opposing aspects of one character – warring, making peace, warring again and, in the end, mutually destructive.

The ugly, misshapen dwarfs, meanwhile, represent greed; they do nothing that is not in their own interests. Master-smiths and magicians, quick to show malice, they lust after fair women, after power and, above all, after gold. Light elves and dark elves and the inhabitants of Niflheim are mentioned in the myths from time to time, but they do not have an active part to play in them. Of the five myths (5, 12, 20, 21 and 25) involving humans, I will have more to say. A glossary of the principal protagonists, places and props can be found on page 237 immediately after the notes.

SOURCES

The greater part of this magnificent mythology, Indo-European in origin, took shape in Germanic Europe between 1000 BC and the birth of Christ. The survival of Bronze Age rock carvings, however, some of them featuring religious symbols, indicates that certain elements in the myths were current in Scandinavia in the previous millennium. But not until Tacitus's *Germania*, written at the end of the first century AD, do we have a written record of ancient Germanic religious beliefs, and our chief sources are much later still, dating from thirteenth-century Christian Iceland, when the old beliefs were largely discredited. We have to rely on poets and antiquarians 'out on the end of an event, waving goodbye'.

There are six primary literary sources (some single, some plural) fundamental to a study of Norse mythology. The notes at the end of the book discuss in some detail the source(s) for each myth and also refer to mythological parallels, literary analogues and archaeological finds.

In 1643 the Bishop of Skalholt in Iceland discovered a manuscript, *Codex Regius*, now thought to have been written in about 1270, consisting of twenty-nine mythical and heroic poems. Confusion over its authorship led to its being called *Saemund's Edda* (the term 'edda' is thought to derive from the Old Norse *oðr*, meaning poem or poetry). A few other poems of the same type were subsequently discovered, notably a group of six in the *Arnamagnaean Codex* of which five appear in the *Codex Regius* and one (*Baldrs Draumar*) does not. The *Elder Edda* or *Poetic Edda* was adopted as the umbrella title for these poems, thirty-four in all, unified by subject matter and form. They appear to have been composed by poets who believed in the old gods, many of them are unique sources for individual myths, and many are highly accomplished poems in their own right. The *Elder Edda*, moreover, possesses in *Voluspa* (The Sibyl's Prophecy) a poem that is by common consent one of the greatest literary achievements of the Germanic world – a powerful and moving account of how the world was created, how it moved from a Golden Age to an age of strife, and how it had to end in total destruction before there could be a new innocence and a new cycle of time.

Although the majority of its poems were probably composed in the tenth century, the *Elder Edda* is actually an anthology of different poets from different places and times; this accounts for the contradictions and many chronological inconsistencies (detailed in the notes) within the myths they recount. There is, of course, no 'right' order or version for the myths (pre-Christian Germanic Europeans were no more uniform in their religious beliefs than any other people) and in retelling the cycle, I have simply attempted to find a psychologically satisfying sequence that reduced difficulties of this kind to a minimum.

Scaldic poems – eulogies and elegies by known poets celebrating their contemporaries – are the other major poetic source for the myths. Their intricate form, which includes syllabics, alliteration, internal rhyme and consonance, resists the most stout-hearted attempts to render them in an acceptable modern poetic translation, but the rich allusive detail they contain is invaluable. The 'shield poems', as a few of them are known, describe mythical scenes painted on the quarters of a shield presented to some king or local chieftain; the poem came along as, so to speak, an ancillary present. These are important sources for a number of the myths, but the greatest pertinence of the scaldic poems lies in the countless kennings, or condensed metaphors, that comprise part of their diction. Many of the kennings are rooted in myths with which the poem's original audience was clearly familiar. So, for instance, four of the kennings for gold are 'Freyja's tears', 'Sif's hair', 'Otter's ransom' and 'Aegir's fire'. As readers of these myths will discover, this is because Freyja wept tears of gold; because when the goddess Sif's hair was cropped by Loki, it was replaced by spun gold; because three gods had to pay a ransom for killing Otter by covering his pelt with gold; and because the sea god Aegir's hall was illumined only by gold that shone like fire. Many of the kennings, then, endorse those myths that have survived and give us tantalising glimpses of those that have not.

The finest man of letters that Iceland has ever produced was Snorri Sturluson (1179–1241). An important political leader and landowner, he was also a great poet, sagaman, historian and critic. His poems include *Hattatal*, a scaldic eulogy for King Hakon and Duke Skuli; his sagas include the brilliantly vivid *Egil's Saga*, while the *Heimskringla* is nothing less than a survey of the whole of Norwegian history from its legendary origins up to his own time. But by far Snorri's most significant work for the student of Norse mythology is his *Prose Edda*.

Iceland had democratically adopted Christianity in 1000 AD, and the accompanying exposure to new European literary modes was eroding both the use of the old scaldic technique and familiarity with the kennings. Snorri's reaction was to write a handbook to encourage poets to compose in the scaldic style – a kind of North European equivalent of Aristotle's *Poetics*. The *Prose Edda*, written in about 1220, includes rules of poetic diction, quotes extensively from scaldic poems that would otherwise be lost to us, displays familiarity with almost all the poems in the *Elder Edda* and retells in full many of the myths that lie behind the kennings in scaldic poetry. One section in particular, 'Gylfaginning', consists exclusively of retellings from the myths.

Snorri Sturluson was writing here both as a Christian and an antiquarian, and we must keep this in mind in using and assessing his work. It would be wrong to suppose that, writing in thirteenth-century Iceland, Snorri Sturluson gives a thoroughly reliable and authentic firsthand view of ancient beliefs. His material fascinated and at times amused or misled him, but above all it fired the storyteller and poet in him (see Note 17 for the complete version of Thor's visit to Hymir). Absorbed by the drama of, and interplay between the nine worlds, he took material from existing sources and, with his own imaginative touch, created in 'Gylfaginning' a superb and delightful work of art – pages that tell many of the myths better than they have been told before or since.

In about 1215, just twenty years before Snorri Sturluson completed *Heimskringla*, a Dane called Saxo, nicknamed Grammaticus, wrote the last words of his sixteen-volume Latin history of the Danes, *Gesta Danorum*. Like *Heimskringla*, this work began with prehistoric times, and the first nine books are a confused medley of myth, legend and religious practice. Saxo Grammaticus knew and used variant versions of many of the myths recorded by Snorri, but his approach is markedly different. Snorri does not sermonise about the gods but lets them stand or fall by their own actions. But, as E. O. G. Turville-Petre writes:

> For Saxo, as for the medieval Icelanders, the gods were not gods, but crafty men of old. With superior cunning they had overcome the primeval giants; they had deluded men into believing that they were divine. But Saxo carried euhumerism further than the Icelanders did. Saxo's gods play a more intimate part in the affairs of men.... Saxo differs from the Icelandic writers chiefly in his bitter contempt of the gods and all they stood for. Snorri sometimes poked fun at them, but it was a good-humoured fun, of a kind which had no place in Saxo's mind.

Nevertheless, *Gesta Danorum* is still the primary source for the Danish and West Norse traditions, just as Snorri Sturluson represents Icelandic tradition. The note to 'The Death of Balder' (Myth 29) includes a detailed comparison of the versions offered by Snorri and Saxo.

The great Icelandic sagas (there are no fewer than seven hundred) together constitute the most surprising and one of the most distinguished achievements in European literature. Written in the thirteenth century by known and unknown hands, some are historical and revolve around the lives and deeds of kings and saintly bishops, some celebrate legendary heroes such as Sigurd the Volsung, some describe the Norsemen's insatiable appetite for exploration and settlement; and perhaps the greatest are the racy, ice-bright family sagas that tell of the lives, loyalties, dilemmas and feuds of individuals and families in Iceland's Heroic Age around 1000 AD.

Inevitably the sagas reflect the religious beliefs and attitudes of their protagonists, and they make available to us a great deal of information about pre-Christian belief and practice – much of which appears to have persisted well into the Christian period in Iceland. In the *Eyrbyggja Saga*, for example, one Thorolf decides to migrate to Iceland. In order to decide where to disembark

> Thorolf threw overboard the high-seat pillars from the temple – the figure of Thor was carved on one of them – and declared that he'd settle at any spot in Iceland where Thor chose to send the pillars ashore.

Thorolf did just that and the saga then describes in detail the building of a temple to Thor, the function of the temple priest, and the use of the temple and its surrounds:

Thorolf used to hold all his courts on the point of the headland where Thor had come ashore, and that's where he started the district assembly. This place was so holy that he wouldn't let anybody desecrate it either with bloodshed or with excrement; and for privy purposes they used a special rock in the sea which they called Dritsker [Dirt Skerry].

In the last category are actual historians and their histories. As mentioned above, Tacitus was the first to write about the religions of the Germanic tribes within the Roman Empire. In the tenth century, the Arab diplomat Ibn Fadlan wrote a detailed record of his prolonged contact with the Norsemen, including a horrifying account of a ship burial in Russia; in the eleventh century, Adam of Bremen offered a sustained description of Swedish paganism and left a very vivid and detailed picture of the greatest of the heathen temples, dedicated to Odin, Thor and Freyr, at Uppsala. The thirteenth-century *Landnamabok* (Book of Settlements), which is a survey of Iceland man by man and inch by inch, contains a significant amount of religious history, including the Icelandic heathen law concerning sacerdotal functions, sacrifices, oath swearing, and so forth. These and many other historical sources, some no less significant than those cited, help us to build up a picture of pre-Christian Scandinavia.

Our principal sources stand only half-way between us and the people who accepted the myths as truths. The filters of literary artifice, fragmented manuscripts, prejudice and contempt occasioned by conflicting religious belief, and hindsight, all obscure our picture. However much we may know, there is far more that we can never know; we are rather like searchers using glow worms to guide us through the darkness.

THE LITERARY STRUCTURE OF THE MYTHS

The majority of the myths are vigorous dramatic narratives. They are also episodes in a slowly developing, panoptic story.

First Odin and his brothers create the worlds and their inhabitants, and then follows a time of peace. Snorri Sturluson characterises this as the Golden Age, metaphorically because it is pure and untarnished and literally because the god's halls and sanctuaries and implements and utensils were made of gold.

This Golden Age ends with a war between the Aesir and the Vanir, the first war in the world. When it becomes clear that neither side will prevail, a truce is called and leaders are exchanged. But no sooner have the Aesir and the Vanir learned to live side by side than, in the third myth in the cycle, the recurring motifs of the myths announce themselves: the antagonism of gods and giants, and the ambivalence of Loki.

A giant masquerading as a mason visits Asgard. He tricks the gods into a wager involving Freyja, the sun and the moon, but Loki's cunning prevails. And the citadel's walls, shattered in the war between the Aesir and the Vanir, are restored into the bargain.

There now follow a number of myths ranging between the worlds in which the gods and giants flex their muscles against one another. Initially worsted (sometimes because of Loki's double dealing), the gods invariably come off better in the end (sometimes because Loki, under pressure, rights the situation). Odin journeys to the world of the giants, Jotunheim, to win the sacred mead of poetry; Loki follows in his footsteps to retrieve Idun and the apples of youth; and in a hilarious burlesque, Thor and Loki travel to Jotunheim together, disguised as bride and bridesmaid, to recover Thor's stolen hammer. In all three myths, the gods achieve their aims and the giants are killed.

But during this time the gods sustain losses too; the wise Kvasir is murdered by two dwarfs and his blood is the basic ingredient of the mead of poetry; in order to fetter the wolf Fenrir, Odin's son Tyr is obliged to sacrifice one hand; and in what is the longest and most picaresque of the myths, superbly told by Snorri Sturluson, Thor suffers very considerable loss of face in the course of a visit to the court of the magical Utgard-Loki. We see here that illusion is not only the tool of the gods but of the giants too.

Running parallel to this motif of antagonism is one of love and friendship. Two gods, Njord and Freyr, marry giantesses, and both Odin and Thor have a number of giant mistresses. The giantess Grid lends Thor her iron gloves, her belt of strength and her staff which enable him to dispose of the giant Geirrod and his two daughters. As already suggested the conflict between gods and giants is all the more tragic because they are also drawn to one another and, in many respects, resemble one another; because, in a sense, they are fighting a civil war in which both sides are inevitably the losers.

The theme of sexual attraction between inhabitants of different worlds persists throughout the cycle: four dwarfs buy the body of the goddess Freyja for four nights; in an intricate and passionate myth, the human Svipdag searches for and wins Menglad, a figure with one foot in Asgard, one in Jotunheim; Odin, so quick to boast of his conquests, is frustrated by a human girl, Billing's daughter; and the dwarf Alvis's journey to claim Thrud, Thor's daughter, as his bride ends when the sun rises and he is turned into a block of stone.

There are elements of playfulness and genial humour in many of the myths in the early part of the cycle. But the time of prodigious contests, of thefts and retrievals, and unexpected love matches, comes to an end with the myth of Thor's visit to the giant Geirrod (Myth 24); here, once again, the giants are bent on destroying Thor and unseating the gods, but here it is also apparent that the greatest threat to the gods is not the giants but one of their own number – Loki.

In the most famous of the myths, certainly one of the world's great tragic stories as it is told by Snorri Sturluson, the beautiful and innocent god Balder is killed by a mistletoe dart – and his return from the world of the dead is prevented by one cynical giantess, Thokk, who refuses to weep for him. Loki's is the hand that guides the dart and Loki is the giantess. From this moment on, it is clear that the world is approaching its end. Loki subjects gods and goddesses to vitriolic abuse; he is pursued and fettered. But the forces of evil cannot long be contained. Odin has already learned the future; he knows it is the destiny of gods, giants, men, dwarfs, and all creation to fight and destroy one another at Ragnarok.

But a shaft of light penetrates the final darkness of this most fatalistic mythology. Odin has also learned that a new cycle of time and of life will begin after Ragnarok. Balder, several other gods, and two humans will survive and return to Asgard and Midgard to repeople the world. The end will contain a beginning.

Interspersed with these colourful and often racy narrative tales are a number of myths whose form is quite different. They are pauses in the development of the cycle somewhat like arias in opera; their function is to reveal mythical knowledge. They are taxing to read in that, although they may have a skeletal narrative framework, they are actually litanies – condensations of a great number of names and facts into the minimum number of words. Three of these myths reflect Odin's unceasing search for, and acquisition of, wisdom. In 'Lord of the Gallows', Odin voluntarily sacrifices himself on Yggdrasill and, as he says, learns nine magic songs and eighteen highly potent charms; we learn what effects they have. In 'The Lay of Vafthrudnir', Odin successfully pits his knowledge against a giant, and in 'The Lay of Grimnir', he reveals a plethora of facts to the boy prince Agnar about both the layout and inhabitants of the mythical universe; both these myths were extensively used by Snorri Sturluson and are unique sources for much information about the cosmology, protagonists and other constituents of the myths.

Two 'flyting' poems – contests of abuse – also furnish many valuable details about the gods. In 'The Lay of Harbard', Odin, disguised as a ferryman, and Thor, anxious to get home, fling taunts at one another across a deep river; and in 'Loki's Flyting', Loki savages one god after another with injurious disclosures and gratuitous insults.

Five myths tell specifically of traditions in Midgard, the world of men. 'The Song of Rig' describes the social structure of the Norse world, 'The Lay of Loddfafnir' lays down a number of rules for social conduct, and 'The Lay of Alvis' is effectively a list of synonyms, an aide-mémoire for poets (put into the mouths of a god and a dwarf); 'Gylfi and Gefion' describes how Sweden and Denmark were given their present shape and 'Hyndla's Poem' is a catalogue of many legendary heroes known to the Norseman. From these myths especially, much information can be elicited about day to day life in the Norse world, the people who believed or half-believed in the gods and who composed, in the tenth century, most of the surviving poems about them.

APPROACH

Non-literate cultures, whether of the Stone Age or the rain forests of the Philippines today, devise potent stories to explain why the sun appears in the morning and disappears at night, why the wind blows, why it thunders, why some men are wise and some foolish, why some have the gift of poetry, why each animal has different characteristics, and so forth. In this way, myth very often relates to some aspect of creation and, in the strict sense, is a dramatic narrative through which humans try to explain to themselves their origins on this planet and the wonders they see around them. A definition of myth is that it is sacred history set in a mythical time, involving supernatural beings who create man and whose actions provide paradigms for men.

Primitive men accepted myths at their face value and believed that the recital of a myth, and the enactment of rites associated with it, gave them divine powers. Within the tribe, there was no one more significant than the myth-teller: he was the poet cum priest cum doctor. If he knew the right words he could, for instance, *cause* rain, necessary for the health and wealth of the land. The great French anthropologist, Mircea Eliade, has written: 'To know the myths is to learn the secret of the origin of things. In other words, one learns not only how things came into existence but also where to find them and how to make them reappear when they disappear.'

Post-Darwinian societies cannot subscribe to myth as being literally true. It is no longer possible to accept that earth and life on earth broke out of an egg or were shaped by some supernatural potter or, as the

Norsemen believed, were made from the bodies of a frost giant and a cow. Perhaps the only real successor to the myth-maker is that poet, philosopher or scientist who is no prisoner of his own methodology but is intent upon discovering origin and function and relationship, a man concerned moreover not only with explicable matter but with spirit. Only he can ever be in a position to recreate the meaning of life for us in the simple yet exalted way that the myth-tellers once did.

This does not imply, however, that the myths have no meaning for us. On the contrary, we recognise in them at once man's age-old anxiety, curiosity and longing, and respond to them. If Sir Philip Sidney's words about 'a tale which holdeth children from play, and old men from the chimney corner' have any application for our society, it is in relation to myth, legend and folktale.

But no collection of straight translations, however good, and whether in verse or prose, could hope to present the Norse myths in a form that would appeal to the wide audience they so well deserve. The multiple and fragmented sources, the condensation, and the assumption of considerable knowledge on the part of the reader, are considerable obstacles. Nonetheless, much of the primary source material does make absorbing reading, and one need not be a specialist to enjoy it. A number of translations are listed in the bibliography.

I decided, therefore, to retell the myths in new versions, and hope that they are both representative of the originals and full-blooded in their own right. I have omitted nothing of any consequence that appears in an eddaic poem or Snorri Sturluson or whatever other source was pertinent, but I have not hesitated to develop hints, to flesh out dramatic situations, and add snatches of dialogue. Above all, I have tried to provide some descriptive background of the nine worlds with their mountains and plains and rivers, their halls and palaces, all united by the World Tree Yggdrasill – the geographical setting for the myths that their original audience would have taken for granted. In doing so, I have (like Snorri Sturluson), drawn regularly on *Grimnismal*, *Vafthrudnismal* and *Voluspa*, and on my own observation of Iceland. I have found it right to use good, blunt words with Anglo-Saxon roots wherever I could do so; the differences in tone between one myth and another are intentional and reflect the disparate voices of the various sources.

It will be clear from the notes, where I have identified the source or sources of each myth, what an immense debt I owe to the *Elder Edda* and the *Prose Edda*; we depend on them for much the greater part of our knowledge of the Norse myths. I have, indeed, only departed from the lines laid down by the *Prose Edda* to include myths ignored by Snorri

Sturluson, or unknown to him, and on the single occasion in which a myth he retells (Myth 17) exists in its entirety in an earlier version. Most of the eddaic poets believed in the old gods and it is our immense good fortune that although he was a Christian, Snorri Sturluson was so fine an antiquarian and so fine a storyteller that he was able to suspend his own disbelief in them.

Although I have referred at times to Saxo Grammaticus, I have seen no reason to use his tortuous versions which are contemptuous of the old gods and relegate them to the status of humans. In addition to identifying the sources, the notes also discuss the protagonists, comment on obscure references, point to parallels, indicate contradictions and chronological inconsistencies that owe to the multiplicity of sources, and suggest some possible directions for interpretation.

The myths teem with unfamiliar and, at first sight, alarming names. You cannot do away with them; to deprive the gods and other characters of their original names would be to deprive them of part of their power. I decided to use the Old Norse originals (simplified where appropriate by omitting the final *r* and by changing ð to *d* and þ to *th*) but have also worked their translations into the fabric of the story wherever I could. Where a name is of little consequence, however, in the sense that it appears in one myth alone (as, for example, with some rivers, the Valkyries, and some of Odin's names), I have occasionally made an exception to this rule, sometimes using the original for its sound value, sometimes using only the translation.

It was W. H. Auden who first encouraged me to look north and immerse myself in the bracing floes of Norse mythology. Having done so, I can only express deep gratitude and say I am astounded that these myths are relatively little known, even to those of us who are geographically and temperamentally of the north. They are part of our tradition and we should be no less familiar with them than with the classical myths which, since the Renaissance, have been such a regular source of inspiration for artists in every discipline. The best of them are no less considerable in their understanding and no less memorable in their wording than any other recorded myths, and the whole of the cycle is greater than the sum of its parts. These myths speak for a dynamic culture and they speak of human longings and mysteries; now let them speak for themselves.

NOTE

A GLOSSARY OF THE PRINCIPAL CHARACTERS IN THE MYTHS THAT FOLLOW APPEARS ON PAGE 237.

THE MYTHS

Hail to the speaker and him who listens! May
whoever learns these words prosper because of
them! Hail to those who listen!

Havamal

1 *The Creation*

BURNING ICE, BITING FLAME; that is how life began.

In the south is a realm called Muspell. That region flickers with dancing flames. It seethes and it shines. No one can endure it except those born into it. Black Surt is there; he sits on the furthest reach of that land, brandishing a flaming sword; he is already waiting for the end when he will rise and savage the gods and whelm the whole world with fire.

In the north is a realm called Niflheim. It is packed with ice and covered with vast sweeps of snow. In the heart of that region lies the spring Hvergelmir and that is the source of eleven rivers named the Elivagar: they are cool Svol and Gunnthra the defiant, Fjorm and bubbling Fimbulthul, fearsome Slid and storming Hrid, Sylg, Ylg, broad Vid and Leipt which streaks like lightning, and freezing Gjoll.

Between these realms there once stretched a huge and seeming emptiness; this was Ginnungagap. The rivers that sprang from Hvergelmir streamed into the void. The yeasty venom in them thickened and congealed like slag, and the rivers turned into ice. That venom also spat out drizzle – an unending dismal hagger that, as soon as it settled, turned into rime. So it went on until all the northern part of Ginnungagap was heavy with layers of ice and hoar frost, a desolate place haunted by gusts and skuthers of wind.

Just as the northern part was frozen, the southern was molten and glowing, but the middle of Ginnungagap was as mild as hanging air on a summer evening. There, the warm breath drifting north from Muspell met the rime from Niflheim; it touched it and played over it, and the ice began to thaw and drip. Life quickened in those drops, and they took the form of a giant. He was called Ymir.

Ymir was a frost giant; he was evil from the first. While he slept, he began to sweat. A man and woman grew out of the ooze under his left armpit, and one of his legs fathered a son on the other leg. Ymir was the forefather of all the frost giants, and they called him Aurgelmir.

As more of the ice in Ginnungagap melted, the fluid took the form of a cow. She was called Audumla. Ymir fed off the four rivers of milk that coursed from her teats, and Audumla fed off the ice itself. She licked the salty blocks and by the evening of the first day a man's hair had come out of the ice. Audumla licked more and by the evening of the second day a man's head had come. Audumla licked again and by the evening of the third day the whole man had come. His name was Buri.

Buri was tall and strong and good-looking. In time he had a son called Bor and Bor married a daughter of Bolthor, one of the frost giants. Her name was Bestla and she mothered three children, all of them sons. The first was Odin, the second was Vili, and the third was Ve.

All this was in the beginning, before there were waves of sand, the sea's cool waves, waving grass. There was no earth and no heaven above; only Muspell and Niflheim and, between them, Ginnungagap.

The three sons of Bor had no liking for Ymir and the growing gang of unruly, brutal frost giants; as time went on, they grew to hate them. At last they attacked Ymir and killed him. His wounds were like springs; so much blood streamed from them, and so fast, that the flood drowned all the frost giants except Bergelmir and his wife. They embarked in their boat – it was made out of a hollowed tree trunk – and rode on a tide of gore.

Odin and Vili and Ve hoisted the body of the dead frost giant on to their shoulders and carted it to the middle of Ginnungagap. That is where they made the world from his body. They shaped the earth from Ymir's flesh and the mountains from his unbroken bones; from his teeth and jaws and the fragments of his shattered bones they made rocks and boulders and stones.

Odin and Vili and Ve used the welter of blood to make landlocked lakes and to make the sea. After they had formed the earth, they laid the rocking ocean in a ring right round it. And it is so wide that most men would dismiss the very idea of crossing it.

Then the three brothers raised Ymir's skull and made the sky from it and placed it so that its four corners reached to the ends of the earth. They set a dwarf under each corner, and their names are East and West and North and South. Then Odin and Vili and Ve seized on the sparks and glowing embers from Muspell and called them sun and moon and stars; they put them high in Ginnungagap to light heaven above and earth below. In this way the brothers gave each star its proper place; some were fixed in the sky, others were free to follow the paths appointed for them.

The earth was round and lay within the ring of the deep sea. Along the strand the sons of Bor marked out tracts of land and gave them to the frost giants and the rock giants; and there, in Jotunheim, the giants settled and remained. They were so hostile that the three brothers built an enclosure further inland around a vast area of the earth. They shaped it out of Ymir's eyebrows, and called it Midgard. The sun warmed the stones in the earth there, and the ground was green with sprouting leeks. The sons of Bor used Ymir's brains as well; they flung them up into the air and turned them into every kind of cloud.

One day, Odin and Vili and Ve were striding along the frayed edge of the land, where the earth meets the sea. They came across two fallen trees with their roots ripped out of the ground; one was an ash, the other an elm. Then the sons of Bor raised them and made from them the first man and woman. Odin breathed into them the spirit of life; Vili offered them sharp wits and feeling hearts; and Ve gave them the gifts of hearing and sight. The man was called Ask and the woman Embla and they were given Midgard to live in. All the families and nations and races of men are descended from them.

One of the giants living in Jotunheim, Narvi, had a daughter called Night who was as dark eyed, dark haired and swarthy as the rest of her family. She married three times. Her first husband was a man called Naglfari and their son was Aud; her second husband was Annar and their daughter was Earth; and her third husband was shining Delling who was related to the sons of Bor. Their son was Day and, like all his father's side of the family, Day was radiant and fair of face.

Then Odin took Night and her son Day, sat them in horse-drawn chariots, and set them in the sky to ride round the world every two half-days. Night leads the way and her horse is frosty-maned Hrimfaxi. Day's horse is Skinfaxi; he has a gleaming mane that lights up sky and earth alike.

A man called Mundilfari living in Midgard had two children and they were so beautiful that he called his son Moon and his daughter Sun; Sun married a man called Glen. Odin and his brothers and their offspring, the Aesir, were angered at such daring. They snatched away both children and placed them in the sky to guide the chariots of the sun and moon – the constellations made by the sons of Bor to light the world out of the sparks from Muspell.

Moon leads the way. He guides the moon on its path and decides when he will wax and wane. He does not travel alone, as you can see if you look into the sky; for Moon in turn plucked two children from Midgard, Bil and Hjuki, whose father is Vidfinn. They were just walking away from the well Byrgir, carrying between them the water cask Soeg on the pole Simul, when Moon swooped down and carried them off.

Sun follows behind. One of her horses is called Arvak because he rises so early, and the other Alsvid because he is immensely strong. The Aesir inserted iron-cold bellows under their shoulder-blades to keep them cool. Sun always seems to be in a great hurry, and that is because she is chased by Skoll, the wolf who is always snapping and growling close behind her. In the end he will catch her. And the wolf that races in front of Sun is called Hati; he is after Moon and will run him down in the end. Both wolves are the sons of an aged giantess who lived in Iron Wood, east of Midgard.

After the sons of Bor had made the first man and woman, and set Night and Day, Moon and Sun in the sky, they remembered the maggots that had squirmed and swarmed in Ymir's flesh and crawled out over the earth. Then they gave them wits and the shape of men, but they live under the hills and mountains in rocky chambers and grottoes and caverns. These man-like maggots are called dwarfs. Modsognir is their leader and his deputy is Durin.

So the earth was fashioned and filled with men and giants and dwarfs, surrounded by the sea and covered by the sky. Then the sons of Bor built their own realm of Asgard – a mighty stronghold, a place of green plains and shining palaces high over Midgard. The two regions were linked by Bifrost, a flaming rainbow bridge; it was made of three colours with magic and great skill, and it is wonderfully strong. All the Aesir, the guardians of men, crossed over and settled in Asgard. Odin, Allfather, is the oldest and greatest of them all; there are twelve divine gods and twelve divine goddesses, and a great assembly of other Aesir. And this was the beginning of all that has happened, remembered or forgotten, in the regions of the world.

And all that has happened, and all the regions of the world, lie under the branches of the ash Yggdrasill, greatest and best of trees. It soars over all that is; its three roots delve into Asgard and Jotunheim and Niflheim, and there is a spring under each. A hawk and eagle sit in it, a squirrel scurries up and down it, deer leap within it and nibble at it, a dragon devours it, and it is sprinkled with dew. It gives life to itself, it gives life to the unborn. The winds whirl round it and Yggdrasill croons or groans. Yggdrasill always was and is and will be.

For note on this myth see page 181.

2 The War of the Aesir and Vanir

ODIN DID NOT EXTEND a friendly welcome to the witch Gullveig when she came to visit him. In his hall the High One and many other Aesir listened with loathing as she talked of nothing but her love of gold, her lust for gold. They thought that the worlds would be better off without her and angrily seized and tortured her; they riddled her body with spears.

Then the Aesir hurled Gullveig on to the fire in the middle of the hall. She was burned to death; but out of the flames she stepped whole and reborn. Three times the Aesir burned Gullveig's body and three times she lived again.

Then wherever she went, and she went everywhere, into every hall, Gullveig was given another name. The awed Aesir and their servants called her Heid, the gleaming one. She was a seer; she enchanted wands of wood; she went into trances and cast spells; she was mistress of evil magic, the delight of every evil woman.

When the Vanir heard how the Aesir had welcomed Gullveig, they were incensed as the Aesir had been by Gullveig's gold lust; they swore vengeance and began to prepare for war. But there was nothing that escaped Odin when he sat in his high seat in Valaskjalf; the Aesir, too, sharpened their spears and polished their shields. Very soon the gods moved against each other and Odin cast his spear into the host of the Vanir. That was the beginning of the first war in the world.

At first the Vanir gained ground. They used spells and reduced the towering walls of Asgard to rubble. But the Aesir fought back and surged forward and caused no less damage in Vanaheim – the world of the Vanir. For a long time the battle raged to and fro, and the longer it lasted the clearer it became that neither side was likely to win.

Then the gods on both sides grew weary of war. Talk and truce seemed better than such turmoil. So leaders of the Aesir and the Vanir met to discuss terms. They argued about the war's origins and whether the Aesir alone were guilty of causing the war or whether both sides were entitled to tribute. The end of the discussion was that the Aesir and Vanir swore to live side by side in peace, and agreed to exchange leaders as proof of their intentions.

So two leading Vanir, Njord and his son Freyr, made their way to Asgard. Njord's daughter, Freyja, journeyed with them, and so did Kvasir, wisest of the Vanir. The Aesir welcomed and accepted them, much as they disliked the fact that Freyr and Freyja were the children of Njord by his own sister. They appointed Njord and Freyr as high priests to preside over sacrifices, and Freyja was consecrated a sacrificial priestess. She soon taught the Aesir all the witchcraft that was well known and in common use in Vanaheim.

For their part, the Aesir sent long-legged Honir and wise Mimir to live in Vanaheim. Honir was well built and handsome, a figure of substance. The Aesir thought he would make an enviable leader in war and peace alike. Mimir, like Kvasir, was held to be second to none in his understanding and wisdom.

The Vanir welcomed and accepted them. They at once appointed Honir to be one of their leaders, and Mimir stood at his right hand, always ready with shrewd advice. Together they were unfailing. When Honir was separated from Mimir, though, things were rather different. Standing alone in a council or meeting, and asked for his opinion, Honir's reply was always the same: 'Well, let the others decide.'

The Vanir began to suspect that the Aesir had tricked them and that they had got very much the worse in the exchange of leaders. And soon their suspicion turned to outright anger and thoughts of revenge. They seized wise Mimir and threw him to the ground and hacked off his head. They told one of their messengers to take it back to those who had so thoughtfully sent it: Odin and the Aesir.

Odin took Mimir's head and cradled it. He smeared it with herbs to preserve it, so that it would never decay. And then the High One sang charms over it and gave back to Mimir's head the power of speech. So its wisdom became Odin's wisdom – many truths unknown to any other being.

For note on this myth see page 183.

3 *The Building of Asgard's Wall*

LONG AFTER THE GOLDEN AGE, it was still very early in the cycle of time. And long after the war between the Aesir and the Vanir, the wall around Asgard that the Vanir had razed with their battle-magic remained a ring of rubble, deserted, the home of eagles and ravens.

The gods were anxious that the wall should be rebuilt, so that Asgard would be safe from evil-doers, but none were eager to take the heavy burden of rebuilding on their own shoulders. This is how matters stood for some time until, one day, a solitary figure on horseback cantered over the trembling rainbow, and was stopped by the watchman Heimdall.

'I've a plan to put to the gods,' said the man.

'You can tell it to me,' said Heimdall warmly. He had felt curious as he watched this man approach from a hundred miles off, and smiled, showing his gold teeth.

'I'll tell all the gods if I tell at all,' said the man from his saddle. 'The goddesses also may be interested.'

Heimdall showed his teeth again in a less friendly manner and directed the man across the Plain of Ida to Gladsheim.

So the gods and goddesses gathered in Gladsheim. Their visitor tied up his stallion and stepped forward under the shining roof, to the middle of the hall. He was surrounded by Odin and the twelve leading gods, each sitting in his high place, and by a throng of gods and goddesses.

Odin eyed him piercingly. 'We are all here at Heimdall's bidding. What do you have to say?'

'Only this,' said the man. 'I'll rebuild your wall round Asgard.'

There was a stir in Gladsheim as the gods and goddesses realised there must be rather more to the builder than met the eye.

'The wall will be much stronger and higher than before,' said the builder. 'So strong and high that it will be impregnable. Asgard will be secure against the rock giants and the frost giants even if they barge their way into Midgard.'

'However,' said Odin, aware that conditions would soon follow.

'I'll need eighteen months,' said the builder. 'Eighteen months from the day I begin.'

'That may not be impossible,' said Odin, the Alert One.

'It is essential,' said the builder.

'And your price?' asked Odin slowly.

'I was coming to that,' said the builder. 'Freyja as my wife.'

The beautiful goddess sat bolt upright and as she moved the Necklace of the Brisings and her golden brooches and armbands and the gold thread in her clothing glittered and flashed. None but Odin could look directly at her, Freyja, fairest of goddesses, more beautiful even than Frigg and Nanna and Eir and Sif. And as she sat erect, the outraged gods all around her were shouting, or waving their arms, deriding the builder, dismissing the builder.

'That's impossible,' shouted Odin. 'Let that be an end to it.'

'I'll also be wanting the sun and the moon,' said the builder. 'Freyja, the sun and the moon: that's my price.'

Loki's voice rose out of the hubbub. 'Every idea has its own merits. Don't dismiss it out of hand.'

All the gods and goddesses turned to look at the Sly One, the giant Farbauti's son, and wondered what was passing through the maze of his mind.

'We must give this plan thought,' said Loki reasonably. 'We owe our guest no less.'

So the builder was asked to leave Gladsheim while the gods and goddesses conferred. And when she saw that the gods were no longer ready to dismiss the idea out of hand but wanted to discuss it in earnest, Freyja began to weep tears of gold.

'Don't be so hasty,' Loki said. 'We could turn this plan to our own gain. Supposing we gave this man six months to build the wall . . .'

'He could never build it in that time,' said Heimdall.

'Never,' echoed many of the gods.

'Exactly,' said Loki.

Odin smiled.

'So what would we lose by suggesting it?' said Loki. 'If the builder won't agree, we lose nothing. If he does agree, he's bound to lose.' Loki slapped his sides and rolled his eyes. 'And we'll have half our wall built, free and for nothing.'

Although the gods and goddesses were a little uneasy about taking Loki's advice, they could see no way to fault the Trickster's scheme. Indeed several of them wished they had thought of it themselves.

'Six months!' said Odin, when the builder had come back into Gladsheim. 'If you build the wall within this time, you can have Freyja as your wife, and take the sun and moon too. Six months.'

The builder shook his head, but Odin continued, 'Tomorrow is the first day of winter. You must agree that no one will come to help you. And if any part of the wall is still unfinished on the first day of summer, you forfeit your reward. Those are our terms, and there are none other.'

'Impossible terms,' said the builder, 'and you know it.' He paused and gazed at Freyja. 'But my longing,' he said. 'My longing . . .' He gazed at Freyja again. 'Then at least allow me the help of my stallion Svadilfari.'

'Those are our terms,' said Odin.

'And those are mine,' said the builder.

'Odin, you're too stubborn,' protested Loki.

'And there are none other,' said Odin firmly.

'What's wrong with allowing him the use of his horse?' shouted Loki. 'How can it possibly affect the outcome? If we refuse, there'll be no bargain, and we'll have no part of the wall at all.'

In the end, Loki's argument prevailed. It was agreed that the builder should begin work on the next morning and have the use of his horse. Odin swore oaths to this effect in front of many witnesses, and the builder also asked for safe conduct for as long as he worked on the wall. He said he was anxious in case Thor, who was away in the east fighting trolls at that time, should return home and fail to see matters in the way the other gods had done.

Long before Early Waker and All Swift set off on their journey across the sky, the builder started work. By the light of the new moon, he led Svadilfari down over a sweeping grassy shoulder and past a copse to a place where the bones of the hill were sticking out, chipped and twisted. There were huge hunks and chunks and boulders of rock there, stuff that looked as though it would last as long as time itself. The builder brought with him a loosely meshed net which he harnessed to his stallion and spread out behind him. Then he began to heave and shove massive slabs on to the net. He gasped and grunted – amongst the gods only Thor could have matched his strength. After some time he had levered and piled up a great mound of rock behind Svadilfari. Then the builder gathered up the net ends in his horny hands, as though he were folding a sheet, and bellowed.

At once Svadilfari bowed his head. He dug his shoes into the earth and began to haul. Mustering his vast strength he dragged the whole quaking mound up the slope. And as day dawned, the builder and his stallion, guffing in the freezing air, brought their load up beside the old broken wall of Asgard.

When the gods and goddesses stirred from their halls, they were astonished and disturbed to see how much rock Svadilfari had hauled up the hill. They watched the mason smash the boulders, and shape them, and set them in place while Svadilfari rested in the shadow of the growing wall; and such was his strength, they began to think that the mason could only be some giant in disguise. But then the gods looked at the great circuit of broken wall that remained; they reassured each other that they had in any case got the best of the bargain.

Winter bared its teeth. Hraesvelg beat his wings and, outside Asgard, the cold wind whirled. The land was drenched by rainstorms and pelted with hailstones, then draped in snow.

The giant mason and his horse gritted their teeth and worked at the wall. Night after night Svadilfari ploughed the long furrow past the copse to and from the quarry. Day after day the mason went on building. And as the days grew longer, time for the mason, and for the gods, grew shorter.

Three days before the beginning of summer the mason had almost completed the circuit of well cut and well laid stone, a sturdy wall high and strong enough to keep any unwelcome visitor at bay. Only the gateway had still to be built. The gods and goddesses were no more able to keep away from the wall than moths from a flame. They stared at it for the hundredth time; they talked of nothing but the bargain.

Then Odin called a meeting in Gladsheim. The high hall was filled with anxious faces and fretful talk. Freyja was unable to stem her tears – the floor around her was flooded with gold.

Odin raised his spear and his voice over the assembly: 'We must find a way out of this contract,' he shouted. 'Who suggested we should strike this bargain? How did we come to risk such an outcome: Freyja married to a brute of a giant? The sky raped of the sun and the moon so that we shall have to grope about, robbed of light and warmth?' Several gods and then every god looked at Loki, and Odin strode across the hall floor towards him. He took a firm grip on the Trickster's shoulders.

'How was I to know?' protested Loki. 'We all agreed.'

Odin tightened his grip and Loki winced.

'We all agreed!' yelled Loki.

'Who suggested the mason should be allowed to have the use of his horse?' Odin asked. 'You got us into this trouble and you must get us out of it.'

There was a shout of agreement from all the gods.

'Use the warp and weft of your mind, Loki. Weave some plan. Either the mason forfeits his wages or you forfeit your life.' Odin squeezed Loki's flesh and sinews until the Sly One, the Shape Changer, dropped to one knee. 'We'll take it all out of you, bit by bit.'

Loki saw that Odin and the other gods were in deadly earnest. 'I swear,' he said. 'No matter what it costs me, I'll see to it that the builder loses the wager.'

That evening the mason led Svadilfari down towards the quarry with a certain spring in his step. It seemed to him as to the gods and goddesses that he would finish the wall within the agreed time, and win rewards rich not only in themselves but also in the sorrow their loss would bring to the gods. He sang a kind of tune, and small birds took shelter in the gloomy copse and listened to his song. Not only the birds. A young mare pricked up her ears and listened intently. Then, when Svadilfari and the mason drew close enough, she sprang out of the thicket. She kicked her heels in the air and, in the moonlight, her flanks simmered.

The mare pranced up to Svadilfari. She danced around him and whisked her tail and Svadilfari began to strain at the long rein by which the mason was leading him.

Then the mare whinnied invitingly and headed back towards the copse. Svadilfari started after her with such a thrust that he broke the rein. He galloped behind the mare into the copse, and the mason lumbered after Svadilfari, shouting and cursing.

All night the two horses gambolled, and all night the enraged mason tripped over roots and tree stumps in the half light. He hurled abuses, he chased shadows, and the light had begun to grow green in the east before Svadilfari returned to him.

So no stone was hauled from the quarry that night and the mason had to make do with the little left over from the day before. It was not nearly enough to build the first part of the gateway and he soon knew that he would no longer be able to complete his task in time.

Then the anger churning inside the mason erupted. He burst out of his disguise and stood before the watching gods and goddesses – a towering brute of a rock giant in a towering rage.

Now that the gods knew the builder was indeed a giant, they revoked

13

their oaths about his safe conduct without a second thought, and sent for Thor.

'A trick!' shouted the rock giant. 'Tricked by a gang of gods! A brothel of goddesses!'

Those were the mason's last words. Then Thor paid him his wages, and they were not the sun and the moon. A single blow from the hammer Mjollnir shattered the giant's skull into a thousand fragments and dispatched him to the endless dark of Niflheim.

A number of months passed before Loki the Shape Changer was seen in Asgard again. And when he returned, ambling over Bifrost and blowing a raspberry at Heimdall as he passed Himinbjorg, he had a colt in tow. This horse was rather unusual in that he had eight legs. He was a grey and Loki called him Sleipnir.

When Odin saw Sleipnir, he admired the colt greatly.

'Take him!' said Loki. 'I bore him and he'll bear you. You'll find he can outpace Golden and Joyous, Shining and Swift, Silver-maned and Sinewy, Gleaming and Hollow-hoofed, Gold Mane and Light Feet, and outrun whatever horses there are in Jotunheim. No horse will ever be able to keep up with him.'

Odin thanked Loki warmly, and welcomed him back to Asgard.

'On this horse you can go wherever you want,' said Loki. 'He'll gallop over the sea and through the air. What other horse could bear its rider down the long road to the land of the dead, and then bear him back to Asgard again?'

Odin thanked Loki a second time and looked at the Sly One very thoughtfully.

For note on this myth see page 185.

# 4 *Lord of the Gallows*

THE AXIS OF THE WORLD was Yggdrasill. That ash soared and its branches fanned over gods and men and giants and dwarfs. It sheltered all creation. One root dug deep into Niflheim and under that root the spring Hvergelmir seethed and growled like water in a cauldron. Down there the dragon Nidhogg ripped apart corpses. Between mouthfuls, he sent the squirrel Ratatosk whisking up the trunk from deepest earth to heaven; it carried insults to the eagle who sat on the topmost bough, with a hawk perched on its brow. And Nidhogg was not content with corpses; he and his vile accomplices gnawed at the root of Yggdrasill itself, trying to loosen what was firm and put an end to the eternal.

Other creatures, too, attacked and preyed off the living tree – four stags nibbled at the new leaves, and goats tugged and tore off the tender shoots. Parts of the huge trunk were peeling, parts were soft and rotten. Yggdrasill whispered and Yggdrasill groaned.

A second root curled into Asgard. Under that root flowed the well of Urd, the spring of destiny, where the gods gathered each day and held a court of justice. The three Norns lived near by, Fate and Being and Necessity. They shaped the life of each man from his first day to his last. And every day they sprinkled water on the branches of Yggdrasill and nourished the suffering tree.

The third root burrowed into that part of Jotunheim held by the frost giants. Under that root bubbled the spring guarded by wise Mimir, and the water in that well gave insight to those who tasted it. The god Heimdall left his shrieking horn there until the day when he would need it to summon every living creature to Ragnarok. And Odin had given one eye for a single draught from it. He won immense knowledge there and with it the thirst for yet greater wisdom. So the Terrible One approached Yggdrasill alone.

Odin said: 'I hung from that windswept tree, hung there for nine long nights; I was pierced with a spear; I was an offering to Odin, myself to myself.

'No one has ever known or will ever know the roots of that ancient tree.

'No one came to comfort me with bread, no one revived me with a drink from a horn. I peered at the worlds below; I seized the runes, shrieking I seized them; then I fell back.

'From Bolthor's famous son, Bestla's father, I learned nine powerful songs. I was able to drain the precious mead from the cauldron Odrorir.

'Then I began to thrive, my wisdom grew; I prospered and was fruitful. One word gained me many words; one deed gained me many deeds.

'The charms I know are not known by the wives of kings or by any man. The first is called Help because it can comfort grief and lessen pain and cure sickness.

'I know a second: any man who hopes to become a healer needs to know it.

'I know a third: if I should sorely need help to hold back my enemy, I can blunt my opponent's blade and soften his staff so he cannot wound me.

'I know a fourth: if anyone should bind me hand and foot, this charm is so great that the locks spring apart, releasing my limbs; I can walk free.

'I know a fifth: if I should see a well aimed arrow speeding to its mark, I can catch it however fast it flies; I have only to fix it with my eye.

'I know a sixth: if anyone thinks to finish me by sending a sapling's roots engraved with runes, that hero – full of spleen – will only destroy himself.

'I know a seventh: if I should see the hall roof burst into flames over the heads of my chosen comrades, I can quench the blaze however fierce it may be; I know the charm.

'I know an eighth: all men would be well advised to learn it: if hatred takes root in men's minds, I can uproot it.

'I know a ninth: if I should need to save my ship in a storm, I can calm the wind that whips off wavecrests and put the sea to sleep.

'I know a tenth: if ever I see witches flying on rafters, I can sing so that they go into a whirl and cannot change back into their day shapes or find their way to their own front doors.

'I know an eleventh: if I have to lead loyal, long-loved friends into a fight, I can sing behind my shield and they will go from strength to strength – unscathed to the battle, unscathed after battle; unscathed they return home.

'I know a twelfth: if I see a hanged man swinging from a tree, with his heels above my head, I can cut and colour the runes so that he will come down and talk to me.

'I know a thirteenth: if I sprinkle water over a child, he will never fall in the thick of battle, nor falter and sink in the sword-play.

'I know a fourteenth: if I so desire, I can tell men the names of the gods and the elves one by one – few fools can do this!

'I know a fifteenth: the dwarf Thjodrorir sang it in front of Delling's doors, a charm of power for the gods, glory for the elves, wisdom for Odin.

'I know a sixteenth: if I long for love-play, I can turn the mind and win the heart of a white-armed woman.

'I know a seventeenth: such a charm that a young girl will be loath to forsake me.

'I know an eighteenth: I will never tell it to a girl or married woman unless I am lying in her arms or she is my own sister! What you and you alone know is always the most potent. And that is the last of the charms.'

These were the words of Odin before there were men. These were his words, after his death, when he rose again.

For note on this myth see page 186.

5 *The Song of Rig*

L ISTEN! Who can hear the sound of grass growing? The sound of
wool on a sheep's back, growing?

Who needs less sleep than a bird?

Who is so eagle-eyed that, by day and by night, he can see the least
movement a hundred leagues away?

Heimdall and Heimdall and Heimdall.

But who could tell it was Heimdall, that figure on the seashore? The
guardian of the gods left his horn Gjall safe in Mimir's spring; he left
Gulltop, his golden-maned stallion, behind the stable door; and he
strode alone across the flaming three-strand rainbow bridge from
Asgard to Midgard.

It was spring and time for sowing. The god walked away from Bifrost
over soft green ground and soon he came to the edge of the earth. All
day, as the sun fled west from the wolf, he picked his way along the wavy
line where the soil meets the deep sea.

At nightfall Heimdall approached a decrepit turfed hut. The evening
air was quite still, but the shack was so rickety that it looked as if it might
collapse if the eagle-giant Hraesvelg gave one flap of his wings. Heimdall knocked and swung open the roughly hewn door. He had to stoop to
get under the lintel and over a pile of sacking on to the shining marl
floor. It took Heimdall a moment to adjust to the rank, smoky gloom;
his eyes smarted and he retched. Then he made out a trestle table, a
bench, more sacking heaped in one corner, a kind of cupboard leaning
against a crumbling wall and in the middle of the room the crouched
figures of Ai and Edda, Great Grandfather and Great Grandmother,
facing each other across the fire.

'Am I welcome?' asked Heimdall.

'What is your name?' said Ai.

'Rig,' said Heimdall.

'You are welcome,' said Edda.

So the god joined Ai and Edda. He spoke honeyed words, as he well
knew how, and in no time he had won the best position by the fire. From
time to time he peered hopefully into the pot hanging over it. After a

while, Edda got to her feet. She shuffled to one corner of the stinking hut, poked about, and dumped a loaf of bread on the table. It was not fully leavened, and was gritted with husks. Then the old woman unhooked the pot of thin broth and put that on the table too. The three of them sat on a rough bench and ate what there was to eat. There was one who was by no means satisfied.

After their meal, Ai and Edda and their guest were ready to lie down and sleep. Again the god spoke honeyed words, as he well knew how, and in no time he had won the best position, in the middle of the bed, with Ai on one side of him, Edda on the other. For three nights the god stayed with Great Grandfather and Great Grandmother. Then he thanked his host and hostess for their hospitality and went on his way.

Every day the two stallions, Arvak Early Waker and Alsvid All Swift dragged the chariot of the sun across the sky. And Day himself rode at ease round the world; the shining mane of his stallion Skinfaxi lit up earth and heaven. But then Night tightened the reins of her mount, Hrimfaxi, and each morning the face of the earth was dewy with foam from his bit. The strength of summer weakened and the length of the days shortened. So grim winter showed his fist, full of frost and snow and ice, and wrestling winds.

Soon nine months had passed and Edda gave birth to a son. He was sprinkled with water and his mother swaddled him. He had raven hair, and Ai and Edda called him Thrall.

If Thrall was less handsome than might be desired, he was certainly striking and all of a piece. From the first, his skin was wrinkled; his hands were chapped, his fingers were stubby and his knuckles were knotted. His face was, in a word, ugly. His back was twisted and his feet looked too large for him.

Nevertheless, Thrall was strong, and as the years passed he made good use of his strength. Day in, day out, and all day long, he sweated in the forest, gathering wood. He bound up bundle after bundle of faggots, and carted them home for burning.

When Thrall was a young man, a girl who was his equal in every way came to his hut. She was bow-legged; the soles of her feet were damp and discoloured; her sun-burned arms were peeling; and she had the squashed nose of a boxer. Her name was Thir the Drudge.

Thrall liked the look of Thir, and Thir liked the look of Thrall. In no time the two of them were sitting near the fire side by side, with eyes only for each other. And in a little more, they had prepared a bed – a bolster and a hairy blanket – and all evening they sat whispering.

That night was not the last that Thrall and Thir slept together. They had a cluster of contented children. The names of their sons were Fjosnir the Cattle Man and Coarse Klur; Hreim and Kreggi, the Shouter and the Horse Fly; Kefsir the Concubine Keeper and Stinking Fulnir; Drumb the Clot and Gross Digraldi; the sluggard Drott and Leggjaldi whose legs were as thick as tree trunks; Lut who was hunch-backed and ashen-faced Hosvir.

These ten sons shored up the structure and repaired the fabric of the hut. They spread loads of dung over the land surrounding it. They took their turn as goatherds and at rounding up the pigs. They all dug for peat.

Thrall and Thir also had daughters. There were oafish Drumba, Dumpy Kumba and hefty-thighed Okkvinkalfa; the best you could say about Arinnefja's nose was that it was homely; there were noisy Ysja and Ambott the Servant; Eikintjasna looked like a peg of oak; Totrughypja was clothed in rags; and bony Tronubeina had legs as long and skinny as a crane.

These were the offspring of Ai and Edda; and from these children stem the race of thralls.

Heimdall continued his journey. He took the shortest way to the next farm, and walked up to the door in the blue hour, just as the light was fading. The god knocked and entered. In the middle of the room, a fire flickered, and sitting near it Heimdall saw Afi and Amma, Grandfather and Grandmother.

Afi had a length of wood laid across his lap and was chipping at it with a knife, shaping a weaver's beam. The knife's blade and the pool of white shavings at his feet gleamed in the gloom. Afi's hair was combed and curled over his forehead; he had a trimmed beard. And his clothes – his leather jacket and breeches – were no less well cut than his hair.

Amma was unwinding flax from a distaff, spinning thread. She stretched and she reached, absorbed in her work. She wore a band round her head and her silver hair was knotted in a bun. She wore a simple frock and a shawl round her shoulders, secured by a handsome clasp.

'Am I welcome?' asked Heimdall.

'What is your name?' asked Afi.

'Rig,' said Heimdall.

'You are welcome,' said Amma.

So the god joined Afi and Amma. He spoke honeyed words, as he well knew how, and in no time he had won the best position by the fire. From time to time he peered hopefully into the pot hanging over it. After a while, Amma stopped working and got to her feet. She padded across the room to a stout oak chest and took out a loaf of rye bread, and a gob of butter, and knives and spoons, and arranged them on the table. She dipped a large jug into the vat of beer standing by the door, and then she unhooked the pot of boiled veal and set that on the table too. Then the three of them sat to eat.

After their meal, Afi and Amma and their guest were ready to lie down and sleep. The god spoke honeyed words, as he well knew how, and in no time he had won the best position, in the middle of the bed, with Afi on one side of him, Amma on the other. For three nights the god stayed with Grandfather and Grandmother. Then he thanked his host and hostess for their hospitality and went on his way.

Every day the two stallions dragged the sun across the sky, and Day himself rode at ease round the world. But then Night tightened the reins of her mount, and each morning the face of the earth was dewy with foam from his bit. Summer's strength weakened, the days shortened. So grim winter showed his fist, full of frost and snow and ice, and wrestling winds.

Soon nine months had passed and Amma gave birth to a son. He was sprinkled with water and his mother swaddled him. His cheeks were ruddy, he had bright eyes, and Afi and Amma called him Karl. Karl was quick to grow, and he was well built and strong. In time he learned how to drive oxen with a goad, and how to fasten the share and coulter to a plough; he discovered how to build huts and barns – how to dig the foundations, and erect a wooden frame, and lay the turf, and pitch a roof; he became a skilful cartwright.

When Karl was a young man, his parents found him a wife as much to their liking as to his – the fair daughter of a freeman living near by. On the appointed day, the bridal party brought her in a wagon to Karl's own farm. She wore a goatskin coat and a veil, and keys jangled at her waist. So Afi and Amma won a daughter-in-law. Her name was Snör. Karl and Snör equipped their farm and arranged things to their liking. They exchanged rings, and laid a colourful counterpane on their bed. That place became their place; it became home.

Karl and Snör had a cluster of contented children. They called their first-born Hal the Man, and their second Dreng the Warrior. And their other sons were Hold the Landowner, the freeman Thegn, and Smith who was a master of every craft; Breid was broad-shouldered and Bondi was a yeoman; when he grew up, Bundinskeggi always wore his beard well trimmed; Bui and Boddi owned a farm and a barn; Brattskegg had

21

a clipped beard too and like his eldest brother, Segg was manly. Karl and Snör also had ten daughters. Their eldest they called Snot the Serving Woman. There was Brud the Bride, slender Svanni and proud Svarri, fair Sprakki and womanly Fljod; Sprund was as proud as her sister Svarri; Vif was born to make a good wife, Feima was bashful and Ristil, the youngest, as graceful as any woman.

These were the children of Karl and Snör; and from these children stem the race of peasants.

Heimdall continued his journey. He took the shortest way to a hall near by and, in the late afternoon, strode up to it. Its wide doors faced south, and on one of the posts was a great wooden ring, intricately patterned.

The god knocked and entered. He strode through the long passageway into the hall where the floor was newly strewn with rushes.

In this spacious, gracious room, the god saw Fathir and Mothir, Father and Mother. They sat gazing into one another's eyes; then they touched, just finger ends.

Unaware of their visitor standing and watching, Fathir then busied himself twisting a new bowstring, sharpening arrows, and working at the shape of the carved elm bowshaft itself.

Mothir, meanwhile, sat and considered her slender arms. She smoothed her pleated chemise and drew the sleeves down to her wrists. Her dress had a train. She wore a flowing blue cape, and a charming cap, and on her breast were two oval brooches. This lady was pale-skinned: her brow was fair, her breast gleaming, and her neck was more white than new-fallen snow.

'Am I welcome?' asked Heimdall.

'What is your name?' asked Fathir.

'Rig,' said Heimdall.

'You are welcome,' said Mothir.

So the god joined Fathir and Mothir. He spoke honeyed words, as he well knew how, and in no time he had won the best position by the fire. Mothir lost no time. She took out an embroidered linen cloth and laid it over the table. She brought white loaves of finely ground wheat; bowls worked in silver filigree, full to the brim with cheese and onion and cabbage; well browned pork and horse and lamb; nicely turned partridge and grouse. The pitcher was full not of mead or ale but wine, and the goblets were made of solid silver. Then the three of them sat to eat. They ate and drank and talked until after dark.

After their meal, Fathir and Mothir and their guest were ready to lie down and sleep. The god spoke honeyed words, as he well knew how, and in no time he had won the best position, in the middle of the bed. Fathir slept on one side of him, Mothir lay on the other. For three nights the god stayed with Fathir and Mothir. Then he thanked his host and hostess for their hospitality and went on his way.

Every day the two stallions dragged the sun across the sky, and Day himself rode at ease round the world. But then Night tightened the reins of her mount, and each morning the face of the earth was dewy with foam from his bit. Summer's strength weakened, the days shortened. So grim winter showed his fist, full of frost and snow and ice, and wrestling winds.

Soon nine months had passed and Mothir gave birth to a son. He was sprinkled with water and wrapped in silk. He had fair hair and colour in his cheeks and the look in his glowing eyes was as grim as a snake. Fathir and Mothir called him Jarl. Jarl was quick to master skills. He learned how to hold and hoist a shining shield, and to wield a lance. Like his father, he twisted bowstrings and shaped bowshafts and loosed quivering arrows. He rode; he unleashed hounds. He learned the art of sword-play, and could swim across sounds.

One day, unannounced, the god walked out of the forest of slender silver birches that stood near the hall. He strode down to the building and found Jarl there, sitting alone.

'Jarl,' he said.

'You are welcome,' said Jarl.

'I've brought you a gift,' said the god. He showed Jarl a bundle of staves carved with signs and coloured red.

Jarl stared at them; he had never seen such things before.

'These are the runes. This is the magic that Allfather learned when he hung on the tree Yggdrasill.'

Jarl looked at the god, then at the runes, then at the god again.

'Do you know the words against pain of the mind, pain of the heart, pain of the body?'

Jarl shook his head slowly.

'Do you know the words that put water on a fire? Do you know the words that put the sea to sleep?' All that day, the god explained the secret meaning of the runes to Jarl, and Jarl felt excited and ready. He thought all his life had been waiting for this moment.

'I have one more thing to tell you,' said the god, as the light failed.

'What is that?' asked Jarl.

23

'My son.' The god took Jarl into his arms. 'You are my son,' he said. And he explained how he had visited the hall so long before. 'You are my son; and as I am Rig the King, so will you be Rig the King. Now is the time to win land, to win great age-old halls, and command a host of followers.'

The god looked piercingly at Jarl, his son, then turned on his heel, and walked out of the gleaming hall into the darkness.

Jarl did not need to be told twice. He thought his father's words explained to him what he had always felt but could not name. He was filled with a sense of release and purpose.

At once Jarl left the hall where he had lived since the day of his birth. He rode through a dark forest, and over passes between frosty forbidding crags; and in a place difficult of access, he established his own hall. He gathered a group of loyal retainers.

Jarl shook his spear and brandished his shield; he spurred his horse and dealt death blows with his sword. He brought his followers to battle and stained the soil red. He slew warriors and won land. Before long Jarl owned no less than eighteen halls. He won great wealth and was generous to his retainers. He gave them finger-rings and armbands, both of gold; he gave them precious stones; and he gave them horses lean and fleet of foot.

In time Jarl sent messengers over the boggy ground to the hall of the chieftain Hersir. And there, on Jarl's behalf, they asked for the hand of his daughter, Erna. She was fair-haired and long-fingered, and accomplished at whatever she put her mind to.

Hersir was delighted. After Erna had made proper preparation, the messengers escorted her to Jarl's hall, wearing a wedding veil. And she and Jarl lived most happily together.

Jarl and Erna had a cluster of contented children. They called their first-born Bur the Son, and their second Barn the Child; there was Jod the Child and Athal the Offspring; Arvi was an Heir and Mog another son; there were Nid and Nidjung the Descendants, Svein the Boy, and kinsman Kund; the youngest was Kon, a nobly born son. Soon all the boys learned to play and swim. As they grew older, they tamed beasts, and made circular shields, shaped shafts and shook spears.

But Kon the Young learned from his father the runes, the age-old meanings. In time he was able to blunt a sword blade and put the sea to sleep. He understood the language of the birds, he could quell flames, and quieten cares – the raging mind and aching heart of an unhappy man. He had the strength of eight men.

Kon and Rig-Jarl shared their secret understanding of the runes, and Kon was even more subtle and wise than his father. He believed it would be his right, too, to be called Rig the King; and he soon won that right.

One day Kon went riding in the gloomy, dark forest. Now and then he reined in his mount and loosed an arrow at a luckless bird. Other birds he lured from their perches, and listened to them.

A crow sat on a branch over Kon's head. 'Kon,' it croaked, 'why do you spend your time seducing birds to talk to you? You would do better to set out on your stallion and show daring in battle.'

Kon listened carefully to the crow's counsel. The darkness seemed to fall back from the clearing where he stood, and to wait in the wings.

'Who have halls more noble than yours?' continued the crow. 'Who have won riches greater than yours – gold and jewels and precious ornaments?'

Kon did not answer; he clenched his fists.

'Who are more skilled than you at steering their ships over the reach of the sea and the stinging saltspray?'

Still Kon did not answer.

'Dan and Danp, Dan and Danp, Dan and Danp,' sang the crow. It looked sideways at Kon. 'They know what it means to temper their weapons with the blood of enemies . . .'

The manuscript breaks off here and so 'The Song of Rig' is incomplete. The poem probably went on to establish the divine descent of the Danish Kings – the names **Rigr, Danr** *and* **Danpr** *occur in early genealogies – and perhaps to celebrate one particular king. For note on this myth see page 188.*

6 *The Mead of Poetry*

WHEN THE AESIR and the Vanir had made a truce, and settled terms for a lasting peace, every single god and goddess spat into a great jar. This put the seal on their friendship, and because the Aesir were anxious that no one should forget it, even for one moment, they carried off the jar and out of the spittle they fashioned a man.

His name was Kvasir. He was so steeped in all matters and mysteries of the nine worlds since fire and ice first met in Ginnungagap that no god nor man nor giant nor dwarf ever regretted putting him a question or asking his opinion. And wherever Kvasir went, news of his coming went before him. When he reached some remote farm or hamlet, sewing and salting and scything and sword-play were laid aside; even children stopped chattering and listened to his words.

What was his secret? It was as much in his manner as in his mine of understanding. Questions of fact he answered with simple facts. But to ask Kvasir for his opinion – What shall I say? What do you think? What shall I do? – did not always mean getting a direct answer. Sitting back in his ill-fitting clothes, as often as not with his eyes closed, he would listen to recitals of problems and sorrows with a kind, grave, blank face. He took in and set everything in a wider frame. He never intruded or insisted; rather, he suggested. Often enough he answered a question with another question. He made gods and men, giants and dwarfs feel that they had been helped to answer their own questions.

The stories of Kvasir's wisdom soon reached the ears of a most unpleasant pair of brothers, the dwarfs Fjalar and Galar. Their interest soon turned to envy and their envy to energy, for they could not admire anything without wanting it for themselves. They asked Kvasir to feast with them and a large gathering of dwarfs in their cave under the earth and, as was his custom, Kvasir accepted. The table was a long slab of uneven rock, the floor was grit and the wall-hangings were dripping stalactites; the talk was chiefly of profit and loss and petty revenge; the food, however, and the tableware, all made of hammered gold, were rather more pleasing.

After the feast, Fjalar and Galar asked Kvasir for a word in private. Kvasir followed them into a gloomy chamber, and that was a mistake. The two dwarfs had knives hidden in their sleeves, and at once they buried them in the wise man's chest. His blood spurted out of his body and Fjalar and Galar caught it all in two large jars, Son and Bodn, and a cauldron called Odrorir. Kvasir's heart stopped pumping and his drained white body lay still on the ground.

When, after a while, the Aesir sent a messenger to ask after Kvasir, the two dwarfs sent back word that he had unfortunately choked on his own learning, because there was no one in the nine worlds well-informed enough to compare and compete with him.

But Fjalar and Galar were delighted with what they had done. They poured honey into the jars and cauldron filled with Kvasir's blood, and with ladles stirred the mixture. The blood and honey formed a sublime mead: whoever drank it became a poet or a wise man. The dwarfs kept this mead to themselves. No one else tasted it; no one even heard about it.

One day the dwarf brothers entertained two gruesome guests, the giant Gilling and his wife. It was not long before they began to quarrel and Fjalar and Galar became more and more spiteful and full of hate. They suggested that Gilling might enjoy the sea breeze, and each taking an oar, rowed far out into the ocean surrounding Midgard. Then the dwarfs rammed their boat into a slimy, half-submerged rock. Gilling was alarmed and gripped one gunwale. His alarm was well-founded; the boat foundered and capsized. Gilling was unable to swim and that was the end of Gilling! The two dwarfs cheerfully righted their craft and rowed back home, singing.

Fjalar and Galar described what had happened to Gilling's wife.

'An accident,' said Fjalar.

'If only he had been able to swim,' Galar said sadly.

Gilling's wife wept and wept and, sitting in their cave, the two dwarfs did not like the feel of the tepid water washing round their ankles. 'I've an idea,' whispered Fjalar to his brother. 'Find a millstone, and go and wait above the entrance to the cave.'

Galar got up and went outside and Fjalar asked the giantess: 'Would it help if you looked out to sea? I could show you the place where he drowned.'

Gilling's wife stood up, sobbing, and Fjalar stepped aside for her as befits a host. And when the giantess stepped out into the daylight, Galar dropped the millstone on to her head.

'I was sick of her wailing,' said Fjalar.

When Gilling and his wife did not return to Jotunheim, their son Suttung set out in search of them. He looked at the dwarfs' dismal faces and listened to their lengthy tales and then he seized both of them by the scruffs of their necks.

Holding one in each hand, a pair of danglers, he angrily waded a mile out to sea, until it was too deep even for him. Then Suttung dumped Fjalar and Galar on a skerry, a sopping rock standing just clear of the water. 'It's much too far for you to swim,' he said. 'Much too far. So when the tide rises . . .'

Fjalar looked at Galar and both brothers grimaced.

'We've a suggestion,' said Fjalar.

'Since it has come to this,' said Galar, 'we're willing to offer you our greatest treasure.'

Then Fjalar described their mead, both its origin and power, with a wealth of words.

'Give us our lives,' said Galar, 'and we'll give it to you.'

'Agreed,' said Suttung.

So Suttung took the two dwarfs back to their cave and, since they clearly had no choice, they handed over Kvasir's blood. The giant stumped back to Jotunheim, carrying Son in one hand and Bodn in the other and Odrorir under his arm. He took the precious liquid straight to the mountain Hnitbjorg where he lived. Suttung hewed a new chamber out of the rock at the heart of the mountain and hid the three crocks in it. And he told his daughter Gunnlod that she had one duty: 'Guard this mead by day and guard it by night.'

Unlike the dwarf brothers, Suttung was boastful about his treasure. So it was not long before the gods learned about the divine mead, and heard how it had fallen into Suttung's unholy hands. Odin himself elected to go to Jotunheim and bring the mead back to Asgard. The Masked God, the One-eyed God, God of the Gods, disguised himself as a giant of a man, and called himself Bolverk, worker of evil. He crossed the river that divided Asgard and Jotunheim and strode across a desert of shifting grey grit where nothing, not even a grassblade, could take root. Bolverk came to a curtain of mountains. He hurried over a snowy pass and at last walked down into a narrow green valley.

Nine thralls were working in a sloping field, men from Midgard with a taste for adventure and handsome reward. They were scything the succulent grass with long, slow sweeps, and seemed very weary.

'Who is your master?' Bolverk asked one thrall who had stopped work entirely.

'Baugi,' said one thrall.

'Baugi?'

'Suttung's brother,' the thrall said, 'the giant who guards Kvasir's blood.'

'Shall I sharpen your scythe?' asked Bolverk affably.

The thrall was rather quick to agree to this, and when Bolverk drew a whetstone from his belt and began to put a new edge on the scythe, the other thralls crowded round in the hope he would hone their scythes too. Bolverk obliged, and the thralls all said that their scythes had never been quite as sharp before; they complained that the giant Baugi was too hard a taskmaster; they pointed to acres of grass, still uncut, that lay before them; coming to the point, the thralls asked whether they could buy the hone.

'I might think about selling it,' said Bolverk, 'but only to one man; and only to the one – if there is such a man here – who will feast me tonight in the manner to which I'm accustomed.'

The air was filled with shouts of agreement. 'Yes,' the thralls shouted. 'Yes . . . Me . . . I will . . . Here . . . All right . . . I'm your man . . . Done . . . Agreed . . . Your hand on it!'

Bolverk looked at them with his one eye. He smiled grimly. Then he threw the whetstone into the air. In the sun it glinted, it looked like silver.

The thralls gasped. They raised their scythes and ran, all of them eager to be under the whetstone when it fell. It seemed to hang in the air, so high had Bolverk tossed it. The thralls jostled, they stepped backwards, they suddenly swung round; and in the end, in their confusion, they all slit one another's throats. The nine of them lay in the long grass they had just cut.

Still smiling grimly, Bolverk caught the whetstone, tucked it into his belt, and walked back the way he had come.

The sun dawdled, and so did Allfather. Not until nearly midnight did he come down from the mountains again, and make his way to Baugi's farm. He said his name was Bolverk and explained that he had been walking all day. Then he asked Baugi if he could give him some kind of a meal and let him stay overnight in one of the huge barns near to the farmhouse.

'A fine time to ask,' said Baugi abruptly.

Bolverk looked pained and asked Baugi what was wrong.

'All my farmhands have been killed. That is what's wrong!' Baugi banged his fist on a trestle table, a blow so powerful it would have flattened a man's head. 'All nine of them. And how can I hope to find any more at this time of year?'

'I've an idea,' said Bolverk. 'You can see I'm strong. Very strong. I can take on the work of nine men.'

Baugi looked Bolverk up and down, and smiled in disbelief, thinking Bolverk was a hollow boaster. 'And if I agreed, what wages would you ask?'

'Only this,' said Bolverk. 'One drink of Suttung's mead.'

Baugi sniffed and shook his head.

'I may be strong,' said Bolverk. 'But to be a poet: that's the finest calling.'

'That mead is nothing to do with me,' said Baugi. 'My brother has it in his safe-keeping; and no one except Gunnlod has ever seen a drop of it. That's how things are.'

'Well,' said Bolverk. 'Those are my terms.'

Baugi shrugged his shoulders and so Bolverk got up to leave.

'I can talk to Suttung,' said Baugi. He had little love for his brother; but he felt sure that, in any case, Bolverk would never be strong enough to keep his part of the bargain. 'Work for me this summer, and I'll tell my brother how you helped me out. That's the best I can do.'

'How far can I trust you?' said Bolverk.

'You'll see,' said Baugi.

For as long as the long days, Bolverk worked for Baugi. As the sun climbed out of the east, Bolverk walked to the green fields still thick with the honey-dew that fell every night from the branches of Yggdrasill. All day he worked under the bright skull of the sky. He worked while the sun hurried west until it seemed to hang, blood red, on the western skyline. Baugi was amazed that Bolverk was as good as his boast, and seemed to need so little rest; he thought now that Bolverk must be more than merely human.

At the end of the summer, Bolverk asked Baugi for his wages. They went together to find Suttung at Hnitbjorg, and Baugi told his brother how Bolverk had helped him and asked for some of the divine mead.

'Never,' said Suttung. 'Not a drop!'

'Well,' said Bolverk as soon as he was alone with Baugi, 'I hope you're not going to accept Suttung's answer. I've worked for you all summer.'

'I've kept my promise,' Baugi said.

'Why should he have it all for himself?' said Bolverk. 'Don't you fancy a mouthful, Baugi? Since your brother won't part with the mead willingly, let us see if we can trick him out of it.'

'Impossible,' said Baugi. 'Do you know where it is hidden?' He was rather nervous of Suttung; but he was also rather nervous of Bolverk. Bolverk pulled an auger called Rati out of his belt, and told the giant that with it he might be able to drill a hole through the mountain. 'This is the least you can do in return for my work.'

Baugi took the auger and pressed the shank against the sheer rock face of the mountain Hnitbjorg; with both hands he turned the handle. He wondered how to get rid of the troublesome farmhand as he wound and wound and the auger sank into the mountain.

'There!' exclaimed the giant. 'Right through!' He withdrew the drill and wiped his brow.

Bolverk peered with his one eye into the dark passage left by the auger. Then he filled his lungs and blew fiercely into it. A shower of rock chippings blew back into his face, and Bolverk knew that Baugi had not, after all, cored the mountain. 'Were you trying to cheat me?' he said.

The giant said nothing. He drilled further into the mountain, vowing silently to dispose of Bolverk as soon as he could.

When Baugi withdrew the auger once more and Bolverk blew down the hole a second time, all the loose chippings were carried forward on the tide of air. Then Bolverk knew that the giant had bored right into the room at the heart of Hnitbjorg. At once he turned himself into a snake and shrithed into the auger hole.

Baugi stabbed at Bolverk with the point of the auger but he was not quick enough; the snake was already half-way down the passage on his way to Gunnlod and the divine mead. As soon as he reached the stronghold, Bolverk changed himself back into a giant of a man – one-eyed but handsome – and stood in front of Suttung's daughter.

Gunnlod was sitting on a stool of solid gold. And at the sight of Bolverk, Suttung's stern warning that she should guard the mead flew right out of her head. She was not sorry to have company. She sat and listened to Bolverk's beguiling words and songs; she wrapped her arms around him; for three days they talked and laughed and for three nights they slept together. In the silent cave under Hnitbjorg, the heartless father of the gods made love to the spellbound daughter of Suttung. Then Gunnlod was drunk with passion and ready to give Bolverk whatever he desired. He asked for three draughts of Kvasir's blood and Gunnlod took his hand and led him to the mead. With his first draught Bolverk emptied Odrorir, with his second draught Bodn, with his third draught Son. The father of the gods held all the divine mead in his mouth.

Then Odin turned himself into an eagle, flapped down the passage out of Hnitbjorg, and headed for Asgard. Suttung saw him and at once murmured the magic words known only to those who have drunk divine mead. Gods and giants and men and dwarfs saw a dark sight – one eagle pursuing another towards the kingdom of Asgard.

The Aesir quickly brought out jars and bowls, and laid them side by side so that they covered the whole courtyard just inside the great wall of Asgard. Anxiously they watched as Suttung came closer and closer to Odin.

The distant rustle became a whirr, and the whirr a terrible flapping and beating of wings. There was only a wingspan between the two birds. Then the eagle Odin dived in over the wall and spat the mead into the crocks assembled beneath him.

In his haste to escape Suttung, Odin could not help letting some mead spill outside the wall, but it was so little that the gods were not bothered about it. They said that anyone who wanted it could have it; and that became the poetaster's portion.

Suttung shrieked and wheeled away and shrieked again. He had lost through cunning what he had won through force, and there was nothing he could do.

And the gods? They had lost wise Kvasir, witness to the friendship between the Aesir and Vanir. But because of the cunning of Allfather, they had won back his blood. Once more Odin drank some of the precious mead. And from time to time he offered a draught to one of the Aesir or to a man or two in Midgard; he offered them the gift of poetry.

For note on this myth see page 190.

7 Loki's Children and the Binding of Fenrir

THE MOTHER OF SLEIPNIR was also the father of three appalling children. Not content with his faithful wife Sigyn, Loki sometimes took off for Jotunheim; the long-legged god hurried east and spent days and nights on end with the giantess Angrboda.

Loki and Angrboda had three monstrous offspring. The eldest was the wolf Fenrir; the second was Jormungand, greatest of serpents; and the third was a daughter called Hel. Even in a crowd of a thousand women, Hel's looks were quite likely to single her out: her face and neck and shoulders and breasts and arms and back, they were all pink; but from her hips down, every inch of Hel's skin looked decayed and greenish-black. Her expression was always the same: gloomy and grim. When the gods heard that the Father of Lies had also fathered these children, they were filled with alarm. They discussed what to do about them at the Well of Urd and the three Norns gave them little encouragement.

'Their mother is evil,' said Urd.

'But their father is worse,' Verdandi said.

'Expect nothing from them but the worst,' said Skuld. 'Expect them to harm you and endanger you. They will be in at the kill.'

And so the gods agreed that Loki's children must be captured. At Odin's behest, a group of gods crossed into Jotunheim by night; they burst into Angrboda's hall and gagged and bound her before she had even rubbed her eyes; then they kidnapped her children and carried them back to Asgard.

Odin was in no doubt as to what should be done with the serpent. He picked up Jormungand and hurled him into the ocean surrounding Midgard, the world of men. He hurtled through the air, smashed through the iron face of the water and sank to the sea bottom. There he lived and there he grew. Jormungand, the Midgard Serpent grew so thick and so long that he encircled the whole world and bit his own tail.

Odin was just as sure what to do about the serpent's sister. He took one look at Hel and hurled her out of Asgard, too. He threw her into the mist and darkness of Niflheim, the world beneath the worlds. And as she fell she heard Odin's decree that she should look after the dead, all those in the nine worlds who died of illness or old age, the condition being that she should share out whatever food she had with whoever came to her.

Hel made herself at home: beyond the sheer rock, Drop to Destruction, she built huge walls around her estate. Her hall Eljudnir, home of the dead, lay within it, behind a massive pair of gates. Hel's manservant and maidservant, Ganglati and Ganglot, moved about so slowly that it was not easy to tell whether they were moving at all; her plate was called Hunger, and her knife Famine. Her bed was Sick Bed, and the bed-hangings Glimmering Misfortune.

Odin thought it would be best if the gods themselves kept an eye on Fenrir. He seemed no different to any other wolf, and all the gods agreed that there would be no harm in letting him roam around the green and golden fields of Asgard. Even so, of all the gods only Tyr, son of Odin, was brave enough to face Fenrir alone, and give him great joints – flesh and gristle and bone – to keep him quiet.

The gods were not slow to change their minds about Fenrir when they saw him growing larger day by day. And when Urd, Skuld and Verdandi renewed their warnings, and said that the wolf would cause Odin's death, their alarm became far greater. They agreed that since they could not kill the wolf there and then and stain the sanctuary of Asgard with his evil blood, they must catch and fetter him. Then the gods made a powerful chain of iron links and they called it Laeding. Several of them went up to Fenrir, showed him the chain, and asked: 'Are you as strong as this?'

The wolf inspected Laeding. 'It's certainly strong, but I'm certainly stronger,' was all he had to say as he let the gods wind the chain round his neck and body and legs, until there was only a small length left for them to hold on to.

'Finished?' snarled the wolf. He planted his massive paws well apart, filled his lungs with air, then flexed every muscle in his body. Laeding's links at once sprang apart, and the gods sprang back alarmed.

The gods lost no time in making another chain. This was called Dromi, and it was twice as strong as Laeding. The links were larger than those of the largest anchor chain; no men could have even moved them. 'If you can break this chain,' the gods told Fenrir, 'you will be known for your strength throughout the nine worlds.'

Fenrir looked at Dromi. He thought it looked immensely strong, but then he thought that he too had grown even stronger since he had snapped Laeding. 'No one wins fame without taking a risk,' was all he had to say as the gods wound the vast chain round his neck and body and legs.

'Finished?' snarled the wolf. He shook so that there was a terrible clinking and clanking and grating; he rolled over and arched his back and banged the chain against the ground; he tightened his muscles until they were as hard as the iron links of Dromi; he stood up again and dug his paws into the earth and strained and strained – and all at once, Dromi snapped. It shattered into hundreds of separate links; the shrapnel flew in every direction. After this, the gods were frightened; they thought they might fail to fetter Fenrir.

'But if anyone can make a fetter that will not break,' Odin said, 'the dwarfs can.' And he sent off bright Skirnir, Freyr's messenger, to the world of the dark elves, Svartalfheim. Skirnir went down under Midgard through gloomy, dank, twilit grottoes. There he found Nar and Nain and Niping and Dain and Bifur and Bafur and Bombor and Nori and hundreds of others, each one as horrible as the next, and promised them gold and more gold if they could make a fetter for Fenrir. In the gloom the dwarfs' eyes gleamed like glow-worms; they whispered and schemed and set to work. They made a fetter as smooth and supple as a silk ribbon, and they called it Gleipnir.

When he returned to Asgard, Skirnir was thanked by all the gods for going on this mission. 'But what is it made of?' asked Odin, fingering the fetter.

'Six things,' said Skirnir. 'The sound a cat makes when it moves; a woman's beard; the roots of a mountain; the sinews of a bear; the breath of a fish; and a bird's spittle.'

The gods were both astonished and sceptical of Gleipnir's power.

'If you doubt it, as I doubted it,' said Skirnir, 'remember the cunning of the dwarfs. After all, have you ever thought why a cat makes no noise when it moves, and why a woman has no beard? You can never prove that a mountain has no roots, but many things that seem not to exist are simply in the dwarfs' safekeeping.'

Then a large group of gods approached Fenrir for the third time. They invited him to go out with them to the island of Lyngvi in the middle of Lake Amsvartnir.

There the gods produced the silken ribbon Gleipnir. They showed it to Fenrir and challenged him to test his strength against it.

'It's a little stronger than it seems,' said one.

'It's as well-woven as the words of a good poem,' said another. 'But you, Fenrir, you'll be able to break it.'

The wolf looked at Gleipnir. 'This ribbon is so slender,' he said, 'that I'd win no fame for snapping it.' He eyed Gleipnir again. 'If, on the other hand, cunning and magic have gone into its making, then slender as it looks, you can keep it for yourselves. I'm not having it wound round my legs.'

'Before this,' said one god, 'you've prised apart massive iron fetters. You'll have no bother with this band.'

'And if by any chance you're unable to break it,' said another, 'we'll set you free again, you can trust us.'

Fenrir showed his teeth and the gods did not like the look of them. 'If you're able to fetter me,' he snarled, 'it will be a long time before I can hope for any help from you.' Fenrir prowled right round the group of gods. 'I don't want to be bound with that ribbon. But neither do I want to be accused of cowardice. So while the others bind me, let one of you put his hand in my mouth as a token of your good faith.'

Tyr looked one by one at all the gods in that company. All the gods there looked at each other and said nothing, wondering what to do. Then Tyr slowly lifted his right arm and put his hand in Fenrir's mouth.

At once the other gods wound Gleipnir round and round the wolf's neck and body and legs, until it was all used up. Fenrir began to struggle against it. He tried to kick and shrug and shake and jerk and roll; but the more he strained the tighter Gleipnir became. Then Fenrir snarled and clamped his teeth; Tyr, bravest of the gods, twisted and cried out, unable and able to bear such pain. The other gods laughed, they knew that Fenrir was bound at last. They all laughed except Tyr: he lost his hand.

The gods fixed the large chain called Gelgja to the end of the silken ribbon. They passed the end of this chain through the hole in a huge boulder called Gjoll, looped it back, and secured it to itself.

The gods drove Gjoll a mile down into the earth. Then they found the vast rock Thviti and dropped that on top of Gjoll to fasten it. Fenrir shook and wrestled. He grated his teeth and gulped and opened his blood-stained jaws immensely wide. Then one of the gods drew his sword. He drove the point hard into the roof of Fenrir's mouth and rammed the hilt against his lower jaw. The wolf was gagged. Fenrir was gagged and Fenrir was bound. His howls were terrible, and slaver streamed from his jaws. It ran from the middle of the island into the lake of Amsvartnir and was called Von, the river of Expectation.

And just as the Midgard Serpent waits at the bottom of the ocean, coiled round the world; just as Hel waits in Niflheim, surrounded by corpses and swirling death-mist; so, gagged and bound on Lyngvi, Fenrir lies and waits for Ragnarok.

For note on this myth see page 192.

8 *The Theft of Idun's Apples*

VERY EARLY ONE SUMMER MORNING, Odin, Loki and Honir crossed into Midgard, happy in one another's company, and intent upon exploring some part of the earth not already known to them.

In the pale blue, almost pale green light that gives an edge to everything, the three friends crossed a desolate reach of grit, patrolled only by the winds. Before men in Midgard had stirred and woken, the gods were striding over scrubby, undulating ground. Then they tramped round a great mass of spiky, dead, dark rock, and headed for the summit of a conical mountain.

All day they trekked and talked and, in the evening, they followed the course of a rapid, milky river from a glacier down into a valley – a jigsaw of fields, yellow and brown and green.

Odin, Loki and Honir had not brought any food with them and were beginning to feel very uneasy about it when they had the luck to come across a herd of oxen. While Loki sized them up, chose one and killed it, Odin and Honir gathered fallen branches from a grove of stunted oaks and made a fire. Then they cut up the ox into huge pieces and put the pieces into the heart of the fire.

The smell ravished the gods; they could barely wait to eat. As soon as they thought the joints were roasted, they scattered the fire and pulled the meat out of the flames.

'It's not ready,' said Odin, surprised. 'We must be so hungry that a little time seemed long to us.'

Loki and Honir raked up the brands and put the meat back into the fire again.

Suddenly a chill wind channelled down the valley. Although the sun still loped across the western sky with the wolf at its heels, all the heat had drained out of the summer day. The three gods wrapped their cloaks around them and sat and waited.

'Do you think it's ready?' asked Honir. 'What do you think? Shall I find out?'

'One of these days, you'll choke on your own uncertainty,' Loki said, leaping to his feet and scattering the fire for a second time. 'It must be cooked by now.'

Odin took a piece out of the flames. 'It's still not ready,' he said. 'And it ought to be.'

'There's nothing wrong with this fire,' Honir said.

'And yet our dinner is as raw now as it was to begin with,' said Loki, looking at the meat and grimacing.

'Well,' said Odin, 'something is working against it.'

'Something sitting up here,' said a voice from above them.

The three gods at once looked up into the leafy branches of the oak tree above the fire. They looked and they saw an eagle sitting there, and it wasn't a small one.

'Let me eat my fill,' said the eagle to the three upturned faces, 'and your ox will be cooked.'

The gods conferred and were of one mind. 'Since we too want to eat tonight,' Odin told the eagle, 'we agree. There is nothing else we can do.' Then the eagle screeched. It flapped its immense wings, swooped down from the tree and settled over the fire. At once it snatched up both the shoulders and both parts of the rump as well. Then it eyed the gods and, crouching at the root of the oak, began to eat. Loki was so angry that he raised his staff and rammed it into the bird's body. The eagle was thrown off balance and dropped the meat. It screeched again and took to the air. One end of the staff was firmly lodged in the eagle's back; and, to his alarm, Loki found that he was unable to let go of the other. He pulled and twisted and yelled to no purpose. His hands were stuck to the staff.

The eagle flew at great speed and it took care to fly close enough to the ground to make sure that Loki did not have a smooth ride. The Trickster was dragged across the floor of Midgard. His knees and ankles banged into boulders; his legs and feet were scratched by gorse bushes and thorns until they were bleeding.

'Mercy!' shouted Loki.

The eagle took no notice. It dragged Loki on his backside across a glacier until he was all but skinned.

'Mercy!' yelled Loki again. He thought his outstretched arms were going to be wrenched from their sockets.

'Only,' said the eagle, rising to give Loki a little respite, 'only if you will swear . . .'

'What?' shouted Loki. 'Anything! Mercy!'

'Only if you will swear to bring Idun and her apples out of Asgard.'

Loki closed his eyes and pressed his lips together and said nothing.

He knew now that the eagle could only be one of the giants, in disguise. The eagle swooped again and Loki could hardly bear the pain as his knee-caps and shins and ankles and toes cracked against rocks and boulders and scree.

'Mercy!' implored Loki. 'I promise you. I swear it.'

'Seven days hence,' said the eagle. 'Lead Idun over Bifrost when the sun is half-way between east and west.'

'I promise,' called Loki.

The Trickster found that his hands were at once set free and he fell to the stony ground. Very slowly he picked himself up and looked at his wounds. Then, in the gathering darkness, he began to limp back towards his companions.

Seven days passed and Loki found Idun wandering through the sloping field above her hall. She was singing softly to herself, and was quite carefree; the sun caressed her. Childlike she moved, untroubled by the world's troubles around her, petty squabbles, suffering, savage wars, and, always, time passing. Her basket of golden apples was looped over one arm.

'Idun!' called Loki.

Bragi's wife paused and turned.

'I've come at once. You can't imagine; I could scarcely believe it myself.'

'Speak more simply,' said Idun.

'Deep in the forest just beyond Bifrost, I came across a tree quite unlike the others. Unlike any tree I've seen in the nine worlds. It stands in a glade and it glows with a soft light.'

Idun opened her grey eyes wide, and Loki went on to describe his find so carefully that anyone less trusting would have known it came straight out of his head.

'Idun, it bears golden apples,' he said, jabbing with his forefinger at one of the apples in the basket. 'The same as yours. And perhaps, like yours, they contain unending youth. We should take them at once for the gods.'

Idun smiled and nodded in agreement.

'Don't forget your own apples. We must compare them,' said Loki, and he led the way over the sunlit field and out of Asgard. They hurried past Heimdall's hall and then Loki took Idun by the hand and walked with her over Bifrost. The flames danced around their feet and they were unharmed.

The eagle was waiting. As soon as Idun set foot in Midgard, it rose from a thicket. It beat its dark wings, swooped on the goddess, and snatched her up. It carried her and her apples straight over the sea to Jotunheim – for as Loki had suspected, the eagle was none other than a giant. It was Thiazi.

Thiazi lifted Idun to his storm-home at Thrymheim, high in the mountains. 'Here you'll stay,' he gloated. 'Without you, without your apples, the gods will age, and I will remain young for ever.'

When they missed Idun, the gods at once grew extremely anxious. They knew that without her magic apples, they would wither and grow old. And, indeed, they soon began to crumple inside their clothes and to seem smaller than they were before. Their skin hung over their bone-houses, bunched or puffy or wrinkled, or stretched so tight that it looked as though the bone would break through. The eyes of one became bloodshot and the eyes of another misty; one god's hands began to tremble, one lost all his hair, and one could not control his bowels. Their joints creaked and ached and they felt utterly limb-weary. The gods felt the spring in their step and the strength in their bodies ebbing from them hour by hour.

Then the minds of the gods lost their skip and started to soften. One became outspoken about the shortcomings of the others and one began to ramble like an idiot, but most of the gods grew quiet and did not trouble to say many things they would have said before. And they were all obsessed by the same concern with time, the same fear. When they did speak, they repeated themselves; or they began sentences and did not complete them. The summer sunlight shone on Asgard, flocculent clouds drifted overhead, and the minds of the gods wandered even as they worried about their old age.

Odin knew he must rally his own strength and summon the gods to council. Everyone in Asgard made his way to Gladsheim, a dismal straggling procession under the sun. Of all the gods and goddesses and their servants, only Idun and Loki were missing.

Allfather looked at the great gathering of stooping, shuffling, mumbling figures. 'We must find Idun,' he called. 'You see how it is without her, without her apples. And it will grow worse. Who was the last to see her?'

'I saw Loki lead Idun over Bifrost,' said Heimdall's servant.

There was a deep silence in Gladsheim. No one doubted then that Loki was the cause of what had happened to them.

'There is only one thing to do,' said Odin. 'We must capture Loki.'

Weary as they were, the gods searched for the Trickster; they looked in every hall and outbuilding, and in every copse and corner of Asgard; they knew their lives depended on it. At last they found him asleep in Idun's own field, and they seized and bound him before he could do anything about it.

Loki was brought to Valaskjalf, protesting, and there Odin at once charged him with leading Idun out of Asgard. 'Bring her back,' said Allfather. 'Your choice is easy to explain and easy to understand. Bring Idun and her apples back. Otherwise we'll put you to death.'

'It is true,' said Loki, 'that I walked out of Asgard with Idun. But then I had no choice.' Loki told them how the eagle that had carried him off when he was trekking with Odin, and Honir was none other than the giant Thiazi. 'And I had to agree to those threats to escape with my life,' said Loki.

'Did you have to fulfil them?' asked Odin.

Loki's eyes gleamed, red and green.

'Since you consort with eagles,' said Odin, 'we'll draw a blood-eagle on your back.'

'No,' said Loki, and he shrank before Odin's savage eye.

'And your rib-cage will spring apart.'

'No,' said Loki, cowering.

'Like wings,' said Odin and his teeth were clenched.

'I will find Idun and her apples,' said Loki. 'If Freyja will lend me her falcon skin, I'll fly at once into Jotunheim. I swear it.'

Then Odin shook and released Loki and Freyja, beautiful Freyja, her face like a pouch now and her hair falling out, went directly to her hall with him. She pulled down the falcon skin hanging over one of the beams.

'You're not quite so beautiful now that you're bald,' said Loki.

Freyja said nothing. Her body shook. She wept tears of gold and handed Loki the falcon skin.

Thrymheim perched on the top of a precipitous sgurr and seemed actually to grow out of the dark rock. The winds whirled round it, and found their way through the walls into the cold, draughty rooms. When Loki reached it in the early evening, he was fortunate enough to find the giant Thiazi was not at home. He had gone off fishing, and his daughter Skadi had gone with him.

Loki discovered Idun in a smoky room, huddled over a fire. She turned to him and at once the schemer extended his falcon wings; he murmured the runes, the magic words, and turned Idun into a nut. Then he picked her up between his claws and flew off as fast as he could.

In a little time, Thiazi and his daughter returned from the day's fishing. When the giant found that Idun was no longer there, he roared and hurled his pails to the ground. He knew there was no way in which the goddess could have escaped from Thrymheim without help.

Then Thiazi donned his eagle skin for a third time and set off across the mountains and the high lifeless wilderness. The distance from Thrymheim to Asgard was immense and the eagle was stronger than the falcon. As Loki drew closer to Asgard, so Thiazi drew closer to Loki.

When he sat in Hlidskjalf looking over the nine worlds, nothing escaped Odin: no movement of man or giant or elf or dwarf, bird in the air or animal on earth or fish in the water. What other gods could not see at all, Allfather fixed and followed with his single eye. Now he saw Loki flying at great speed towards Asgard and the eagle Thiazi chasing him. At once he ordered all the gods and goddesses and their servants, worn out and short-winded as they were, to hurry out of Asgard with bundles of plane shavings, all the wood that the servants of the gods prepared to kindle fires in their great halls. 'Pile them up against the walls,' said Odin. 'Loki is coming.'

The still summer air began to hum, as if an unseen storm were near and about to burst on them. It began to throb and then the gods and goddesses saw the falcon, and the huge eagle close behind it. From a great height the falcon dived down over the walls of Asgard, still holding the nut between its claws. 'Light the shavings!' cried Odin. 'The shavings!'

The flames leaped up, almost unseen in the bright sunlight. The eagle was so close behind the falcon that he could not stop himself; he flew straight through the flames; his wings caught fire. Thiazi blundered on into Asgard, and fell to the ground in torment. Then the gods stumbled back through the gates into their citadel and quickly killed him there.

Loki threw off Freyja's falcon skin. He looked at the grey, aged, anxious ones pressing around him, and scornfully laughed in their faces. Then the Sky Traveller bent over his trophy; he cradled it between his hands and softly spoke the runes.

Idun stood there, young and supple and smiling. She moved innocent among the ailing gods. She offered them apples.

For note on this myth see page 194.

9 *The Marriage of Njord and Skadi*

BEYOND THE GIRDLE of flint-grey water and the loveless lava flows, beyond the burning blue crevasses, lay Thrymheim, the storm-home of Skadi and her father Thiazi. It was a wonder that the hall withstood the charges of the wind and the batteries of hail.

Thiazi was not there; he had gone in pursuit of his prisoner Idun, the goddess who had escaped him. Skadi waited for them to return and, as the sun slipped over the horizon, the sky in the west seemed to catch fire and blazed.

The white night dallied and yielded; another dawdling day passed and still Thiazi and his captive did not come back. Then Skadi was alarmed and thought the gods must have ambushed him; even as she waited, she knew in her heart that she would never see her father again.

Skadi's pale eyes gleamed. She grew cold with anger, then icy with fury. She swore vengeance on his murderers.

Skadi walked from chill room to chill room in Thrymheim. She donned a coat of mail and a helmet and chose the finest of her father's weapons: a sword engraved with magic serpentine patterning, a spear with a shaft of ash, a circular shield covered with hide and inlaid with birds of prey – gleaming gold eyes and gaping red beaks. Then she set out for Asgard.

Now that Idun walked among them again and the giant Thiazi was dead, now that they had recovered the apples of youth, the Aesir were carefree once more. They were aware of the clement sun as if they had never felt it on their backs before; they listened to each note of each birdcall, and watched every grassblade growing. They felt at peace with themselves again, and at peace with each other.

When Heimdall saw Skadi nearing the walls of Asgard and raised the alarm, the gods had no wish to see more blood spilt, or to prolong the feud. Some of them gathered and met the giantess and asked her, 'Will you take gold for your father's death?'

'What good would that be?' asked Skadi. 'Have you never heard of my father's wealth? When his father Olvaldi died, he and his brothers Idi and Gang came into a gold hoard. They measured it out in mouthfuls, so as to share it fairly. And whatever belonged to my father now belongs to me. No, I will not take gold.'

'What will you take?' asked the gods.

'A husband,' said Skadi, and she looked long at Balder, fairest, most gentle and wise of the gods. 'I'll settle for a husband and a bellyful of laughter.'

Then the gods conferred and agreed that Skadi could choose a husband from amongst them as payment. They did, however, make one condition. 'You must choose him by his feet,' said Odin. 'Until you've chosen, that is all you'll be able to see of him.'

Skadi was not unwilling and Odin arranged for all the gods to gather in a courtyard so that the giantess could make her choice. Shielding her eyes from all but the gods' feet, Skadi lost no time but at once chose the most shapely pair of feet, believing that they would naturally belong to Balder, the most handsome of the gods.

'A good choice,' said Odin.

Skadi quickly looked up and gazed into the friendly, knowing eyes not of Balder but of the lord of seafarers and sea harvests, the god Njord. His skin was weathered and he had the clear gaze of one who has spent long at sea; he even smelt of salt.

Skadi was startled. She stepped back, and her icy look killed Njord's smile. 'I thought . . .' she began.

'Think carefully,' said Njord. 'Remember the words you speak now are the beginning of a marriage.'

'I've been tricked,' said Skadi bitterly.

'You might have chosen Loki,' replied Njord unperturbed.

'So you have your husband then,' said Odin. 'A fair reward for your father's death; many would say, indeed, the better of the bargain.'

'You've forgotten the laughter,' said Skadi.

'That's easily put right,' said Odin.

Skadi shook her head. 'Since my father died, I've brimmed with anger or been drained by fatigue. I'll never laugh again.'

'Where's the Trickster?' asked Odin.

Loki stepped forward rather less jauntily than usual. He wondered whether Skadi knew that he had not only helped her father to steal the apples, but helped the gods to recover them too, and so brought about her father's death.

'Can you make this lady laugh?' said Odin. 'If anyone can you can.'

'Not I, sir . . .' stammered the Sly God, as if he were some peasant standing before the High One. 'Not before I've told you what happened, sir . . .' Loki produced a long leather thong from behind his back. 'It was like this. I was going to market and I wanted to take that goat there along with me.' Loki winked at Skadi. 'You know how goats are, don't you, lady? They have ideas of their own.'

Loki stumbled across the courtyard where all the gods and Skadi were assembled, and tied one end of the thong to the goat's beard. Both my hands were full, lady. I was carrying produce to the market. So I tied this goat to a tegument . . .'

'A tegument?' said Skadi.

'Lady,' said Loki, 'my testicles!' And he looped the thong behind his scrotum. The goat moved a little further off to nibble at new grass, and the thong linking them tightened.

'Early in the morning it was, lady,' said Loki. 'Ah! Very early. The goatsuckers were still singing . . .' The Trickster cupped his hands to his mouth, closed his eyes, and made a magical soft whirring sound. 'Rrrr . . . rrrrrrr . . . rrrrrrr . . . OWK!' squawked Loki, as the goat suddenly yanked the thong.

'Owk!' squawked the goat as Loki pulled back. It was a tug of war. And when the goat gave way, it gave way so completely, bounding towards Loki, that he fell backwards into Skadi's arms.

And Skadi laughed; despite herself she laughed, and for a while she forgave Loki everything because of her laughter.

'Playing the goat,' said Loki, panting.

'Enough,' said Allfather. 'I've a mind to please Skadi further.' Then Odin took two liquid marbles from his gown and Skadi recognised her father's eyes.

'But look!' cried Odin.

He hurled the balls into heaven. 'Two stars,' he said. 'Your father will look down on you and on us all, for as long as the world lasts.'

Then Njord asked Skadi to go with him to his hall, the shipyard Noatun, but Skadi said she would only live with Njord in her old home, Thrymheim. 'Since neither of us is going to get his way entirely,' said Njord, 'we had better agree to take turns: nine nights in one place, then nine nights in the other.'

Then Njord and Skadi left the courtyard and the kingdom of Asgard, and made their way to Jotunheim. They climbed over rock and scree, and through sheets of snow too bright for the eye when the sun shone on them, a dreary uniform wasteland when clouds masked the sun. And the higher they climbed into a frozen world as still as death itself, the happier Skadi became. In Thrymheim, she gave herself to Njord. After nine nights, however, Njord admitted that he had no love for the icy mountains. 'And,' he said, 'I think the howling of wolves sounds ugly compared to the hooping of swans.'

Then Njord and Skadi came back to Asgard and passed nine nights at Noatun, and Skadi's dislike of the fertile, rocking sea was no less great than Njord's dislike of the barren mountains. 'I cannot even sleep here,' she said. 'There's too much noise in the shipyard, and too much noise from the harbour – boats putting out, boats coming in, the unloading of fish. And the mewing gulls disturb me, flying in at dawn from deep waters.'

It was not long then before Njord and Skadi decided that the gap between their taste was so great that, although they were married, they must live apart. Njord stayed at Noatun and Skadi returned to Thrymheim.

The giantess covered great distances on her skis; her quiver was always at her side and she hunted and shot wild animals. The ski goddess, that crouched dark shape sweeping across the desolate snow-scapes, took injury and death wherever she went. She had been touched by the god of plenty; she had yielded a little, and then frozen again.

For note on this myth see page 195.

10 *The Treasures of the Gods*

SOMEHOW THE SHAPE-CHANGER got into Sif's locked bedroom. Smiling to himself, he pulled out a curved knife and moved to her bedside. Thor's wife was breathing deeply, evenly, dead to worldly sorrows. Then Loki raised his knife. With quick deft strokes he lopped off Sif's head of shining hair – her hair which as she moved rippled and gleamed and changed from gold to gold like swaying corn. Sif murmured but she did not wake; the hair left on her cropped head stuck up like stubble.

Loki scooped up the skeins. He dropped Sif's sheen hair to the floor, a soft glowing mass. The Trickster looked at it and grinned; then he left Sif's bedroom.

'A joke,' protested Loki, dangling a foot off the ground.

'What kind of a joke?' shouted Thor, not loosening his grip for one moment.

'Only a joke,' whined the Sky Traveller.

All morning Sif had sobbed and sobbed. She knew and Thor knew that only Loki would have shorn her hair. 'Well, what are you going to do about it?' demanded Thor.

'I'll replace it,' yelped Loki. 'I'll get help from the dwarfs. I promise to replace it.'

'Or else,' said Thor, and he dumped Loki on the ground.

Loki raised both hands and cautiously explored the top of his head.

'Or else,' Thor said, 'I'll smash every bone in your body.'

Loki straightened his clothes and smoothed his hair and then suddenly he winked at Thor. He hurried out of Asgard, over Bifrost, and down into the land of the dark elves. He picked his way through a chain of chilly potholes, and he skirted dark and shining pools, until he reached a great cave, the home of the sons of Ivaldi.

The sly god explained to the two dwarfs the reasons for his journey, without finding he need describe just how Sif had lost her hair. 'Only you dwarfs are skilled enough smiths,' he said, 'and only the sons of

48

Ivaldi could spin gold as fine as Sif's hair and imbue it with such magic that it will grow on her head.'

'What will we get out of this?' was all that the sons of Ivaldi wanted to know.

'The thanks of Sif and Thor and the friendship of the gods,' said Loki. 'That counts for a great deal. And, above that, I give you my oath that I'll repay you in full measure when you have need of me.'

The dwarfs could see that although Loki offered nothing but promises, they were likely to get the better of the bargain, since the most they could lose was a little effort and a few ounces of gold. They piled wood on to the furnace in the corner of their cave, and while one dwarf worked the bellows, the other began to hammer and spin the gold. Loki watched and marvelled, and his eyes flickered red and green in the firelight.

The sons of Ivaldi made a long wave of fine golden strands and, as they worked, they murmured spells over them. The hair hung over Loki's outstretched arm like a single shining sheet and yet a breath of air was enough to ruffle it.

'To waste this blaze is to no one's advantage,' said one of the dwarfs.

'We can please the gods at no further expense,' said the other.

So the sons of Ivaldi set to work again and, before the furnace had begun to lose any of its heat, they fashioned a marvellous ship for Freyr called Skidbladnir and forged for Odin a spear called Gungnir, as strong as it was slender. Then the two dwarfs gave Loki the ship and the spear and explained their magic power. As usual Loki was at no loss for words – his mouth was full of air, thanks and compliments and promises to hurry back with news of what the gods thought of such gifts.

On his way back through the dismal underground caverns, Loki had an idea. He did not head straight for the welcoming light of Midgard, but turned down a long aisle studded with rock pillars and, carrying his three treasures, walked into the hall of Brokk and Eitri.

The dwarf brothers stood up to greet Loki. But when they saw the skein of hair and the ship and the spear, they ignored him entirely. Their hearts quickened and their fingertips tingled. Loki let them take the treasures out of his hands and turn them over and over, watching their scorn and envy grow.

'Have you ever seen such work?' exclaimed Loki. 'Such perfect craftsmanship?'

'Yes,' said Brokk.

'Whose?' asked Loki.

'My own,' said Eitri bluntly.

'Well then,' said Loki slowly, as if the thought were just forming in his mind, 'you think you could make treasures as fine as these?'

'Not as fine . . .' Brokk said.

'Finer,' said Eitri.

'No,' said Loki craftily. 'Surely not. I'll stake my head on it. Brokk, I'll stake my head that your brother can't forge treasures the like of these.'

Brokk and Eitri were very eager to take up this challenge. It occurred to them that if they were as good as their boast, not only would they be rid of the schemer Loki but the treasures made by the sons of Ivaldi would be theirs for the taking.

Leaving Loki with a horn full of mead and with orders only to wait, Eitri and Brokk stumped across their hall and through an arch into the rocky alcove that was their smithy. At once Brokk began to pile wood on to the furnace while Eitri hammered and rolled a length of gold wire and cut it into hundreds of short pieces. Then Eitri laid a pigskin on the roaring fire and said to Brokk, 'Pump the bellows now. Whatever happens, keep pumping until I pull this treasure out of the forge.'

A little while after Eitri had walked out of the smithy, a fly alighted on Brokk's leathery hand. It stung him. Brokk glanced down but did not pause; he kept pumping the bellows, and when Eitri returned he pulled Gullinbursti out of the forge, a boar with bristles of gold.

Now Eitri picked a great block of unflawed gold. He heated the metal until it was glowing and malleable. Then he hammered it into shape and put it back into the furnace. 'Pump the bellows now,' said Eitri. 'Whatever happens, keep pumping until I pull this treasure out of the forge.'

A little while after Eitri had left the smithy, the same fly returned and settled on Brokk's neck. It stung him twice as sharply as before. Brokk winced and flinched but he did not pause; he kept pumping the bellows, and when Eitri returned he took Draupnir out of the forge, an arm-ring of solid gold.

Now Eitri humped a great hunk of iron across the smithy and into the furnace. He heated it and hammered it. He struck at it and shaped it, he reshaped it, he tapped and tapped at it. His body ached, he streamed with sweat and, when he was ready, his head and heart were both banging with his own efforts. 'Pump the bellows now,' said Eitri. 'It will all be wrecked if you stop pumping.'

Very soon after Eitri had walked wearily out of the smithy, and looked around for their visitor, the fly buzzed through the arch into the alcove. This time it settled between Brokk's eyes, and at once it stung him on both eyelids. The dwarf was blinded with blood. He could not see what he was doing. For a moment he took a hand off the bellows, so that they caught their breath, to brush the fly off his forehead and the blood out of his eyes. Then the Shape Changer, Loki, for the fly was none other, returned to his waiting place and his horn of mead.

At this moment Eitri hurried back into the smithy. 'What has happened?' he shouted. He peered into the furnace. 'So nearly,' he said. He peered into the flames again and his glittering grey eyes did not even reflect them. 'So very nearly spoiled.' Then Eitri pulled from the forge an iron hammer, massive and finely forged, but rather short in the handle. He called it Mjollnir. Eitri and Brokk stared at it, they stared at each other, they slowly nodded.

'Take this hammer and this ring and this boar,' said Eitri. 'Tell the gods the mysteries of these treasures. Go with Loki to Asgard and claim that schemer's head.'

Brokk and Eitri walked out of the alcove and found the Sly One, the Shape Changer, waiting for them, smiling. He cast an eye over their three treasures. 'Ready?' he said.

Loki and Brokk made their way slowly across the shining fields of Asgard, laden with their treasures. Word of their coming ran ahead of them, and they were met in Gladsheim by all the gods, sitting in their high places. Loki at once told of his visit to the world of the dwarfs, and boasted that he had been able to exploit the dwarfs' envy and greed to secure six gifts for the gods.

'Talk while you can,' said Brokk. 'Soon you'll have no tongue.'

It was agreed that Odin and Thor and Freyr should decide whether Eitri or the sons of Ivaldi were the finer smiths, and Loki began to display his treasures.

'This spear,' he said, 'is for you, Odin. It is Gungnir. It differs from other spears in this way: it never misses its mark.' The Father of Battle took the spear and raised it and looked around the hall. Nobody could withstand his terrible gaze. 'You may want to use it,' Loki said, 'to stir up warfare in the world of men.'

Then Loki turned to Freyr. 'This vessel is for you, Freyr. It is Skidbladnir. As you can see, it's large enough to hold all of the gods, fully armed. As soon as you hoist its sail, a breeze will spring up and fill it, and urge the boat forward. But when you have no need of it, you can take it apart.' Loki swiftly dismasted and dismantled the boat until the pieces were together no larger than a piece of cloth. 'You can fold it up like this,' said Loki, 'and put it in your purse!'

'My third gift,' said the schemer, 'I owe to you, Sif.' He showed the skein of flowing golden hair to the goddess. 'As soon as you lift this to your head, it will take root and grow. You'll be no less beautiful than you were before.'

Thor's wife took the hair from Loki. She fingered it, she turned it over and over, then she slowly raised it to her head. There was a shout of joy in Gladsheim; it was just as Loki said.

Now Brokk produced his gifts. 'This gold arm-ring is for you, Odin,' he said. 'It is Draupnir. There is a little more to it than it seems. Eight rings of its own weight will drop from it on every ninth night.'

Then Brokk turned to Freyr. 'This boar is for you. He is Gullinbursti. He can charge over earth, air and sea alike, and no horse can keep up with him. And no matter where he goes, running through the night or plunging into the gloom under all the worlds, he'll always be surrounded by brilliant light. He carries it himself because his bristles shine in the dark.'

'My third treasure,' said Brokk, 'is for you, Thor. This is the hammer Mjollnir. You can use it against anything, and use it with all your strength. Nothing can ever break it.' The Storm God eagerly grasped the hammer and listened. 'Even if you hurl it, you'll never lose it. No matter how far you fling it, it will always return to your hand. And should you need to hide it, you can make it small enough to tuck inside your shirt.' All the gods stared at Mjollnir, astounded, and knew what powerful magic must have gone into its making. 'It has only one small flaw,' added Brokk, 'not that it matters. Its handle is rather short.'

Odin and Thor and Freyr wasted no time in giving their answer. All three were of one mind, that wondrous though all the treasures were, the hammer Mjollnir was the most valuable because it alone could guard the gods against the giants.

'You, Brokk,' said Odin, 'have won the wager.'

'Loki's head,' shrieked Brokk.

'Wait!' cried Loki. 'What would you do with my head? I'll give you its weight in gold instead.'

'There's no future in that,' said Brokk. 'And no future for you.'

The gods in Gladsheim laughed to see the Trickster cornered.

'Well,' said Loki slowly, 'well . . . catch me then!' He darted through the doors of the hall and made off as fast as he could. By the time Brokk had made a move to stop him, the Sky Traveller was already well on his way, wearing his shoes with which he could fly over land and water. The gods in Gladsheim laughed all the louder.

'If you had any honour, you'd help me,' shrieked the dwarf. 'Thor, help me!'

Thor was in no mood to see Brokk humiliated. He leaped up from his high seat and stormed out of Gladsheim. The gods and Brokk waited, and after a while Thor returned, dragging Loki after him.

'Not so fast!' said Loki, raising a hand, as Brokk started towards him. 'It's true you have a claim on my head. But of course you can't have any part of my neck.'

The gods grinned and nodded, and Brokk saw that Loki had got the better of him.

'In that case,' said Brokk, 'since your head is mine, at least I'll stop your sweet talk. I'll sew your lips together.'

Loki shrugged his shoulders. 'Nothing but fine words!' he said.

Brokk unwound a thong from round his waist and tried to skewer Loki's lips with his knife. That was no good. Sharp as the point was, the dwarf could not even draw a drop of blood.

'I could certainly do with my brother's awl,' said Brokk. No sooner had he spoken than Eitri's awl lay at his feet. Brokk picked it up, and it proved sharp enough to pierce Loki's lips. The dwarf drew the leather thong through the holes and sewed up the Trickster's mouth.

Loki ran out of Gladsheim. He ripped the thong out through the holes, and yelped at the pain of it. Then for some while the Schemer stood listening to the hum inside the hall – the hive of happiness. He began to dream of revenge, and slowly his lips curled into a twisted smile.

For note on this myth see page 196.

11 *Skirnir's Journey*

FREYR HAD NO BUSINESS to be in Odin's hall, Valaskjalf. And he had no right at all to sit in the high seat Hlidskjalf and look out over all the worlds. That was the right only of Odin and his wife Frigg.

Freyr narrowed his eyes and looked north into Jotunheim. What did he see? A large handsome hall belonging to the giant Gymir. And what did he see next? A woman coming out of this hall. Her name was Gerd – she was Gymir's daughter. She seemed to be made of light, or clothed in sparkling light. When she raised her arms to close the hall doors, the dome of the sky and the sea surrounding the earth at once grew brighter. Because of her, all the worlds were hidden in a flash of brilliant icy light.

Freyr looked and longed. The more he looked, the more he was unable not to look. His eyes burned like fireballs; his only desire was to win Gerd. Freyr gazed at her until she had crossed a courtyard into her own hall. The worlds grew shadowy and the god lowered his eyes; then he left Hlidskjalf and crept out of the hall.

The God of the World paid for presuming to sit in Hlidskjalf. He ached with an endless sad longing. He spoke to no one and wanted no one to speak to him. He could not sleep. He did not want to eat. He did not want to drink. He could neither escape his fierce desire, nor see how to satisfy it.

Njord, Freyr's father, became concerned about his son. He called for Freyr's servant, shining Skirnir, and told him: 'Go and ask my son what has upset him. Why is he so angry, or else so sad, that he will not even share his feelings and set them free?'

'I will ask him that,' said Skirnir, 'but I won't like the answer.'

Skirnir approached Freyr and said to him, 'First of the Gods, why must you stay here in your hall, day in and day out, without food or drink or sleep? Why do you shun company?'

'What good would it do?' said Freyr. 'No amount of talk can help, nothing can blunt this anguish. And what if the elf-beams do shine every day? My mind is full of gloom.'

'There is no grief so great you cannot tell it to me,' said Skirnir. 'We were children together. We've always trusted one another.'

Then Freyr unlocked his word-hoard. He told Skirnir how he had seen Gerd from Hlidskjalf, and how she brightened the nine worlds with her radiance, and how he longed for her. 'No man,' he said, 'has ever loved a woman as I love her. And no god would ever agree to our union.'

Skirnir listened and nodded.

'Go!' said Freyr. 'Whether her father likes it or not, bring her to me here, and I'll give you great rewards.

Skirnir smiled. 'Give me the horse that follows its nose through the dark, and will not bridle at magic, flickering flames. And give me the sword that will fight against giants of its own accord.'

Then Freyr handed over two of his greatest treasures. He lived to regret that: at Ragnarok, a sword to ward off the fire-demon Surt would have been handy.

Skirnir mounted and made off at once. As he galloped out of Freyr's courtyard, his horse's hooves struck fire from the paving stones. He came to the banks of the Iving in the early evening. Skirnir was ferried across the river into Jotunheim, and then night fell. 'Can you feel this darkness pressing against us?' said Skirnir to the horse, and they galloped across lifeless flatland. 'Now we must head for the fells, where the frost giants live. You and I share the same fate. We'll either get home again quickly, or we'll fall into the hands of some dreadful troll.'

Skirnir rode through the night, and during the night he and his mount galloped up a mountain pass and came to a curtain of fire. Freyr's horse did not even break its pace and galloped straight through the searing magic flames. At daybreak Skirnir, the Shining One, came down into a saucer of land covered with sour grey grass. It was a loveless kind of place, surrounded by desolate hills that welled like breasts and were pocked by outcrops of rock. In the middle of this depression stood Gymir's hall and, next to it, his daughter Gerd's hall, guarded by a fence. A pair of hounds were chained to the gateposts, and they were not pleasant.

Skirnir looked around and saw a single herdsman sitting way up on the hillside. He turned away from the halls and rode up to him. 'Nothing escapes your eye,' Skirnir said, 'sitting here on this hill. Tell me, how can I muzzle those hounds and enter Gerd's hall?'

The herdsman looked at Skirnir and said stonily. 'Are you doomed to die? Or are you dead already? There's no way in which you can talk to Gymir's daughter, this year or next year or ever.'

Skirnir could see that the herdsman did not mean to help him. He wheeled away without more ado and, as he galloped down the slope again, called out over his shoulder, 'Fearlessness is better than a faint heart for any man who puts his nose out of doors. The length of my life and the day of my death were fated long ago.'

In her hall, fair Gerd heard the coming and going, barking and shouting, and asked her servant, 'What is all that noise that echoes round these walls? The ground shakes; the hall itself shudders.'

'A man outside the fence. He's dismounting now. And now he has set his horse to graze.'

'Welcome him, then,' said Gerd coldly. 'My heart says this visitor is my brother's murderer. Nevertheless tell him a horn of mead awaits him in this hall.'

So Skirnir passed unharmed between the disappointed hounds and walked into the hall; it was colder in there than he would have wished.

Dressed entirely in white, Gerd came forward to welcome him. 'Are you one of the elves? Or one of the gods? How were you able to pass through the flickering flames to these halls?'

'I'm no elf,' said Skirnir, 'and I'm no god, though it's true that I've come through the fire curtain.' He looked at Gerd and dipped his hands into the pockets of his cloak. 'These,' he said, 'these are eleven of the apples of youth. They're yours, Gerd. I'll give them all to you if you'll promise yourself to Freyr and call him your darling dear.'

'Never,' said Gerd icily. 'No one is going to buy my love with golden apples and promises of youth. And however long we live, Freyr and I will never share one roof.'

Skirnir reached into the pocket of his cloak again. 'I've brought you this arm-ring,' he said. 'It is Draupnir. Long ago Odin placed it on Balder's pyre. Eight rings of its own weight drop from it on every ninth night.'

'Be that as it may, I have no wish for it,' said Gerd, and her voice chilled Skirnir to the marrow. 'There's wealth enough in Gymir's hall.'

Skirnir continued to smile. 'You see this honed and gleaming sword here in my hand? I'm going to hack off your head unless you do as I ask.'

'Force will get Freyr nowhere,' said Gerd. Her cold eyes glittered. 'Neither Freyr nor anybody else. But if my father Gymir finds you here, I'm sure he'll be glad to flex his muscles.'

Skirnir was undaunted. 'Look again at this honed and gleaming sword. The old giant will fall to his knees before this blade; your father is doomed to die.' Then Skirnir laid down Freyr's sword and raised his own staff. Gerd gazed at it spellbound. 'I will touch you, Gerd, with this magic staff. I will teach you and tame you. You must make your way to the place where you'll never meet and never talk to any man again. You will sit on the eagle's hill at the end of heaven and stare down at Hel's gates. And although you must eat, all food will seem as vile to you as the sallow snake seems to men.

'You'll become a sight to make our blood run cold. The frost giant Hrimnir will gape at you. You'll become better known than the watchman of the gods as you peer out, bleakly, from your windy penthouse.

'Rage and longing, tears and torment will rack you. However you twist and turn, you'll not escape your fate: a troubled heart, a double portion of misery.

'Here in Jotunheim, spiteful spirits will pick at you and prick you every day, and every day you will crawl to the halls of frost giants – crawl for no purpose, and crawl without even hope.

'While others are glad, you will grieve, your body will shake with sobs. You'll live always amongst three-headed giants and never once sleep with a husband. May lust grip you! May despair sap you! Be like thistle tossed into the hayloft and trampled underfoot!

'I went to the dark wood, the dripping forest, to find a magic branch. I found this staff. The greatest of the gods, Odin, is enraged with you. Freyr will lose no love for you. Gerd, worst of women, you have unleashed the wrath of all the gods.

'Frost giants, listen! Rock giants, listen! Sons of Suttung, listen! And hear me, gods in Asgard! I forbid this woman to meet with any man. I forbid this woman joy of any man.

'Hrimgrimnir, pale and unearthly in his shroud of frost, is the giant who will enjoy you in the gloom near Hel's gates. Under the roots of Yggdrasill, foul corpses will press on you horns full of piss. However great your thirst, that is the best drink there will be for you. That is my curse!

'Gerd, I have inscribed a charm for you, sealed with three runes: longing and raving and lust. But what I have written, I can erase, if I have good reason.'

As she listened to Skirnir's spells, Gerd began to tremble terribly. At length she raised her eyes, slowly, and gazed at her guest.

'Skirnir,' she said, 'you are welcome here. Drink from this frost-cup filled with mead for you.' Now her eyes no longer glittered like broken ice; they were filled with tears. 'I never believed,' she said, 'that I should swear to love one of the Vanir.'

Skirnir lowered his staff and took the frost-cup. 'Before I ride home, I must know everything. When will you meet the son of Njord?'

'There is a forest, Barri, that we both know well. It is beautiful there, and peaceful. And there Gerd will give herself to the son of Njord nine nights hence.'

Then Skirnir bowed. He took his leave of Gerd and walked out of her chilly hall. He called his horse to him, remounted and rode swiftly back to Asgard before it was morning.

Sleepless, Freyr heard him coming. He stood outside his hall, impatient and anxious.

Skirnir smiled and, taking his time, dismounted.

'Skirnir! Before you unsaddle, before you go a foot further, tell me! Were you successful? Have you brought ecstasy or anguish out of Jotunheim?'

The god and his servant stood in a shaft of soft orange light near the entrance to Freyr's hall. Skirnir gathered his cloak around him and looked at Freyr. 'There is a forest, Barri, that we both know well. It is beautiful there, and peaceful. And there Gerd will give herself to the son of Njord nine nights hence.'

'One night is long,' cried Freyr, 'and two nights are longer. How can I bear three? How can I . . .' He raised his arms and threw back his head and closed his eyes. 'Often enough I've thought a whole month shorter than half one such night, charged with this desire.'

For note on this myth see page 199.

# 12 *The Lay of Grimnir*

H RAUDUNG, KING OF THE GOTHS, had two sons, Agnar and Geirrod. One day when Agnar was ten winters old and Geirrod eight, the brothers gathered their tackle and went out rowing in the hope of landing some fish. But soon the wind began to bluster, and the boys were driven so far out to sea that they lost sight of land. The night-shadow grew long, and in the darkness the small boat tossed and spun and was smashed to pieces on a rocky shore. Standing bedraggled in the darkness, with waves breaking around them, Agnar and Geirrod had not the least idea where they were.

Next morning the two boys found a poor peasant and stayed with him and his wife through the winter. The woman busied herself with Agnar, and the man looked after the younger, Geirrod, and taught him many things. They often walked over the land together, and what they said to each other only they knew. When the spring came, the peasant gave Geirrod the new boat that he had carved, carpentered and pitched during the winter.

Then one day the man and his wife walked with the boys down to the shore and the man took Geirrod aside, put an arm round his shoulders, and had a few words with him. Agnar and Geirrod stepped aboard and, helped by a fair wind, and acting on the advice the couple had given them, they had the good fortune to fetch up again at their father's landing stage.

Geirrod was in the prow of the boat. He snatched the oars and jumped out. Then he gave the boat a great shove, and yelled 'Go where the trolls will get you!' His elder brother Agnar and the little boat drifted back out to sea.

When Geirrod walked into King Hraudung's hall, he found that his father had died during that winter. He was surrounded by a great company, eager to know where he had been, marvelling that he had come back, shaking their heads when they heard from Geirrod that his elder brother Agnar, heir to the throne, had been drowned months before. Then Geirrod was acknowledged as king of the Goths; his father's retainers now swore loyalty to him. And great things were

59

expected of him as Hraudung's son – all the more so after such a wondrous return. But the older Geirrod grew, the greater his faults became. It was not long before his nature – his sudden fits of anger and his cruelty and tyranny – became known throughout the Norse lands.

Odin and Frigg sat in the high seat, Hlidskjalf, and looked out over the worlds.

'Do you see Agnar?' said Odin, 'your foster-son? He's coupling with a giantess in a cave. He's fathering brutes. But my ward, Geirrod, is a king. He rules over a great country.'

'He's so miserly,' Frigg replied, 'that if guests visit him when he is already entertaining, he pretends to welcome them and then has them tortured.'

'That is nothing but vile slander,' said Odin.

Odin and Frigg agreed to put things to the test and Frigg swiftly sent her maidservant Fulla to Midgard with a message for Geirrod.

'Beware,' said Fulla, 'of a magician who has come to your country and means to lay a spell on you. You will know him in this way: even the fiercest dog will not leap at him.'

Now, in fact, it was a slander that Geirrod was unwelcoming. For all his untrustworthiness, his moods and his violence, he was generous and kept an open house. All the same, he heeded Fulla's warning and told his followers to detain the traveller whom no dog would attack. It was not long before this man turned up at Geirrod's hall; he wore a dark blue cloak and said his name was Grimnir, the Hooded One. That, however, is all Grimnir would say. When he declined to explain where he had come from or where he was going, or to declare his purpose, or to exchange any other common courtesies, Geirrod became angry. He remembered Fulla's warning. 'If you will not speak,' he said, 'you must have reason not to.'

Still Grimnir said nothing.

'If you will not speak of your own free will,' he said, 'I will make you speak.'

And still Grimnir said nothing.

Then the king had Grimnir trussed and slung between two roasting fires, like a pig on a spit. 'Until you talk,' said Geirrod.

Grimnir hung between the fires for eight nights, and said nothing.

King Geirrod had a son ten winters old, called Agnar after his brother. Everyone loved him: his father, the king; the retainers and their ladies; the servants in the court. When he saw how Grimnir was suffering, he suffered with him. And when everyone else in the hall was drunk and snoring, Agnar approached Grimnir and offered him a brimming horn. He said his father was wrong to torture Grimnir without cause.

Grimnir gratefully drained the horn. The fires had crept so close that they singed the cloak on his back. Then Grimnir began to talk. 'Fall back, fire! You are too fierce. My cloak is smouldering, flames scorch the fur. For eight nights now I've waited here, and I've been ignored by all except Agnar. Geirrod's son will be hailed as ruler of all the Goths and Burgundians.

'Greetings, Agnar! The Lord of Men greets you. You'll never be better rewarded for the gift of a single drink.

'Listen now! Where gods and elves live the land is hallowed; and Thor will live in Thrudheim until all the gods are destroyed. The other gods have halls too. The first is called Ydalir, dales where yews grow, and Ull lives there. The second is Alfheim, where the light elves live. The gods gave that place to Freyr when he cut his first tooth. The third is called Valaskjalf, Hall of the Slain; one god built it for himself, and with their own hands the others thatched it with silver. The fourth is Sokkvabekk, the sinking floor – it is lapped on all sides by cool murmuring water and there, every day, Odin and Saga drink joyfully from gold goblets.

'The fifth is Gladsheim, home of gladness, and Valhalla stands near by, vast and gold-bright. Odin presides there, and day by day he chooses slain men to join him. Every morning they arm themselves and fight in the great courtyard and kill one another; every evening they rise again, ride back to the hall, and feast. That hall is easily recognised: its roof is made of shields and its rafters are spears. Breast-plates litter the benches. A wolf lurks at the western door, and an eagle hovers over it. Andhrimnir the cook, smutty with soot, boils the boar Saehrimnir's flesh in a great blackened cauldron. That is the finest of all food, though few men get to taste it. The War Father feeds his wolves, Freki and Geri, with hunks of meat; but wine alone is always enough for Odin's own needs. Every morning the two ravens, Huginn and Muninn, are loosed and fly over Midgard; I always fear that Thought may fail to wing his way home, but my fear for Memory is greater. The torrent Thund roars beside Valgrind, Valhalla's outer gate, and the sun – the fish of the wolf – dances in the water. The river looks so deep and wild that the slain fear they will not be able to wade across it. Behind Valgrind are the sacred inner doors; and although the gate is age-old, few know how to bolt it. Valhalla itself has five hundred and forty doors, and when the time comes to fight against Fenrir, eight hundred warriors will march out of each door, shoulder to shoulder.

' 'The sixth is Thrymheim, the place of uproar set in the mountains. That's where the great giant Thiazi lived. Now it's owned by his daughter, fair Skadi – she was Njord's bride. The seventh is Breidablik, Broad Splendour: Balder has set up his hall there in beautiful country, blessed and untainted by any evil.

'The eighth is Himinbjorg, the Cliffs of Heaven, and Heimdall is master of it. The watchman of the gods sits in his fine hall, drinking mead. The ninth is Folkvang, the Field of Folk, and Freyja decides who shall enter Sessrumnir, the hall there. Every day she shares the slain with Odin.

'The tenth is Glitnir. It has pillars of red gold and its roof is inlaid with silver. That's where Forseti is most often found, sitting in judgement and resolving strife. The eleventh is the harbour Noatun, and Njord, blameless ruler of men, presides there in his high-timbered temple. The twelfth is Vidi where Vidar lives, a land of long grass and saplings. But that brave god will leap down from his steed when he has to avenge his father's death.

'The goat grazing outside Valhalla is called Heidrun. She nibbles the shelterer Laerad's branches and every day she is milked and fills a great pitcher with fine, clear mead; that pitcher seems quite bottomless. And the deer wandering outside Valhalla is Oak-thorned; he nibbles the branches of Laerad too, and from his horns a stream drops into Hvergelmir, the Roaring Cauldron. That is the spring from which runs every river in the nine worlds.

'Listen to their names! Slow and Broad, Sekin and Ekin, Cool and Loud-bubbling, Battle Defiant, Fjorn and Rin and Rinnandi, Gipul and Gopul the torrent, Old and Spear-teeming, Vin and Holl and Tholl, Grod and Gunnthorin: these are the rivers that make their way across the fair fields of Asgard.

'But that is not all: Vin and Vegsvin that knows where to go, Nyt and Naut and the river that sweeps people away, Nonn and Hronn, Slid and Hrid, Sylg and Ylg, Vid and Van, Vond and Strond, Gjoll and Leipt; they are the rivers that course through Midgard, and cascade from Middle Earth straight into Hel.

'When the gods go each day to meet in council at the Well of Urd, Thor has to wade across the rivers Kormt and Ormt and the two Kerlaugs. All the other gods gallop over Bifrost and their steeds are called Joyous and Golden, Shining and Swift, Silver-maned and Sinewy, Gleaming and Hollow-hoofed, and Gold Mane and Light Feet.

'The ash tree Yggdrasill has three roots. One is embedded in Niflheim, another in the world of the frost giants, the third in Midgard. All day and every day the squirrel Ratatosk scurries up and down its trunk; he is carrying insults between the eagle perched in the topmost branches and the serpent Nidhogg, the Corpse Sucker, in Niflheim. Four harts throw back their heads and stretch to nibble the tender topmost twigs; they are Dain and Dvalin, Duneyr and Durathror. And underneath Yggdrasill are more serpents than a slow-witted man would dream of: Goin and Moin, the sons of the gnawing wolf; Grabak and Grafvolluth; the Bewilderer and the Bringer of Sleep. They will gnaw at the roots of the tree until the end of time. Yggdrasill suffers greater hardship than men realise: the deer crop its crown, Nidhogg gnaws the roots, and the trunk itself is rotting.

'In Valhalla, Shaker and Mist, Axe Time and Raging take it in turns to bring me my brimming horn. And nine other Valkyries bring ale to the slain warriors. Their names are Warrior and Might, Shrieking, Host Fetter and Screaming, Spear Bearer, Shield Bearer, Wrecker of Plans and Kin of the Gods.

'Arvak the Early Waker and Alsvid, All Swift, are the names of the steeds whose wearisome work is to drag the sun across the sky. Long ago the gods took pity on them, and put bellows under their yokes. And in front of the sun, like a shield, stands Svalin. Should he let his guard slip, the mountains and the sea would burst into flames. Skoll is the wolf on the tail of the sun, and he will chase her until at last he runs her down in Iron Wood; and Hati, Hrodvitnir's son, is the wolf in pursuit of the moon.

'The earth was made from Ymir's flesh and the oceans from his blood. The gods made the hills out of his bones, and trees from his hair, and the sky dome is his skull. They used his eyebrows to build the mountain wall, Midgard, as a safeguard for men; and out of his brain they shaped the welling dark clouds.

'Ull and the other gods will smile on the first man to reach into these flames. They could all look through the vent, and see my plight, if someone would move that cauldron aside.

'Long ago the sons of the mighty dwarf Ivaldi made Skidbladnir, best of all ships; it was a gift for Freyr. Likewise, Yggdrasill is the finest of trees, Odin the greatest of gods, and Sleipnir the swiftest of steeds; Bifrost is the bridge of bridges and Bragi the best of word-smiths; Hobrok is the finest hawk, and Garm the fiercest hound. I have raised my face to the gods and they have heard me, all those who sit and drink at Aegir's banquet.

63

'I will tell you my names: I am Grim; I am Gangleri; I am Raider and the Helmeted One, I am the Pleasant One and the Third; I am Thud and Ud; I am Death Blinder and the High One; I am Sad and Svipall and Sangetall; I am Glad of War and Spear Thruster; I am One-eyed, Flame-eyed, Worker of Evil; I am Fjolnir and Grimnir, the Hooded One, I am Glapsvid and Fjolsvid; I am Deep Hood and I am Long Beard; I am Sigfod and Hnikud; I am Allfather; I am Atrid and the Cargo God. I have never been called by one name alone since I first showed myself in Midgard.

'In Geirrod's hall I am known as Grimnir, and Asmund knows me as Gelding. I was called Keel Ruler when I travelled on a sledge, and at the council of the gods I am called Thror. Vidur is my name when I go into battle, and the gods have known me as Just as High, Fulfiller of Desire, Shouter, and Spear Shaker, Gondlir the Wand Bearer and grey-bearded Harbard. I took the names of Svidur and Svidrir to deceive the giant Sokkmimir; I slew him, Midvitnir's famous son.'

The god turned his head from the young prince Agnar and turned his terrible gaze on King Geirrod.

'You are drunk, Geirrod! You've drunk yourself stupid. Think of all you've lost. Neither I nor any of my slain warriors will raise a hand to help you now.

'How little you have acted on all I once told you. The messenger you trusted betrayed you. And now I see my friend's sword bared and shining with blood. Ygg, the Terrible One, will soon lay claim to your pierced body, for your life has come to an end. The Norns have nothing but death to offer you. Look at me – I am Odin! Draw your sword against me if you dare!

'Now I am Odin. Once I was the Terrible One, the Thunderer, the Wakeful, the Shaker; I was the Wanderer and the Crier of the Gods; I was Father and Bewilderer and Bringer of Sleep. All these names are one name; they are names for none but me.'

King Geirrod sat and listened. His sword lay across his lap, half-sheathed. When he heard his guest reveal that he was Odin, he leapt up to release him. But the sword slipped from the King's hand and fell hilt first to the ground. Then Geirrod stumbled and fell on his sword so that it skewered him and killed him.

Odin vanished then. And Agnar became king and ruled for a long time.

For note on this myth see page 200.

13 *The Necklace of the Brisings*

THE NIGHT WAS ALMOST OVER; the sky was green and grey in the east, and snowflakes were ghosting around Asgard.

Loki and only Loki saw Freyja leave Sessrumnir. Her cats slept undisturbed by the hearth; her chariot lay unused; in the half light she set off on foot towards Bifrost. Then the Sly One's mind was riddled with curiosity; he wrapped his cloak around him and followed her.

The goddess seemed not to walk so much as drift over the ground. She glided through sleeping Asgard, her hips swaying as she made her way over the rainbow that trembled and danced around her.

The snow veils of Midgard beneath were dazzling in the rising sun. Dreaming of gold, lusting after gold, Freyja crossed a barren plain (and Loki hurried behind her). She picked her way across a twisting river, silenced by ice; she passed the base of a great glacier, chopped and bluish and dangerous; and at the end of the short hours of daylight she came to a group of huge rounded boulders, jostling under the shoulder of an overhanging cliff.

Freyja found the string-thin path that led in and down. Her eyes streamed from the cold and her tears fell as a small shower of gold in front of her. The path became a passage between rock and rock and she followed it until it led into a large dank cavern. There the goddess stood motionless; she could hear water dripping into rock pools and the movement of a small stream coursing over rock; she listened again and then she heard the sound of distant tapping, and her own heart began to beat faster, to hammer with longing.

The goddess sidled through the dismal cave. The sound of the tapping, insistent yet fitful, grew stronger and stronger. Freyja stopped, listened again, moved on; at last she stopped, eased her way down a narrow groin, and stepped into the sweltering smithy of the four dwarfs, Alfrigg and Dvalin, Berling and Grerr.

For a moment Freyja was dazzled by the brilliance of the furnace. She rubbed her eyes, and then she gasped as she saw the breathtaking work of the dwarfs – a necklace, a choker of gold incised with wondrous patterns, a marvel of fluid metal twisting and weaving and writhing.

She had never seen anything so beautiful nor so desired anything before.

The four dwarfs, meanwhile, stared at the goddess – she shimmered in the warm light of the forge. Where her cloak had fallen apart, the gold brooches and jewels on her dress gleamed and winked. They had never seen anyone so beautiful nor so desired anyone before.

Freyja smiled at Alfrigg and Dvalin and Berling and Grerr. 'I will buy that necklace from you,' she said.

The four dwarfs looked at each other. Three shook their heads and the fourth said, 'It's not for sale.'

'I want it,' said Freyja.

The dwarfs grimaced.

'I want it. I'll pay you with silver and gold – a fair price and more than a fair price,' said Freyja, her voice rising. She moved closer to the bench where the necklace was lying. 'I'll bring you other rewards.'

'We have enough silver,' said one dwarf.

'And we have enough gold,' said another.

Freyja gazed at the necklace. She felt a great longing for it, a painful hunger.

Alfrigg and Dvalin and Berling and Grerr huddled in one corner of the forge. They whispered and murmured and nodded.

'What is your price?' asked the goddess.

'It belongs to us all,' said one dwarf.

'So what each has must be had by the others,' said the second, leering.

'There's only one price,' said the third, 'that will satisfy us.'

The fourth dwarf looked at Freyja. 'You,' he said.

The goddess flushed, and her breasts began to rise and fall.

'Only if you will lie one night with each of us will this necklace ever lie round your throat,' said the dwarfs.

Freyja's distaste for the dwarfs – their ugly faces, their pale noses, their misshapen bodies and their small greedy eyes – was great, but her desire for the necklace was greater. Four nights were but four nights; the glorious necklace would adorn her for all time. The walls of the forge were red and flickering; the dwarfs' eyes were motionless.

'As you wish,' murmured Freyja shamelessly. 'As you wish. I am in your hands.'

Four days passed; four nights passed. Freyja kept her part of the bargain. Then the dwarfs, too, kept their word. They presented the necklace to Freyja and jostled her and fastened it round her throat. The goddess hurried out of the cavern and across the bright plains of Midgard, and her shadow followed her. She crossed over Bifrost and returned in the darkness to Sessrumnir. And under her cloak, she wore the necklace of the Brisings.

The Sly One made straight for Odin's hall. He found the Terrible One, the Father of Battle, sitting alone in Valaskjalf. His ravens perched on his shoulders and his two wolves lay beside him.

'Well?' said Odin.

Loki smirked.

'I can read your face ...'

'Ah!' interrupted Loki, his eyes gleaming wickedly, 'but did you see hers?'

'Whose?' said Odin.

'Did it escape you? Didn't you see it all from Hlidskjalf?'

'What?' insisted Odin.

'Where were you, Odin, when the goddess you love, the goddess you lust after, slept with four dwarfs?'

'Enough!' shouted Odin.

Loki ignored him altogether and Odin was possessed with such jealousy that he found it impossible not to listen. With unfeigned delight at shaming Freyja and angering Odin at the same time, Loki launched into his story. He left out nothing and he saw no need to add anything.

'Get that necklace for me,' said Odin coldly, when Loki had at last brought Freyja home to Asgard.

Loki smiled and shook his head.

'You do nothing that is not vile,' cried Odin. 'You set us all at one another's throats. Now I set you at her throat: get that necklace.'

The Sly One sniffed. 'You know as well as I – indeed surely far better than I – that there's no way into that hall against her wishes.'

'Get that necklace,' shouted Odin. His face was contorted; his one eye was burning. 'Until you get it, let me never see your face again.'

Then Loki looked at the Terrible One. Odin's face was a mask now, grim and sinister. The Sly One's arrogance turned to cold fear; he recognised the danger.

Then Odin's wolves got up, and so did Loki. He ran out of the hall, howling.

Later that same night, the Sly One walked across the shining snow-field to the hall Sessrumnir. Boldly he made his way up to the door. It was locked.

He drew his cloak more closely round him; he shivered as the night wind picked up snow and grazed his face with it. He felt the cold working its way into his body and into his blood.

Loki remembered Sif – her locked bedchamber, her shorn shining hair, his own lips pierced with an awl. He scowled and inspected the door again. The Shape Changer shook his head; he muttered the words, and turned himself into a fly.

Sessrumnir was so well built that he was still unable to find a way into the hall – a chink between wood and plaster, or plaster and turf. He buzzed around the keyhole, but that was no good; he examined the top and bottom of the door, and they were no good; he flew up to the eaves and they were no good; then he flitted to one gable end and there, at the top, right under the roof, he found an opening little larger than a needle's eye. Loki, the Shape Changer, squirmed and wriggled his way through. He was at large and inside Sessrumnir. After making sure that Freyja's daughters and serving maids were asleep, he flew to Freyja's bedside but the sleeping goddess was wearing the necklace and its clasp lay under her neck; it was out of sight and out of reach.

So Loki changed shape again, this time becoming a flea. Then he amused himself crawling over Freyja's breast, across the necklace, and up on to one cheek. There he sat down; he gathered his strength and stung her pale skin.

Freyja started. She moaned and turned on to her side and settled again. But now the clasp of the necklace was exposed just as the Shape Changer had intended.

As soon as he was certain that Freyja was sleeping soundly once more, Loki resumed his own form. He looked swiftly around and then with light fingers released the clasp and gently drew the necklace from Freyja's throat. No thief in the nine worlds was as nimble and skilful as he. With no movement that was not necessary and without making a sound, he stole to the hall doors, slid back the bolts, turned the lock, and disappeared into the night.

Freyja did not wake until morning. And as soon as she opened her eyes she put her fingers to her throat . . . she felt the back of her neck . . .

The goddess looked around her; she leaped up and her face coloured in anger. When she saw the doors of Sessrumnir were open and had not been forced, she knew that only Loki could have entered the hall, and knew that not even he would have risked such an undertaking and such a theft unless Odin himself had sanctioned it. What she did not know and could not fathom was how her secret – her greed and her guilt and her gain – had been discovered.

Freyja hurried to Valaskjalf and confronted Odin. 'Where is that necklace?' she demanded. 'You've debased yourself if you've had any part in this.'

Odin scowled at Freyja. 'Who are you,' he said, 'to speak of debasement? You've brought shame on yourself and shame on the gods. Out of nothing but sheer greed you sold your body to four foul dwarfs.'

'Where is my necklace?' repeated Freyja. She stormed at Odin; she took his rigid arm and pressed herself against him; she wept showers of gold.

'You'll never see it again,' said the Terrible One, Father of Battle, 'unless you agree to one condition. There is only one thing that will satisfy me.'

Freyja looked at Odin quickly. And whatever it was that passed through her mind, she bit her tongue.

'You must stir up hatred. You must stir up war. Find two kings in Midgard and set them at each other's throats; ensure that they meet only on the battlefield, each of them supported by twenty vassal kings.' The Father of Battle looked grimly at the goddess. 'And you must use such charms as give new life to corpses. As soon as each warrior is chopped down, bathed in blood, he must stand up unharmed and fight again.'

Freyja stared at Odin.

'Those are my conditions. Whether they wish it or not, let men rip one another to pieces.'

Freyja inclined her head. 'Then give me my necklace,' she said.

For note on this myth see page 201.

14 *The Lay of Thrym*

WHEN THOR AWOKE and reached out to grasp his hammer, it was not there. The Hurler leaped up. He tousled and tangled his red beard; his hair bristled as he searched for Mjollnir. 'Listen, Loki!' said Thor. 'No god in Asgard has seen my hammer; no man in Midgard has seen my hammer: it has been stolen.'

Then Thor and Loki hurried to Folkvang, and into Freyja's hall Sessrumnir. They well knew that if the hammer were not found, it would not be long before the giants stormed Asgard's walls and brought the bright halls of the gods crashing to the earth.

'Will you lend me your falcon skin,' asked Loki, 'so that I can search for Thor's hammer?'

'If it were fashioned of silver,' cried Freyja, 'you could use it. I would lend it even if it were spun out of gold.'

Then Loki donned the falcon skin. The feather dress whirred as he climbed into the moving air, and left the world of the gods behind him. He flew until Asgard became no more than a bright haze away to the west; he flew as fast as he could until at last he reached the world of the giants.

Thrym, king of the frost giants, felt at ease with the world. He had unteased and combed his horses' manes; he was sitting on a green mound, plaiting gold thread, making collars and leashes for his horrible hounds.

When the Sky Traveller saw Thrym, he swooped down beside him.

'How are things with the gods?' said Thrym. 'How are things with the elves? And what brings you to Jotunheim alone?'

'Things are bad for the gods,' said Loki. 'Things are bad for the elves. Have you stolen Thor's hammer?'

Thrym laughed, and the sound was like the chuckle of broken ice. 'I've hidden Thor's hammer eight miles deep in the earth. No one is going to touch it unless he brings Freyja here to be my bride.'

Loki grimaced and the sound of Thrym's freezing laughter followed him as he climbed again into the sky. The feather dress whirred. He left the world of the giants behind him and flew as fast as he could until at last he returned to the world of the gods.

Thor was waiting in the courtyard of Bilskirnir and at once asked the Sky Traveller, 'What's in your head and what's in your mouth? Real news or mere nuisance?' The Thunder God's eyes blazed and it was clear that he would brook no nonsense. 'Stand here and tell me the truth at once. A sitting man forgets his story as often as not, and a man who lies down first lies again afterwards.'

'I bring nuisance and I bring news,' said the Sly One, the corners of his crooked mouth curling. 'Thrym, king of the frost giants, has your hammer. And no one is going to touch it unless he brings Freyja to be his bride.'

Then Thor and Loki hurried to Sessrumnir for a second time and found Freyja there.

'Well, my beautiful!' said Loki, narrowing his eyes. 'Put on your bridal veil.'

'What?' retorted Freyja.

'We two must hurry,' answered Loki, grinning. 'You and I are going to Jotunheim. Thrym, king of the frost giants, has taken a fancy to you.'

Freyja was so angry that the walls of Sessrumnir shuddered. The gold-studded benches started from the floor. Then Freyja snorted; her face became fiery; her breasts rose and fell; her neck muscles bulged. Then suddenly the marvellous Necklace of the Brisings burst apart – the links snapped and a shower of precious stones rolled around the hall. 'How would it look if I went with you to Jotunheim?' demanded Freyja. 'Everyone would say the same. A whore! Just a whore!'

Loki raised his eyebrows; Thor sniffed and smirked and shifted from foot to foot and did everything except look Freyja in the eye.

'Go away! said Freyja. 'Both of you.'

Then every god headed for Gladsheim, the hall with the silver thatch, to sit in solemn council and discuss how to recover Mjollnir. The goddesses joined them there. The watchman Heimdall had left Himinbjorg and the trembling rainbow bridge. Like the other Vanir, he could read the future. The White God said, 'Let us swaddle Thor ...' He paused and looked around '... swaddle Thor in the bridal veil!'

There was a moment of silence and then a howl of laughter from the assembled gods and goddesses.

Heimdall waited until the uproar had died down and then he went on: 'Let us repair the Necklace of the Brisings and secure it round his ... his pretty neck.'

Once again Gladsheim erupted and Thor looked across at Heimdall with profound distaste. But the White God was unabashed. 'He must be decked as befits any bride. A bunch of jingling keys must hang from his waist. And he must wear a becoming dress – as long a dress as possible! We mustn't forget to pin well-wrought brooches on her ... on his breast.'

This care for detail delighted the gods and goddesses; and they also saw the force of Heimdall's argument.

'And he'll need a charming cap,' concluded Heimdall in a sing-song voice, 'a charming cap to crown it all.'

Thor scowled. 'You'll all mock me and call me unmanly if I put on a bridal veil,' he said.

Then Loki, the son of Laufey, called out insolently, 'Silence, Thor! There's no argument. Giants will live in Asgard if we don't retrieve your hammer.'

So the gods and goddesses swaddled Thor in a bridal veil. They repaired the Necklace of the Brisings and clasped it round his neck. They hung a bunch of jingling keys from his waist, and he wore a becoming dress down to his knees; they pinned well-wrought brooches on his breast, and they crowned it all with a charming cap.

'I'll be your maidservant,' warbled Loki. 'We two will hurry to Jotunheim.'

The Thunderer's goats were rounded up and driven to Bilskirnir. There they were harnessed, and impatiently bucked and wrestled with their halters.

Gaping fissures opened in the fells, flames scorched the earth, and Thor, the son of Odin, galloped with Loki to Jotunheim.

'She will come!' shouted Thrym in a frenzy. 'She's coming! Stir your great stumps! Spread straw on the benches! They're bringing Freyja, Njord's daughter from Noatun, to be my bride.'

Thrym strode up and down his chilly hall, checking the arrangements. Then he sat on a bench and said to himself: 'I've cattle in my stables with horns of gold; I've jet black oxen – beasts to gladden the heart of any man. I've piles of precious stones, and mounds of silver and gold.' Thrym's thoughts evaporated in the cold air, and he sighed, 'I've had everything I wanted – everything except Freyja.'

When the travellers from Asgard arrived at Thrym's hall in the early evening, they were welcomed with great ceremony. The same giant servants who had spread straw on the benches now served up a fine supply of good food and drink.

Thrym ushered Thor, in his bridal veil, to the feasting table. With all the courtesy he could command, he pointed out the fine fare drawn from earth, sea and air alike in her honour. Then he led his intended bride to one high seat and himself sat in the other. Loki promptly ensconced himself next to Thor on the other side.

Thor felt hungry. He devoured an entire ox, and followed that with eight salmon. Then he scooped up and scoffed all the delicacies set apart for the women. And to round things off, he downed three horns of mead.

Thrym watched this feat with growing surprise and anticipation. 'Who has ever seen a bride with such hunger, such thirst?' he exclaimed. 'I've never met a woman who took such huge mouthfuls or who drank so much mead.'

The subtle bridesmaid sitting at Thor's side took it upon herself to answer Thrym. 'Freyja has not eaten for these past eight nights, so wild was her desire for her wedding night.'

Thrym leaned forward and peered under the veil; he could not wait to kiss her. The giant king was so startled that he leaped back the whole length of the hall. 'Her eyes!' he shouted. 'Why are Freyja's eyes so fearsome? They're like burning coals.'

The subtle bridesmaid sitting at Thor's side took it upon herself to answer Thrym. 'Freyja has not slept for these past eight nights, so wild was her desire for her wedding night.'

Now Thrym's luckless sister walked up to the bride and bridesmaid, and she was not half-hearted about asking for a dowry. 'If you want my love,' she said, 'and my loyalty, give me the rings of red gold on your fingers.'

'Bring forward the hammer!' called the king of the giants. 'Bring forward the hammer to hallow the bride. Put Mjollnir between her knees now so that Var will hear our marriage oath and give us her blessing.'

The Thunder God's unsparing heart sang and danced when he saw his hammer. As soon as it was placed between his knees, he snatched it up in his mighty grasp, swept off his veil and stood revealed as the god, Thor, the Hurler.

Thrym leapt up from his high seat and his companions leapt up from their benches.

Thor's eyes were as red as his beard. He glared at the company of giants and growled. Then he raised his hammer, took one massive step towards Thrym, and crushed his skull. Thor showed no mercy: he felled all the other giants and giant women at that bridal feast. The hall floor was strewn with a host of bodies. Thrym's luckless sister had dared ask for gold rings but the iron hammer rang on her skull.

And so Thor, the Son of Odin, won back his hammer.

For note on this myth see page 204.

15 *The Lay of Vafthrudnir*

'SUCH FEVER IN MY BLOOD!' cried Odin. 'I so long to range far and wide.' Allfather prowled up and down Valaskjalf as if he were caged. 'What do you think, Frigg? I've a mind to visit Vafthrudnir in his high hall.'

'I would rather the Father of Warriors stayed in Asgard, home of the gods,' said Frigg. 'So far as I know, Vafthrudnir has no equal amongst the giants.'

'I've roamed far and I've learned much and all that the gods know I know,' replied Odin. 'I want to match my wits against the riddle-master, the wise giant Vafthrudnir.'

'Go safely then,' said Frigg. 'Return safely. And may the way you're taking be safe. Father of Men, your mind must be needle-sharp when you pit yourself against that giant.'

Then Odin left Asgard to plumb the wisdom of the giant. He ferried himself across the wild and the wide and the whispering rivers and made his way over the trembling rainbow. He pulled down his wide-brimmed hat so that no one would see he lacked one eye, smiled grimly, and walked into Jotunheim.

The further Odin went, the colder it grew. He strode over a ribbed and silent plain, bright with snow, and past plumes of steam that issued from whistling fissures. And at the mouth of a valley, surrounded on three sides by the purple mountains, Odin found the hall of Im's father, Vafthrudnir. The Terrible One entered it.

'Greetings, Vafthrudnir!' Odin called out. 'I've heard so much about you that I wanted to meet you. Is it true that you're wise? Can it possibly be true that there's nothing you do not know?'

'Who are you?' demanded Vafthrudnir. 'What man thinks he can slight me in my own high hall? You'll not leave this place alive unless you're wiser than I am.'

'My name is Gagnrad,' said Odin. 'A bringer of fortune; a walking charm! It has been a hard journey to your hall, and I'm thirsty. I must say I had hoped for a warmer welcome after such a haul.'

'What are you standing there for?' said the giant. 'There's no need

75

to hold the floor. Choose a seat, make yourself at home. Then we'll soon find out who knows more – the guest or his time-proven host.'

'A poor man does best to speak to the point or to say nothing at all in a rich man's hall,' Gagnrad said. 'Tough-minded men brook little bragging.'

'All right, Gagnrad,' said Vafthrudnir, 'answer from the floor if you can answer at all. What's the name of the stallion that, every morning, draws Day across the world?'

'That is Skinfaxi. He is the stallion who draws shining Day to gladden the eyes of men. To heroes he seems the very best of horses, and his mane is fiery.'

'All right, Gagnrad,' Vafthrudnir said, 'answer from the floor if you can answer at all. What's the name of the stallion that, over and over again, brings Night from the East for the noble gods?'

'Hrimfaxi is the name of the stallion that, over and again, brings Night for the noble gods. Foam falls from his bit at dawn, and that's the source of dew in the dales.'

'All right, Gagnrad,' said Vafthrudnir, 'answer from the floor if you can answer at all. What's the name of the river that divides the world of the gods from the world of the giants?'

'Iving is the river that divides the world of the gods from the world of the giants. In time past it has never frozen, in time to come it will flow freely.'

'All right, Gagnrad,' said Vafthrudnir, 'answer from the floor if you can answer at all. What's the name of the plain where Surt and the fine gods will meet and fight?'

'Vigrid is the plain where Surt and the fine gods will meet and fight. It's a hundred miles long and a hundred miles wide.'

Vafthrudnir stared at his guest. 'You know much,' he said. 'Sit here at my bench and let us talk further. Here and now, my guest, in this hall, we'll wager our heads – your life or my life – on the outcome of this contest.'

Then Odin sat down and began to pose his questions.

'First tell me then, Vafthrudnir, if in your wisdom you know the answer: at the beginning of time, wise giant, where did the earth and the sky come from?'

'The earth was shaped from Ymir's flesh, and the mountains were built from his bones. The sky was made from that frost giant's skull and the salt seas were streams of his blood.'

'Second, tell me then, Vafthrudnir, if in your wisdom you know the answer: where did the moon and the burning sun come from, those travellers over the world of men?'

'Mundilfari fathered the moon and the burning sun. Each day they run along the arc of heaven to tell the time for men.'

'Third, tell me then, Vafthrudnir, if you're so wise and know the answer: where does Day come from, and from where does Night come with its waning moon, travellers over the world of men?'

'Delling is Day's father and Nor the father of Night. New moon and old moon were shaped by the gods to tell the time for men.'

'Fourth, tell me then, Vafthrudnir, if you're so wise and know the answer: where did winter and warm summer first come from for the fine gods?'

'Vindsval the Wind Cold was winter's father, and gentle Svosud fathered summer.'

'Fifth, tell me then, Vafthrudnir, if you're so wise and know the answer: who was the first of the giants and what were the names of the first-born?'

'Bergelmir was born countless winters before the making of the earth. That mighty giant was Thrudgelmir's son and Aurgelmir's grandson.'

'Sixth, tell me then, Vafthrudnir, if you're so wise and know the answer: where, wise giant, did Aurgelmir and his issue come from, so long ago?'

'Venom dropped from the stormy waves of Elivagar. It clotted and rose until it was a giant. That is how the race of giants began, and that's why we're all so fierce.'

Seventh, tell me then, Vafthrudnir, if you're so wise and know the answer: how did the grim giant conceive children since he never slept with a giantess?'

'It's said that a boy and a girl grew in the frost giant's armpits. And with one leg and the other leg that wise giant begat and bore a son with six heads.'

'Eighth, tell me then, Vafthrudnir, if you're so wise and know the answer: what is your first memory? There can be nothing you do not know!'

'Bergelmir was born untold winters before the making of the earth. My first memory is of that wise giant in a boat's rocking cradle.'

'Ninth, tell me then, Vafthrudnir, if you're so wise and know the answer: from where does the wind come that travels over the waves and yet is never seen?'

'The eagle Hraesvelg, the Corpse Eater, is said to sit at the end of the world. When he flaps his wings, wind moves over the world of men.'

'Tenth, tell me now, if you know everything, about the fates of the gods. How can Njord be one of their number – for he presides over many temples and wayside shrines – although he was not begotten by gods?'

'The Vanir created him in Vanaheim. At the end of the world he'll return to his own people.'

'Eleventh, tell me then, if you know everything, about the fates of the gods. Who are the men in Odin's hall who go out to fight each day?'

'All the dead heroes in Odin's hall go out to fight each day. They fell each other, and then soon return healed from the fight, to sit at the feast.'

'Twelfth, tell me now how you know all about the fates of the gods. You are indeed able to read the runes of the gods and the runes of the giants.'

'I am indeed able to read the runes of the gods and the runes of the giants, because I know and have visited the nine worlds and Niflheim below, the place where dead men dwell.'

Then Odin said: 'I've roamed far and I've learned much and all that the gods know I know: what will survive when, at the end, the terrible winter afflicts men?'

'Lif and Lifthrasir will hide themselves in Hoddmimir's Wood. The dew each dawn will be their food; that will be their meat then.'

'I've roamed far and I've learned much and all that the gods know I know: from where will the sun come back to the smooth sky after Fenrir has torn her apart?'

'Alfrothul, the Elf Beam, will bear a fair daughter before Fenrir tears her apart. This maid will walk in her mother's ways after the gods have been destroyed.'

'I've roamed far and I've learned much and all that the gods know I know: who are the wise maidens who will wing over the sea?'

'Three times three maidens will fly over Mogthrasir's Hill. And although they have giants' blood, they will guard the children of men.'

'I've roamed far and I've learned much and all that the gods know I know: who will rule over the world of the gods when Surt's fire dies out?'

'Vidar and Vali will live in the home of the gods when Surt's fire has abated. Modi the Wrathful and Magni the Mighty will own the hammer Mjollnir after Vingnir the Hurler has fallen in the fight.'

'I've roamed far and I've learned much and all that the gods know I know: what will cause Odin's death when the gods fight at Ragnarok?'

'The wolf will swallow the Father of Men. Vidar will avenge him. He will tear apart those terrible jaws and Fenrir will be slain.'

'I've roamed far and I've learned much and all that the gods know I know: what did Odin himself whisper in the ear of his son Balder before he burned on the pyre?'

Vafthrudnir looked long at his guest, and recognised him. He said in a low voice, 'No one can tell what, long ago, you whispered in the ear of your son. Before I told of the first giants and the doom of the gods, I was already fated.' The giant spoke his final words in this life. 'I've pitted myself against Odin. You will always be wiser and wisest.'

For note on this myth see page 205.

16 *Thor's Journey to Utgard*

THOR SAID SUMMER was the open season and he announced his plan of making a journey east into Utgard and flexing himself against the giants. 'However few they are,' he said, 'they are too many.'

'In Utgard,' said Loki, 'you'll need sharp wits.'

'Sharp wits,' repeated Thor seriously.

'And yours are as blunt as your hammer,' said Loki, winking at Thor. 'Why not take me?'

Thor ignored the insult and accepted the offer. 'Evil creature: good companion,' he said.

Loki's eyes gleamed, now brown, now green, now indigo. His scarred lips parted a little and twisted into a wolfish smile.

'Tomorrow, then,' said Thor.

Very early in the morning, before the sky turned blue and before a cock crowed, Thor had his goats brought in from Thrudvang and harnessed to his chariot. Thor and Loki took their seats and Thor grasped the reins of twined silver. The chariot rattled across the plains of Asgard, still soaked with dew, and Thor looked lovingly at the halls of the sleeping gods and goddesses – towering hulks, all of them silent and dreamlike in the ashen light.

They passed through the great gate and headed for Midgard, the home of men. All day the Charioteer and the Trickster rode and talked, at ease with each other and the world. And early in the evening they came to a lonely farm, the only building for miles around. It was low-slung and almost as green as the fields surrounding it; the turfed roof seemed to grow out of the ground.

'A very poor place,' said Loki.

'What they cannot provide I will,' said Thor. He pulled up his goats and climbed out of the chariot.

The farmer and his wife and their children, Thialfi and Roskva, stepped out of their farmhouse and then started to tremble when they recognised their visitors.

'What we want,' said Loki, 'is food and shelter for the night.'

'We will gladly give you shelter,' said the farmer.

'And we can offer you the little food we have,' said the wife. 'Vegetables, potage; but there's no meat.'

'Not even a chicken?' said Loki, looking around him.

The farmer slowly shook his head.

'We'll use my goats then,' said Thor. Without ado he slaughtered both animals, and skinned them; then he cut them into joints and jammed them into the wife's large cauldron.

The farmer and his wife, their long-legged son and fair daughter felt almost sick with hunger at the thought of such a feast; they kept looking at the meat to see whether it was cooked. Thor spread the skins of his two goats some way from the fire. 'As you eat,' he said, 'throw the bones on to the skins.'

They all sat down together under the stars. 'Mind what I said,' Thor enjoined them. 'Be careful with the bones and throw them all on to the skins.' Then they all began to eat.

The farmer's son, Thialfi, had gone hungry for so long that he could not bear the thought of wasting good marrow. While Thor was talking to his father, he grasped one thigh bone and quickly split it with his knife and sucked the rich juice from it. Then he tossed it on to the heap of bones covering the skins.

After they had eaten Thor and Loki and the farmer's family were ready to sleep. And they all slept soundly after such a fine meal. Thor was the first up; just before daybreak he rose and dressed and went out of the farmhouse. Then he took his hammer, Mjollnir, raised it over the goatskins and hallowed them.

At once the goats stood up, fully fleshed and bleating. But as they began to move about, Thor noticed that one goat had a lame hind leg. He hurried back into the farmhouse. 'Who?' he shouted, and the walls of the farm trembled so much that they nearly collapsed.

The farmer and his wife were shocked out of their sleep and sat straight up in their bed. 'Who disobeyed me?' roared Thor. 'I can see a thighbone has been broken.'

Thor's eyebrows beetled and the farmer and his wife and Thialfi and Roskva cowered. His eyes burned like orange flames and the family thought their days in Midgard had come to an end. Then, when the Thunderer grasped his hammer, so that his knuckles turned white, the farmer's wife and Roskva screamed in terror. 'Mercy!' pleaded Thialfi, screwing up his eyes. 'Mercy! Mercy!' And the farmer begged, 'My land, my farm, everything I own. Take them. Take everything I own and spare our lives.'

If Thor was sometimes furiously angry, he was never angry for long. When he saw how the whole poor family were panic-stricken, the blood stopped racing round his body. 'I'll take Thialfi and Roskva to be my servants,' he said roughly. 'And that's an end to the matter.'

Now Thor and Loki were ready to resume their journey. Thor gave the goats and the chariot into the farmer's care. He said he would collect them on his way back, and told Thialfi and Roskva to come with them to Utgard.

For a long time they walked across gently falling land until at last they came to the girdle of water dividing the world of men from Jotunheim. They stared at the fretful grey water and the mountains beyond – squat tubs and barrels of unfriendly land suppressed by leaden sky.

'They can wait until the morning,' said Thor.

Then they busied themselves with putting most of the contents of their knapsack into their stomachs. And filled with the remains of the previous night's meal, and a helping of porridge as well, they slept in the sand beside the rocking ocean.

Thor and Loki, Thialfi and Roskva did not have to walk far along the strand next morning before they found an old boat, beached and disused. They took it over and hauled it down to the water. The boat reared and kicked forward every time Thor pulled the oars and by midday they reached the shore of Utgard, a broad strip of land that lay between the water and the mountains.

The four travellers beached their boat and, as there was no sign of life along the coast, they headed inland. After a while they came to a forest that stretched so far in both directions that there seemed to be no way round it. So they made their way into it and began to pick their way through it. All afternoon they walked through the shadows, light-headed with hunger and the sweet-smelling pine; the ground was springy underfoot.

By the time that the light began to fade, late in the evening, they had still seen no sign of life and knew that they would have to go without much food that day, for their own stocks were running low.

'We must at least find somewhere to stay for the night,' said Loki. 'I wouldn't care to end up as carrion.'

'Is Fenrir's father so afraid of wolves?' said Thor, and smiled to himself.

Restless and fleet of foot, Thialfi ran ahead again and again, scouting out the forest for Thor and Loki and his sister. Now he came back with the news that he had found a glade not far ahead, with a curious kind of hall standing in the middle of it. When they reached the glade, Thor and Loki walked round the hall. It puzzled them too. Although there seemed to be no door, the whole of one end of the hall was open; the opening was as high as the hall was high and as wide as it was wide. And the hall itself was enormous; any of the halls in Asgard, even Valhalla, could have fitted inside it.

'This place will keep the rain off our backs,' said Loki. 'And here at least the damp will not seep into our bones.'

The gods and Thialfi and Roskva were so worn with travelling all day that, hungry though they were, they very quickly settled and fell asleep.

At midnight, however, all four of them were shocked out of their sleep. They heard a terrible growling. The noise grew louder, it grew so loud that the hall began to rock and sway. Thor and Loki and Thialfi and Roskva started to their feet and the ground shuddered under them.

'An earthquake,' shouted Thor.

Thialfi and Roskva stood wide-eyed; then they hugged one another. 'Let's get out,' said Loki. 'I don't want to be flattened and stiff as a plank.'

At this moment, however, the ground stopped shaking. The earth-thunder ceased as abruptly as it had begun, and the night was as silent as it had been before.

'Outside is no safer than inside,' said Thor.

'There must be somewhere better than this,' replied Loki.

'Let us at least get the hang of this place,' Thor said. 'The known is always better than the unknown.'

So the four of them groped their way towards the far end of the hall. But the darkness seemed to grow thicker and more stifling with every step they took. They did, however, make one find: a smaller side-room led off to the right, about half-way down the vast main hall.

'This is better,' said Thor. 'At least we can make a fight of it here if a man or monster shows its face. Earthquakes, however, are something else.'

So Loki and Thialfi and his sister Roskva felt their way into the pitch dark recess of the side-room, and Thor sat down in the doorway. He gripped the handle of his hammer and vowed to guard them against allcomers. Even now, the travellers did not enjoy unbroken sleep. They were woken several times by a muffled roaring, and lay awake for most of the night in a state of dread.

As soon as it began to get light, Thor cautiously made his way out of the hall. At once he saw a man lying full length in the glade and he was by no means a dwarf. He was asleep, and in his sleep he suddenly snorted. Then he began to snore, and Thor understood the nature of the noise that he and his companions had heard during the night. He looked at the giant grimly and buckled on the belt given to him by the giantess Grid. He felt his strength grow, and surge like a spring tide within him.

At this moment the giant woke and, seeing Thor standing almost over him, sprang to his feet. He was as tall as the pine trees around them, and Thor was so taken aback at his height that he did not hurl Mjollnir at him but asked, astonished, 'Who on earth are you?'

'Skrymir,' boomed the giant. 'Big Bloke.'

'No one is going to quarrel with that,' muttered Thor.

'I don't have to ask who you are,' said Skrymir, eyeing Loki, Thialfi and Roskva who had now crept out of their sleeping quarters. 'I know you're Thor. Have you moved my glove?'

Skrymir bent down and picked it up – the glove that Thor and the others had seen as a vast hall. Thor now saw that what they had taken for the main hall was the cavity for Skrymir's hand and four fingers, and that the side-room was the opening for his thumb.

'What would you say to my company today?' said Skrymir.

'We'd welcome it,' Thor said. 'We're on our way to Utgard.'

'Eat and drink with me first,' said Skrymir.

Thor and his companions were far from unhappy about that, for their own knapsack was now almost empty. When they had eaten as much as they wanted, Skrymir said, 'Let's pool our provisions.'

'Very well,' said Thor.

So Skrymir simply dropped their knapsack into his own larger bag, tied it up and slung it over his back. Then he set off through the forest, taking huge strides, so that Thor, Loki and Roskva were soon left behind. Even Thialfi, as fleet of foot as any man in Midgard, was hard put to keep up with him. The travellers, however, could always tell which way to go by stopping to listen to the sound of Skrymir crashing through the forest ahead of them. In the evening, they caught up with the giant at the very edge of the forest. He was sitting under a large oak.

'There are no buildings here,' he said, 'but these oaks will give us shelter for the night. I'm tired after such a trek, and all I want to do is sleep.'

Thor looked pained and Loki ravenous; Thialfi and Roskva thought of their father's farm and their mother's cauldron. 'A lack of meat seems little hardship now,' said Roskva forlornly.

'But you can take my bag,' said Skrymir. 'Prepare yourselves some supper.' Then he lay down and rolled over and, within a minute, he was asleep. The oak tree shook at his snoring, and the birds perched in its branches took themselves off for a better place. Thor grasped the bag of provisions. 'You can make the fire,' he told the others, 'and I'll undo it.'

But that is just what he could not do. The straps keeping the travellers from their supper were as adamant as the rope Laeding that bound the wolf Fenrir, and Thor was unable to work a single one loose. His companions each took a turn and the prospect of having any supper that evening slowly receded.

Thor grew more and more frustrated. His beard bristled at the thought that Skrymir had not meant them to be able to open the bag. Then he lost his patience altogether. He gripped Mjollnir with both hands and took a couple of steps forward so that he stood right over Skrymir. Then he brought the hammer down on the giant's forehead.

Skrymir sat up. 'What was that?' he said. 'Did a leaf fall on my head?' He looked around him. 'And you, have you had your supper and are you ready to sleep?'

'As a matter of fact,' said Thor hurriedly, 'we were just about to turn in.' The travellers slowly made their way to the shelter of a second massive oak tree standing near by. They lay down there but, now that Thor's hammer had failed him for the first time since it was forged by Brokk and Eitri, they were all too anxious as well as too hungry to be able to sleep.

At midnight Skrymir was snoring again. The trees near by shuddered, and the ground shook under their bodies. Thor decided he had heard enough. Without a word he got up and quietly made his way over to Skrymir. Then he raised Mjollnir quickly and fiercely, and slammed it down on the middle of the giant's crown. He could feel that the head of the hammer had sunk well into Skrymir's brains.

Skrymir sat up. 'Now what was that?' he said. 'Did an acorn fall on my head?' He looked around him. 'And you, Thor, what are you doing over here?'

'Like you,' Thor said hastily, 'I've just woken up. But it's the middle of the night, and we should both go back to sleep.' As he talked, Thor backed away and lay down again beside his companions under the second oak. His brows beetled and he vowed to himself that when he got the chance to hit Skrymir again, the giant would see stars and plunge to the depth of Niflheim. He lay very still, waiting for Skrymir to go back to sleep.

Shortly before daybreak, Thor was sure his victim was fast asleep. His ears could scarcely withstand the racket of his snoring. Once more he got up, and quietly made his way over to Skrymir. He raised Mjollnir and, with all his immense might, crashed it into the giant's upturned temple. He buried the whole hammer head in Skrymir's brains; it sank in up to the handle.

Skrymir sat up and rubbed his cheek. 'Are there any birds up there in that tree?' he said. 'Just as I was waking, I thought some droppings fell on to me.' He looked around him. 'And you, Thor, are you well and truly awake?'

Thor was dumbstruck.

'It's time your companions stirred themselves. Tell them to get up and dress. It's not far from here to the stronghold of Utgard.' Skrymir narrowed his eyes. 'I've heard you whispering to each other that I'm no dwarf, but wait until you get to Utgard. You'll see men there much bigger than I am.'

Whether he was aware of it or not, Thor was slowly shaking his head. Loki and Thialfi and Roskva stirred under their oak, and listened to the giant.

'And let me give you a bit of advice,' said Skrymir. 'Keep your pride for your own kind; keep your mouths shut. Utgard-Loki's men won't stand for bragging from small fry like you.'

Thor seethed at such an insult, but there was nothing whatsoever he could do about it. He stood and listened.

'Your other course of action,' said Skrymir, 'would be to head straight home and, in my view, that would be the right one. But if you insist on going on, walk east from here.' Skrymir pointed out the way. 'As for me, I have to head north for those distant mountains.'

Then Skrymir picked up his bag of provisions, threw it over his back and, without a friendly word, without even a nod, he stumped away along the hem of the wood. Thor and his companions watched him go. 'I don't imagine we'll miss him much,' said Loki, 'or long to see him again.'

The four travellers left the forest behind. All morning they walked until it was no more than a blur on the horizon. They pressed on over rising ground and, when the sun stood almost directly overhead, crossed a saddle-back with three strange square-shaped valleys, and climbed down into a plain where stood a massive stronghold. The walls were so high that they had to throw back their heads to see the top of the buildings beyond.

Thor and his companions were happy to be near their journey's end. They hurried along a well-worn track that led up to the great gates fashioned from wrought iron. But they were locked and no one attended them. They peered through the bars and marvelled at the size of the halls inside the stronghold.

'The bigger they are, the heavier they fall,' said Thor, fingering Mjollnir. But then he remembered Skrymir again and felt uneasy. He rattled the gates but he was unable either to prise them open or to make himself heard.

'Whenever was brawn as good as brain?' said Loki. 'I said you'd need sharp wits.' Then he slipped between the bars and stood, grinning, inside Utgard. Slender Roskva and long-limbed Thialfi followed him at once, but Thor had a less easy time of it. In the end, however, he worked his way through: two of the iron bars gave way for him.

The travellers made for the huge hall before them. The door was open, and so they walked in. A large number of giants, male and female, old and young, most of them as vast as Skrymir had described, were lounging on the benches lodged against the walls. They stared at Thor and Loki and Thialfi and began to sneer; they ogled Roskva and began to leer. One giant sat alone in a chair at the end of the hall and judging him to be Utgard-Loki himself, Thor and his companions made their way up to him and courteously greeted him.

The giant king took not the least notice. That is to say, he did not look at them but through them. He made no move and he said nothing. Thor frowned and turned to Loki.

Loki yawned.

'Greetings!' repeated Thor much more forcefully, even though the king of the giants was not deaf. 'We have . . .'

'News,' boomed Utgard-Loki, rudely interrupting Thor, 'travels slowly from other worlds. An event, or visit, overtakes word of it.' He smiled a knowing smile. 'Or am I mistaken in taking this whippersnapper to be Thor the Charioteer?'

Thor bridled but, surrounded by giants, he was unable to call the tune.

For the first time Utgard-Loki looked at Thor. 'Well, maybe you're stronger than you look,' he said. 'At what skill would you say you excel? And what can your companions do? We never allow anyone to stay with us unless he is master of some craft or pastime.'

Loki was standing a couple of steps behind the others. Seeing that Thor had no answer on the tip of his tongue, he took up the challenge. 'I've a certain gift,' he called out, 'and I'm ready to prove it. There's no one in this hall who can eat faster than I.'

The giant king considered Loki. 'If you're right that will certainly be an accomplishment,' he said. 'We'll put it to the test.' Utgard-Loki looked along the benches and pointed at a giant sitting at the far end of the hall. 'Logi,' he shouted. 'Come up here and pit yourself against Loki.'

Then the giant king's servants carried a trencher into the hall and set it down before the throne. They heaped it with hunks of chopped meat, and it reminded Thor that rather too long had elapsed since they had last eaten. A chair was provided for Loki at one end of the trencher, and for Logi at the other, and at the word from the giant king, they both began to eat.

They gobbled and consumed and devoured. Each of them ate as fast as he could, edging his chair forward as he ate, and they met in the middle of the trencher. Loki had eaten every scrap of meat and left nothing but the bones. But Logi had not only eaten the meat; he had eaten the bones and the trencher as well.

'I would say,' proclaimed the giant king, 'that Loki is the loser.'

An unpleasant shout from his followers indicated that this was what they thought too.

Loki narrowed his eyes and viewed Utgard-Loki with deep mistrust.

'So what can this young lad do?' asked the giant king.

'I'll run a race against anyone you care to name,' said Thialfi.

'That's a singular skill,' said Utgard-Loki, 'and you must be a fine athlete if you think you can outstrip anyone here. We must put it at once to the test.'

Then the giant king and his followers and the four travellers made their way out of the hall to an open place where there was a level of grass that made a good running track.

'Hugi!' called the giant king.

One of the younger giants ambled up to Utgard-Loki.

'You're just the one to run against Thialfi. Go to your marks for the first race.'

Then, on a sign from the giant king, Thialfi and Hugi sprinted over the grass as fast as their legs could carry them. They scarcely seemed to touch the ground. And Hugi reached the end of the track so far ahead of Thialfi that he was able to turn round and welcome him.

'Well, Thialfi,' said the giant king, 'if you mean to win this contest you'll need to exert yourself. I must say, though, that I've never seen a man from Midgard with such a turn of speed.'

Then Thialfi and Hugi made their way back to the start again and, on a sign from the giant king, they sprinted over the grass as fast as their legs could carry them. They scarcely seemed to touch the ground. And by the time Hugi reached the end of the track, Thialfi was tailing him by the distance of a well-drawn crossbow shot.

'Thialfi is certainly fast on his feet,' said the giant king. 'But I think that victory has slipped from his grasp now. The third race will settle things.'

Thialfi and Hugi made their way back to the start once more and, on a sign from the giant king, they sprinted over the grass as fast as their legs could carry them. They scarcely seemed to touch the ground. And this time Hugi ran twice as fast at Thialfi. By the time he got to the end of the track, Thialfi had still not reached the half-way mark.

After this there was no argument. It was agreed that enough ground had been covered to settle the matter.

'Now, Thor,' said the giant king, 'you're well known for your boasting. I've heard that you brag endlessly about this and that and the other. Which of all your skills will you deign to show us?'

Thor ignored Utgard-Loki's insults, as he had to. 'I'll drink,' he said. 'And I very much doubt whether anyone here can sink as much as I can.'

'Very well,' said the giant king.

Then the four travellers and all the giants made their way back into the cavernous hall, and Utgard-Loki asked his cup-bearer to fetch the sconce-horn used by all his followers. The cup-bearer put the brimming horn into Thor's hands.

'We think a man who can drain this in one draught is a good drinker,' said the giant king. 'Some men take two draughts to empty it, but no one here is so feeble that he cannot finish it off in three.'

Thor had a look at the horn. He thought he had seen larger, although it seemed a bit on the long side. He was, moreover, very thirsty, for the giant king had not offered him or his companions so much as a drop since they first reached the hall. He raised the horn to his mouth, closed his eyes, and began to swill the liquid down in enormous gulps; and, as he drank, he felt sure that he would drain the whole horn in one draught. But Thor ran out of breath before the horn ran out of liquid. He raised his head, looked into the horn, and was startled to see that the level of the drink was little lower than before.

'You drank plenty,' boomed Utgard-Loki, 'but nothing like enough.'

The Thunder God scowled at the sconce-horn.

'If I'd been told that Thor could only drink that much, I'd never have believed it,' said the giant king. 'Still, I know you'll empty it with your second draught.'

Thor said nothing. He simply raised the horn to his mouth again, and opened his throat and poured a tide of drink down it until he was gasping for breath. But he was still unable to tilt the horn back and drain it. Thor raised his head and peered into the horn. He thought that although there was now some space between the rim and the drink and it was possible to carry the horn without spilling liquid, he had made rather less headway with his second draught than with his first.

Utgard-Loki shook his head and sighed. His breath was like an unsavoury warm wind swirling around Thor and Loki and Thialfi and Roskva. 'What's going on, Thor?' he asked. 'Haven't you left rather too much for comfort? It seems to me that if you're going to empty this horn, your third attempt will have to be your best.'

Thor glared at the sconce-horn and his red beard bristled.

'I know you're much admired in Asgard. But you won't be admired by any of us here, you know, not unless you do better in some other contest than you've done in this one.'

Thor was fretful at his own shortcoming and wrathful at the giant king's words. He raised the horn to his mouth, and opened his throat and drank and drank. He drank as much as he could stomach, and still he could not drain it. At last he raised his head and peered into the horn; and he saw that it was at least somewhat lower than before. Then Thor thrust the horn into the cup-bearer's hands, and angrily shook his head at the laughing invitations from all around him to drink more and drink again.

'It's clear enough,' remarked the giant king, 'that your prowess is not all that we supposed. Still, do you want to try your hand at some other kind of contest? Your drinking doesn't really do you much justice, does it?'

'I can prove myself in countless ways,' Thor said gruffly. 'But let me say I'd be surprised if anyone in Asgard called such huge draughts trifling.'

Utgard-Loki smiled down at Thor and said nothing.

'So what have you got in store for me now?' said Thor.

The giant king shook his head and sighed. 'Young giants here perform the feat of lifting my cat from the ground. I can't pretend it's very highly rated. Indeed, I'd never have dreamed of suggesting it to great Thor unless I'd seen with my own eyes that you're not half as strong as I thought you were.'

As if it had been waiting on its master's words, a grey cat under the giant king's throne uncoiled and sprang on to the floor. It was no kitten.

Thor stumped forward, put one massive arm under the cat, and began to lift. As he lifted, the cat simply arched its back. Now Thor used both hands and with a mighty effort he heaved at the cat. But the animal only arched its back still more so that its body formed a steep rainbow over the god's head; its four feet remained on the ground.

All the watching giants laughed at the way in which the cat, with its effortless movement, frustrated Thor's muscular attempts on it. Now Thor stood under the cat, between its legs, and rocked forward on to his toes in an attempt to lift it. And when he stretched his hands and the cat's belly as high above his head as he could, the cat was finally obliged to raise one paw. That was as much as Thor could manage.

'Much as I thought,' said Utgard-Loki. 'It's rather a big cat, and Thor is a midget compared to the mighty men at this court.'

'Call me what you like!' shouted Thor. 'But just let someone come and wrestle with me here. Now I'm really angry.' The Thunder God glared at the giants around him. He was beside himself with his own failures and the giant king's string of taunts and abuses.

Utgard-Loki looked along the benches and rubbed his bush of a beard. 'I can't say I see anyone here to wrestle with you,' he said. 'They'd all feel it was beneath them.'

Now Thor was wondering how he could bring Mjollnir into action. He fingered the hammer and grated his teeth.

'Wait!' said the giant king. 'I've an idea. Go and find Elli, my old foster-mother. Thor can wrestle with her if he wants to.'

The giants chuckled.

'She's thrown men who have struck me as stronger than Thor,' said Utgard-Loki.

After a little while, a horrible old crone hobbled into the hall and made her way towards the throne. The giant king got up to greet his foster-mother and asked her if she would consider coming to grips with Thor.

Elli agreed and threw away her stick. Then Thor fairly hurled himself at the old woman. But the moment he laid hands on her he knew she was far stronger than she seemed. Thor heaved and strained and grunted and the old woman stood firm and unshaken; the greater his pressure, the more easily she withstood it.

Now Elli won the upper hand and tried a hold or two. Suddenly she took Thor by surprise. She caught him in a lock and threw him off balance. Thor bared his teeth and clung to Elli desperately. He tried to take her down with him, but after a struggle, he was forced on to one knee.

'That's enough!' cried Utgard-Loki. 'Quite enough! You've shown us your strength as a wrestler, and there's certainly no need for you to take on any more of my followers.'

After the eating and the running, the drinking and the wrestling, it was late in the evening. Utgard-Loki himself found places for Thor and Loki, Thialfi and Roskva on the crowded benches. And there they were brought as much food and drink as they wished and were made most welcome. Then the floor was padded with bedding and pillows. In that high hall, the four weary travellers and the concourse of giants lay down and fell asleep.

Thor and his companions were the first to wake. They dressed and made ready to leave Utgard. But then the giant king stirred. He picked his way over the trunk-like bodies of his sleeping followers and set up a table beside the travellers. Then he woke his servants and, in a little while, Thor and Loki and Thialfi and Roskva were regaled once more with food and drink.

Now there was no limit to the giant king's courtesy. He made his way past the sleeping giants and out of the hall with his guests, and showed them through the massive gates of Utgard.

For a time they walked across the green plain in the early morning sunlight. The giant king was as genial as can be imagined, but after the previous night's experiences Thor was still chastened and Loki was unusually silent. Thialfi and Roskva, on the other hand, were glad to be away and alive – their spirits rose and they chattered gaily.

'Well,' said Utgard-Loki, 'this is where I must leave you.'

Thor looked up at him.

'How do you feel things have turned out?' asked the giant king. 'Were they as you thought? And tell me, have you ever met anyone more powerful than I?'

Thor shook his head. 'I can't deny,' he said, 'that I've come off second best. You've put me to shame. What's more, I know you'll bandy it about that I'm nothing to reckon with, and I don't like that.'

'Listen, Thor!' said the giant king. 'I'm going to tell you the truth now that we're outside the walls of Utgard – for as long as I live, and people listen to me, you'll never see the inside of those walls again.'

Thor looked baffled.

'If I'd known how strong you are, you wouldn't have got in at all,' continued Utgard-Loki. 'I can promise you that. Do you know you were very nearly the end of us all?'

Not a word escaped Loki. But he pressed his scarred lips together and began to smile secretly.

'I've used spells to trick you,' said the giant king. 'It was I who met you in the forest. You remember that bag packed with provisions? I fastened it with wires and so it's no wonder you could find no way of undoing it. Then you hit me three times with your hammer. The first blow was the lightest, but if it had touched me, it would have been enough to kill me. That saddle-backed hill not so far from my stronghold, and those three square-shaped valleys, one of them so deep – those were the dents you made with your hammer. I set that saddle-back between you and me, but you never knew it.'

Thor listened to Utgard-Loki's explanation. He listened with mixed feelings: wonder, relief, frustration, and slowly rising anger.

'I used spells, too,' said the giant king, 'when you and your companions vied with my followers. Loki was ravenous and ate very, very fast, but the man called Logi was wildfire itself. He burned up the trencher as well as the meat. And when Thialfi ran against Hugi, he was running against my own thought. He couldn't be expected to keep up with the speed of thought.'

Loki grinned maliciously at Thor. Thor saw nothing to smile about.

'And you,' said the giant king, 'when you drank from that horn you thought you were found wanting. But I tell you, I could scarcely believe my eyes. You didn't realise the other end of the horn was in the sea. When you get back to the ocean, you'll see just how much it has ebbed.' The giant king mused for a while. 'And that cat,' he boomed, 'that was a wonder! Everyone was appalled when you made it lift one paw off the ground. For of course it was not what it seemed to be: it was Jormungand, the Midgard Serpent that encircles the world and bites on its own tail. You reached up so high that it all but grazed its back on the sky.

'And it was a marvel, Thor, that you withstood Elli for so long, and even then only fell on to one knee. Elli is old age. Even if his life is not cut short by the sword or illness or by some accident, no one can withstand old age in the end.

'And now,' said the giant king, 'this is where our ways part. It will be better for us both if you do not visit me again. I have used magic, and I'll use it again to protect Utgard so that you'll never be able to harm me in any way.'

Thor was seething. When he heard the giant king's words, he gripped his hammer Mjollnir and raised it over his head. He summoned all his strength.

In vain, all in vain: Utgard-Loki had vanished.

Then Thor swung on his heel with the aim of smashing the walls of Utgard, the halls, the lounging giants. But there was no stronghold there – nothing but a sweeping, shimmering plain. No Utgard; no giant-king; except for the dents in the saddle-backed hill, it was all as if it had never been.

Thor turned to join his companions. The four of them slowly made their way back to the sea, and crossed it into Midgard. Thor retrieved his chariot and goats from the farmer and his wife. Then, with Loki, Thialfi and Roskva, he returned at last to Thrudvang, galloping over the green and gold fields of Asgard.

For note on this myth see page 206.

17 *The Lay of Hymir*

THE GODS HAD PLENTY OF FOOD but they had run out of mead and ale. They began to feast but the more they ate, the less they felt like eating, with no drink to wash the food down.

They sacrificed a small animal and dipped twigs into its blood. They shook them and the runes scored on them began to shine; they shook them again and divined that Aegir, god of the sea, could help them. So a group of gods and goddesses left Asgard and made for the island of Hlesey; and there they found Aegir and his wife Ran in their hall beneath the waves, lit only by gleaming gold.

The sea god was sitting at peace with the world and as blithe as a child. Thor, son of Odin, soon put an end to that. He looked Aegir in the eye and almost blinded him. 'Brew some ale for the gods,' he commanded. 'Brew it at once and brew plenty of it!'

Thor's abrupt tone angered Aegir. He lowered his eyes and considered how to repay him. 'I've no cauldron that would hold enough,' he said. 'Bring me a cauldron, Thor, and I'll brew ale for all the gods.'

The gods and goddesses looked at each other. None of them owned a cauldron that was large enough, nor did they have the least idea where they could get one. Then one-handed Tyr, always truthful, turned to the Thunder God and volunteered, 'My father, the giant Hymir, lives away to the east, beyond the stormy waves of the Elivagar. I know he has a cauldron – a huge cauldron five miles deep.'

'Do you think we could lay hands on it,' asked Thor, 'this water-whirler?'

'We can,' said Tyr, 'but only if we're cunning. Do not reveal who you are; call yourself Veur.'

So Thor and Tyr set off at high speed and that same day they reached Egil's farm, where Thor left his high-horned goats, Tanngnost Tooth Grinder and Tanngrisni Gat Tooth. Then the gods headed east and crossed the Elivagar; they travelled almost to the end of the earth and the sky above, and at last they came to Hymir's hall. It stood on a mountain quite close to the sea.

The first person they came across was Tyr's grandmother for whom

Tyr had very little love. She was a monster with nine hundred heads.

Thor shook his head and marvelled greatly.

But then Tyr's mother walked into the hall. She had the most beautiful pale skin and wore a necklace and armbands of gold. She welcomed her son and Thor and brought them goblets of ale. 'Giant blood runs in my veins,' she said. 'I know what's what. Brave as you both may be, I think you'd better hide beneath one of the cauldrons. My husband has rather a brusque way of greeting his guests.'

As might be expected, Thor had little liking for this suggestion, but Tyr sided with his mother and asked Thor what he stood to lose by being a little cautious. And so they waited in safety until ugly Hymir came in late from hunting. As he walked into the hall, the icicles hanging from his frozen beard clinked and chinked.

Hymir's wife got up to meet him. 'Greetings, Hymir! You've got good reason to be happy. Your son is here in the hall – how long we've waited while he journeyed far and wide. And he has brought a companion with him, the foe of Hrod and friend to all men. He is called Veur.' Hymir's gentle wife tried to soften the heart of her husband. 'Look at them sitting at the end of the hall under the gable, hiding behind one of those supports and hoping it will guard them.'

The giant glared balefully at the support and at once the gable's crossbeam cracked. Then eight well tempered cauldrons toppled and fell from the shelf there: they crashed on to the hall floor and smashed into smithereens. Only one did not break, the one under which Thor and Tyr were sheltering.

The two gods crawled out from under the rim and Hymir faced them. The old giant's eyes glittered and he pierced them with his gaze. But when he saw Hrod's sworn enemy step into the open, he felt uneasy himself and knew no good could come of his visit. All the same, he made due provision for his guests; he gave orders to his servants that no less than three oxen should be slaughtered and flayed and boiled.

At once his servants lopped off the heads of the cattle and carried them to the cauldron hanging over the fire. The meal was prepared. And before he went to sleep that night Sif's husband, Thor, astonished Hymir by devouring two whole oxen.

Hymir, the friend of Hrungnir, said, 'If the three of us want to eat again together, we'll have to go out hunting.'

'Let us go out rowing, then, and see what we can get,' said Veur to the savage giant. 'All I need from you is bait.'

'Help yourself from the pasture where my herd is grazing,' said Hymir. 'I've no doubt, giant killer, that you'll find a turd or two there easily enough.'

The god at once made his way out of Hymir's hall into the steep pasture surrounding it. There he found a splendid black ox, Himinhrjot the Heaven Bellower. The giant killer grabbed its high horns and wrenched them apart until they snapped, and then he broke the beast's neck. 'What you ate was bad enough,' said Hymir grimly. 'But it seems to me that you're even more of a nuisance left at large than sitting by my fire.'

Hymir and Thor left the others behind in the hall and went down to the sea. They launched the giant's boat and, to begin with, Thor manned the oars. Then Hymir took over. The giant, kinsman of apes, rowed well out from the land and then shipped his oars so that he could start to fish.

'Further!' urged Thor. 'Row further!'

'I don't want to row one stroke further,' Hymir replied.

The fierce giant began to prepare his tackle. He fixed hooks to his line and cast it over the gunwale. Almost at once the line tightened and Hymir hauled up two whales, hissing and sighing and churning the water into a maelstrom.

Odin's son, Veur, was sitting in the stern, and he prepared his gear with great care. The slaughterer of monsters and guardian of men baited his hook with the head of the ox Heaven Bellower. Then he cast his line into the dark water.

Under the waves the enemy of the gods, the serpent surrounding Midgard, let go of its own tail and gaped and took the bait.

Thor did not hesitate. Fist over fist, he quickly pulled in his line. Jormungand, the Midgard Serpent, lashed the sea into a frenzy. The water fizzed and frothed but the Thunder God did not loosen his grip. He dragged the monster up under the keel and then began to haul it over the gunwale.

Then Thor raised his hammer and it sang a grisly song on the hairy head of that terrible serpent, brother of Fenrir.

The serpent roared and the mountains of Jotunheim heard and replied. Midgard shuddered. Jormungand tugged at the great barb piercing the roof of its mouth. It twisted and wrenched and, at last, with a tearing of flesh, it set itself free; the serpent sank once more to the bottom of the sea.

Shaken and appalled by what he had seen, Hymir had no heart for words and made heavy weather of the homeward journey. First he pulled strongly on one oar, then on the other, in the hope of picking up a following wind to carry them closer to land and into calmer water. When the keel finally scraped the shingle, and the boat lodged, Hymir said, 'There's enough work here for two pairs of hands. Will you drag the boat up beyond the tide mark and secure it? Or would you rather pull the whales back to my hall?'

Without even bothering to reply, the Charioteer stood up and stepped out of the boat. He grabbed the prow with his massive fists and began to raise it – the bilge water slopped and swilled back to the stern. Then the god began to drag the boat with the two whales, the oars and the great bailer still inside it; he hauled it across sand, on through a birch wood, and over a hill until he reached Hymir's hall.

Tyr and his mother welcomed them there, and marvelled at Thor's feat in bringing the boat and the cargo up from the sea.

Even now, stubborn Hymir would not own that he had come off second best, and he resolved on another test of strength. 'You're a fair oarsman, certainly,' he said, 'but so are many others. I'd only call a man strong if he were able to smash this glass goblet.'

The Charioteer took the goblet from Hymir and promptly hurled it against one of the stone pillars supporting the gable. The hall was filled with bits and pieces of flying masonry. Then one of the giant's servants hurried down to the end of the hall and picked up the goblet from a heap of rubble. It was unbroken and he brought it back to Hymir.

Hymir's wife bent her head towards Thor. 'Throw it at his head,' she whispered. 'He eats so much that it's almost solid. However hard that glass is, his head must be harder.'

Then the Charioteer stood up again. He turned to face Hymir and, with all his divine strength, threw the goblet straight at the giant's forehead. Hymir's skull remained intact; but the wine goblet fractured and fell to the floor in two pieces.

Hymir bent down and picked them up and put them on his knees and stared at them. 'With the loss of this goblet,' he said sadly, 'I lose far more than a goblet.' The giant shook his head as if suddenly all his strength had ebbed from him. 'What's mine is yours now. My last cauldron is yours,' he said. 'I can't stop you from taking it. Even so, it will be a mighty task to cart it out of this hall. I'll never be able to say again, "Brew for me cauldron, cauldron, brew me ale!"'

Tyr did not need to be invited twice. He jumped up and took hold of the cauldron and began to pull, but he was unable to move it.

Hymir looked at him and smiled sourly.

Then Tyr tried again. He filled his lungs and pulled, but the cauldron only rocked and settled back into its original position.

Now Thor seized the rim. The cauldron was so massive and Thor exerted so much pressure that his feet splintered the wooden planks and broke right through the hall floor. Then the god hoisted the vast cauldron on to his shoulder and strode out of the hall. Its handles yapped at his ankles.

Thor and Tyr had not gone far before Thor turned round, wanting to have a last look at Hymir's hall. It was just as well that he did. The first thing he saw was Hymir and a whole throng of many-headed giants who had left their lairs in the east and were coming after them. Thor eased the massive cauldron from his shoulder and set it down on the ground. Then his hands were free to take a grip on Mjollnir. He stood his ground and swung his hammer; not a single monster, not one prowler of the wilderness, was able to withstand it.

Now Thor shouldered the cauldron again and the two gods hurried on. It was not long before they reached Egil's farm, where Thor had left his chariot and goats though one – thanks to Loki – was lame and limped in its harness.

Thor returned home while the gods were meeting in solemn assembly at the Well of Urd, under the branches of Yggdrasill. All the gods gazed at the cauldron, amazed; and they acclaimed Thor and his companion Tyr.

So Aegir was outwitted. Thor gave him the cauldron and took away his pride. And that winter and every winter the gods drank tides of warming ale brewed for them in the sea god's gleaming hall.

For note on this myth see page 208.

18 *Hyndla's Poem*

THE GIANTESS HYNDLA was asleep. She was growling in her gloomy cave, and it wasn't a pleasant sound.

Freyja and her boar stood in the cave's mouth, listening. Then Freyja called out: 'Hyndla, my friend! Hyndla, my sister! Wake up! Come out of your hole in the hill.'

The growling gave way to a sound like a bitch howling at the moon. The giantess was yawning.

'It's dark in there and it's getting dark out here,' Freyja called. 'And we must go to Valhalla together. We must win Odin's favour – he's always open-handed with his followers. He gave a helmet and a coat of mail to Hermod and he gave a sword to Sigmund.'

Now there was only silence within. Hyndla was listening.

'To some he gives gold, to others glory in battle,' said Freyja. 'To many he gives wisdom, and to many wordskill; fair winds to the sailor, craft to the poet and a stout heart to many a hero.' Freyja paused. 'I'll pay court to Thor as well,' she called out. 'And I'll ask him always to look kindly on you, and support you, although he has little love for giant women.'

A large unwholesome face loomed out of the gloom and Hyndla slouched out of the cave. She was dressed in something like sacking.

'Bring one of your wolves from its lair,' said Freyja, 'and let him and my boar run in harness. My boar cannot carry us both or hurry on the way to Asgard. He's a marvel and I don't want to ride him into the ground.'

Hyndla looked at the goddess with beady eyes. 'Nonsense!' she said. 'Pretence and promises! You can't even look me straight in the eye. Well, I'll tell you straight: that's no boar, that's your lover, young Ottar, thè son of Instein. You're riding your lover on the road to Valhalla.'

'And you,' said Freyja, 'are full of wild ideas. My lover beneath me on the road to Valhalla! This is my battle-boar, Hildisvini. His golden bristles show him the way in the dark. He was made by mastersmiths, the dwarfs Dain and Nabbi.'

100

Hyndla said nothing; she just sniffed, and started to back away into her cave.

Freyja would not give up and would not go away. She wrangled, she wheedled and cajoled, she threatened, she made promises and in the end she won the giantess's half-hearted agreement that they should journey to Asgard together.

'Little choice,' said the giantess, 'if I want any peace.'

As Freyja had suggested, the giantess rode a wolf and the goddess mounted her boar; the two animals ran in harness and at last the travellers reached the gates of Valhalla. They reined in beside Valgrind, the outer gate, and the deer Heidrun who was grazing there – water streaming from his horns – bounded away to safety.

Freyja and Hyndla dismounted, and walked down to the banks of the torrent Thund. 'Let us talk of the ancestry of two heroes,' Freyja said, 'Ottar the Young and Angantyr, two men fathered by gods.'

Hyndla smiled the half smile of one who knows the truth always comes out in the end.

'Ottar raised an altar to me,' cried the goddess. 'He built up the stones, and now they have turned to glass. He reddened the altar again and again with the blood of oxen; Ottar always put his faith in goddesses.' Freyja took a step towards the giantess. 'Now tell me the names of the ancients and their kindred. Which men are Skjoldungs, which are Skilfings, Othlings and Ylfings? Who are the first-born and who are the high born, the most noble men in Midgard?'

Hyndla looked at Freyja. Then she looked at the boar and took a deep breath. 'You, Ottar,' she said, 'are the son of Instein, and he was the son of Alf the Old; Alf sprang of Ulf, Ulf of Saefari, and Saefari's father was Svan the Red.'

The boar had pricked up his ears and was listening carefully.

'Your mother,' said the giantess, 'adorned with gleaming gold bracelets, was the priestess Hledis; her father was Frodi and her mother Friaut. Her lineage was peerless. Friaut's mother was Hildigun, who was the daughter of Svava and Saekonung. They're all your kinsmen, Ottar, you fool! It's a lot to remember – do you want to hear yet more?'

The boar was listening and so was Freyja.

'Hildigun's husband was Ketil,' the giantess resumed. 'So he was your mother's grandfather on her mother's side. Frodi came before Kari and Hoalf sprang of Hild. Nanna, the daughter of Nokkvi, came next; and her son married your father's sister. That lineage is long, and even longer, and they're all your kinsmen, Ottar you fool!'

'Isulf and Osulf, the sons of Olmod – whose wife was Skurhold, the daughter of Skekil: they should be counted among the noblest of heroes, and they're all your kinsmen, Ottar, you fool!

'Then,' said the giantess, 'there are the twelve Berserks: Hervard and Hjorvard, Hrani and Angantyr, Bui and Brami, Barri and Reifnir, Tind and Tyrfing and the two Haddings. These were the sons of Arngrim and Eyfura, born long ago on the island of Bolmsö. Howling and foaming in frenzy, they left a trail of terror and leaped like wildfire over land and water. And they're all your kinsmen, Ottar, you fool!'

The giantess narrowed her eyes and raised a horny finger. 'Long, long ago, all the sons of Jormunrek were given to the gods in sacrifice. Now Jormunrek was one of Sigurd's kinsmen – mark my words carefully – Sigurd who could stand against all, slayer of the dragon Fafnir. The hero Sigurd was Volsung's grandson, and his mother was Hjordis of the Hraudungs; her father was Eylimi of the Othlings. And they're all your kinsmen, Ottar, you fool!

'The sons of Gjuki and Grimhild were Gunnar and Hogni and his daughter was their sister Gudrun, Sigurd's wife. The third son, Gotthorm, was not fathered by Gjuki. And they're all your kinsmen, Ottar, you fool!

'Hvedna's father was Hjorvard and Haki was the best of his sons. Harald War Tooth was the son of Aud and her husband Hrorek the Ring Giver. Aud the Profound was Ivar's daughter, but Rathbard was the father of her son Randver. And they're all your kinsmen, Ottar, you fool!'

Freyja looked at the giantess in triumph. 'Ottar and Angantyr have made a wager,' she said, 'they have staked their whole inheritance on the matter of their lineage. Now give my boar the memory-beer so that, when Ottar and Angantyr meet three days hence, he'll remember your fine recital – every word of it. We must protect Instein's well earned wealth, his family heirlooms, so that the young hero can enjoy them.'

The giantess opened her rotting cavernous mouth and yawned. 'Go away!' she said. 'I want to sleep again. I'm not doing you any more favours.' She gave Freyja a withering look. 'My noble goddess,' she said, 'you leap around at night like Heidrun cavorting with a herd of goats.'

Freyja slowly raised her arms. 'I will girdle you with flame so you cannot leave this place without catching fire.'

Hyndla laughed in contempt. 'You've gone running to Od,' she said, 'who always loved you; and many another has wormed his way under your apron. My noble goddess, you leap around at night like Heidrun cavorting with a herd of goats.'

There was fire in Asgard, dancing in the air. A band of flame, a quivering halo, surrounded the giantess. Her limbs tightened; she pressed her arms against her side.

'Flames about me!' cried the giantess. 'The earth is on fire, and I must pay the full price or forfeit my life.' Hyndla flinched as the girdle began to tighten. 'Ottar's draught of memory-beer,' she called. 'Take it! It's full of venom. It will bring him to an evil end.'

'Stuff!' said Freyja. 'Nonsense! It is you who are full of bitterness and rancour. Your threats will do no harm, though.' The goddess was smiling and douce. She trailed her fingers down the boar's back. 'Ottar will drink nothing but the best if I get my way with the gods. Ottar will prosper.'

For note on this myth see page 210.

19 *Thor's Duel with Hrungnir*

ODIN, GOD OF GODS, was not content with being able to see everything that happened in the nine worlds. He was not content even with being able to understand all that he saw. His blood raced and he longed to test life's winds and tides for himself.

While Thor was away fighting trolls and troll women and their wolfchildren in Iron Wood, Odin bridled at his own lack of action. He became so restless that he donned his golden helmet and leaped on to Sleipnir, hungry for some happening.

Sleipnir vaulted the torrent Thund beside Valhalla and then the old river that snaked through a canyon; he spring-heeled over the broad gleaming river and the river teeming with spears, and his eight hooves clattered as he galloped over scree. For hour after hour Odin rode towards Jotunheim across utterly dreary country, at first flat and tussocky and pocked with small deserted lakes, then flat and stony – a sea of slabs where nothing lived and nothing grew. At last, where the land began to swell and in some places to smoke, leavened by fires far below the earth crust, Odin came to the hall of Hrungnir, strongest of all the giants.

'Who are you?' demanded Hrungnir.

The Raider pulled his blue cloak close about him, tilted his wide-brimmed hat forward, and said nothing.

'I've been watching. I saw you coming, your gold helmet flashing under the sun. You seemed to be riding as much through the air as on the ground.' Hrungnir rubbed his enormous nose. 'That's an uncommonly fine horse you've got there.'

'Better than any in Jotunheim,' retorted Odin. 'That's for sure.'

'That's what you think,' replied the giant.

'That's what I know,' said Odin.

'What do you know of Jotunheim, little man?' said Hrungnir, his temper rising. 'Don't be so certain.'

'I'm certain enough to wager my head on it.'

'You fool!' bellowed Hrungnir. 'Have you never heard of Gold Mane?'

'Who?' said Odin.

'My horse!' shouted Hrungnir. 'Gold Mane. Fast as your horse may be, Gold Mane will gallop him into the ground.'

'Gab!' spat Odin. 'All gab!'

'Gold Mane!' boomed Hrungnir, and his voice bounced back off the mountain wall.

'My head, Hrungnir,' called Odin, spurring Sleipnir into a gallop. 'Come and collect it!'

By the time Hrungnir had sprung on to Gold Mane, the Helmeted One was already on the other side of the smoking hill. The god and the giant raced across the flatlands and neither gained ground on the other; they raced into the uplands, and Hrungnir had no thought for anything but the chase; they crossed the nineteen rivers and before the thick-headed giant had taken stock of where he was, he found himself inside the walls of Asgard. Then at last he realised who his visitor had been.

Odin was waiting for Hrungnir beside Valgrind, the outer gate of Valhalla. 'That's an uncommonly fine horse you've got there,' he said.

Hrungnir glared at Odin, angry but unable now to do anything about it.

'You must be thirsty after such exertion,' Odin said. 'Let Gold Mane drink from this torrent Thund. And you, Hrungnir, come and drink in Valhalla.'

Odin led the way in under the roof of shields and spears, and his wolves Freki and Geri at once got up and loped towards him. Ranks of warriors filled the benches, feasting and drinking after the day's slaughter, and when they saw the giant, they began to shout. It was an awesome noise, as if the sea itself were caught in the mighty hall and waves were breaking on a strand of stones.

The Father of Battle raised one hand and as the clamour began to die down he called out, 'Hrungnir comes unarmed. He comes in peace. Let him drink and leave in peace.'

'How can I drink,' said Hrungnir, 'without a horn in my hands?'

Then the Valkyries Axe Time and Raging brought out the two massive horns from which Thor was used to drink. Both were brimming with ale.

'Drink!' said Odin. 'Test your thirst against our finest trenchermen.'

All the company in Valhalla watched as Hrungnir tossed off one horn without taking a breath, and then did the same with the other – such a tide of ale that even Thor might have had trouble with it. It was not long before the giant began to feel the effects. 'I will!' he shouted suddenly.

Odin looked at Hrungnir and his one eye glittered. 'Surely not,' he murmured.

'I will,' the giant shouted again. He waved his arms and, thrusting his head forward, glared at Odin. 'I'll pick up this piffling hall and carry it home to Jotunheim.'

The warriors sitting at the benches roared with laughter. Hrungnir swung round to face them. He meant to take steps towards them, but his balance was wrong and he reeled sideways. 'I'm going to shink Ashgard in the shea,' he bellowed.

Odin folded his arms. His mask-like face hid his thoughts. After a while he asked rather casually, 'Then what is to become of us?'

'You,' shouted Hrungnir. 'I'm going to kill you, you gods and warriors. Shmash you!' The giant brought his fist down on a trestle table; its end leaped up and the table danced and fell flat on its face.

There was not so much noise in the hall then. Everyone was watching Hrungnir. 'All except you two,' said the giant, pointing at Freyja and Sif, fairest of the goddesses. 'I'll take you back with me. I can find a use for you.'

Odin nodded and Freyja sidled forward. As she moved, all the jewels she was wearing flashed and glimmered, and Hrungnir tried to rub the stars out of his eyes. 'Drink again,' said Freyja. She poured a lot more ale into one of the horns.

'Is jat all the ale in thish hall?' demanded the giant. 'I'll drink every drop of ale in Ashgard.'

But although the giant drank more and more, he did not fall into a stupor as Freyja had planned; he simply assaulted the company with a stream of boasts. The gods and warriors soon became tired of them and Odin sent a messenger to find Thor in Iron Wood and ask him to return to Asgard at once.

It was not at all long before Thor burst into the hall, swinging his hammer. 'What's this?' he shouted. 'What next?' No one had seen him more angry, even when Loki had cut off Sif's hair. 'What next when sly devils of giants can hope to drink in Valhalla?'

Hrungnir looked at Thor blearily, and hiccuped.

'Who says you can drink here?' demanded Thor. 'And why is Freyja waiting on you? Is this a feast in honour of the giants?'

The giant waved an arm in the direction of Odin. 'His shafe conjuct,' he burbled. 'Ojin, he invited me in.'

106

'Easier to get in than out,' said Thor, tightening his hold on his hammer and raising it again.

'If you kill me unarmed,' said the giant, 'it won't add much to your fame – except for foul play.' Drunk as he was, he well understood he still had to escape from Valhalla unscathed and he knew, too, what would touch Thor most closely. 'It would be a better tesht,' he began, 'a much better tesht of your bravery.'

'What?' said Thor.

'If you dared fight me.'

'Dared,' repeated Thor between his teeth.

'I challenge you to meet me,' said Hrungnir. 'On the borders of Jotunheim and Ashgard. We'll fight at Grjotunagardar, the Stone Fence House.'

Thor looked at the giant and saw that he was in earnest.

'What a great fool I am to have left my hone and shield at home,' said Hrungnir. 'If I had my weapons, we could shettle the matter here and now. But if you mean to kill me unarmed, you're a coward.'

No one had dared challenge Thor to a duel before and the Thunder God was eager to accept. 'You can count on it,' he told the giant. 'I do not break faith. Do not break faith with me.'

Then Hrungnir barged out of Valhalla without a backward look. He heaved himself on to Gold Mane's back and galloped away to Jotunheim as fast as he could.

When the giants heard about Hrungnir's journey to Valhalla and his forthcoming duel with Thor, they thought he had won great honour. 'And,' they said, 'you have won the first part of a famous victory.' But for all that the giants were uneasy and anxious. They knew that if Hrungnir lost the duel, and was killed, that would be a bad hour for Jotunheim. 'If you do not win,' they said, 'what can we expect? You're the strongest of us all.'

At Grjotunagardar there was a river with a bed of clay.

'Let us dredge it,' said the giants. 'Let us mould a man so vast that Thor will shake at the sight of him.'

Then the giants worked night and day and piled up the clay and made a mountain of a man: he was nine leagues high, and measured three leagues across the chest from armpit to armpit.

'He may be so tall that the clouds gather round his head,' said the giants, 'but he is nothing but clay. What are we going to do about his heart?'

The giants were quite unable to find a heart anything like large enough. In the end they killed a mare and put her heart into his body. Its pump was enough to give the clay life, but rather too unsteady to inspire much confidence. They called this clay giant Mist Calf, and told him to wait by Grjotunagardar.

On the appointed day Hrungnir headed for the Stone Fence House. And unlike Mist Calf, his heart gave others heart. It was made of unyielding stone, sharp-edged and three-cornered. Hrungnir's head was made of stone, too, and so was the great shield he held in front of him as he waited for Thor. With his other hand, he grasped a huge hone; he shouldered it and was ready to hurl it. Hrungnir looked very nasty and very dangerous.

Then Thor, the Son of Earth, angrily sprang into his chariot and Thialfi leaped in beside him. It rocked beneath them. The Charioteer bawled and at once his two goats strained at their harnesses; the chariot rattled out of Thrudvang. The moon's path quivered and echoed. Lightning flared and flashed and men on middle earth thought the world itself was about to catch fire. Then hail lashed the ground; it smashed frail stooks and flattened fields of grass and men quailed within their walls. Headlands were shaken by such storms that gullies and rifts and gashes and chasms opened underfoot, and rocks and boulders cascaded into the curdling sea.

They rolled into Jotunheim towards Grjotunagardar. Then Thialfi jumped out of the chariot and ran ahead of it until he could see Hrungnir and Mist Calf. They stood side by side, and Mist Calf's heart thumped inside him.

'Thor can see you,' shouted Thialfi. 'Can you hear me? Thor can see you with your shield raised before you.' Thialfi cupped his hands to his mouth. 'Can you hear me, Hrungnir? Put it on the ground. Stand by your shield. Thor will come at you from below.'

Then Hrungnir laid his stone shield on the ground and stood on it; he grasped his hone with both hands.

The moment he saw Hrungnir standing at the Stone Fence House, Thor brandished his hammer and hurled it at him. The giant was assaulted by blinding forked flashes and claps of thunder.

Hrungnir saw the hammer flying towards him. He drew back his hone and aimed it straight at Mjollnir. The hammer and the hone met in mid-air with a dazzling flash, followed by a crack that was heard through the nine worlds. The hone was smashed into hundreds of fragments.

The shrapnel flew in every direction. One piece flew to Midgard and splintered again as it crashed into the ground – and every bit is a whetstone quarry. Another piece whistled through the air and lodged in Thor's head. The strongest of all the gods was badly wounded. He fell out of his chariot, and his blood streamed over the earth. But Thor's hammer found its target. Despite the hone, Mjollnir still struck Hrungnir on his forehead and crushed his skull. The giant tottered and fell. One of his massive legs pinned Thor down by the neck.

When Mist Calf saw Thor, he was terrified; he sprang a leak and peed uncontrollably. Then Thialfi swung his axe and attacked Mist Calf, the giant with feet of clay. Thialfi hacked at his legs and Mist Calf did not have enough strength in his body to fight back. He lurched and toppled backwards, and his fall shook Jotunheim. Every giant heard him fall; they knew what had happened at the Stone Fence House.

'My head!' growled Thor.

Thialfi inspected the piece of whetstone stuck in Thor's head.

'It's in better shape than Hrungnir's head,' said Thialfi. He seized the giant's leg and tried to lift it and release Thor. But for Thialfi it was like trying to lift the trunk of a tree; he was unable to move it an inch.

'Get help,' said Thor.

Thialfi put his fleetness of foot to good use. It was not at all long before many of the gods hurried out of Asgard and came to Grjotunagardar, rejoicing at Thor's great victory and anxious to release him. One by one the strongest of the gods tried to lift the giant's leg but none of them – not even Odin himself – was able to do anything about it.

The last to reach Stone Fence House was Magni, the son of Thor and the giantess Jarnsaxa. He was three years old. When he saw how the gods were unable to release his father, he said, 'Now let me try!' Magni stooped, grasped Hrungnir by the heel, and swung the giant's foot away from his father's neck.

All the gods cried out in wonder and Thor quickly got to his feet.

'It's a pity I didn't come sooner,' said Magni. 'If I had met this giant, I'd have struck him dead with my bare fist.'

'If you go on as you've begun,' said Thor warmly, clamping an iron-gloved hand on to his son's shoulder, 'you'll become quite strong.'

'My mother is Iron Cutlass,' Magni said. 'And I am the son of Thunder.'

'What's more,' said Thor, 'I'm going to give you Gold Mane. Take Hrungnir's horse as a reward.'

'No,' said Odin sharply. 'You shouldn't give such an uncommonly fine horse to the son of a giantess instead of to your own father.'

Thor took no notice. He clapped his hands to his banging head and rode back to Asgard, followed by the Aesir. Only Odin complained; the other gods gave thanks that good had prevailed over evil and that they seemed quite safe again, as safe as they had ever been.

When Thor got to Thrudvang, and walked into his own hall Bilskirnir, the whetstone was still stuck in his head. So he sent to Midgard for the sybil Groa, the wife of Aurvandil the Brave. The wise woman hurried up over Bifrost and all night she chanted magic words over Thor – charms and spells known only to her. As she sang, the hone began to work loose, and the hammering in Thor's head began to fade. It seemed less like pain than the memory of pain.

Thor was so thankful that he wanted to make Groa happy. 'I have a surprise for you,' he said.

'Nothing could surprise me,' said Groa.

'This will,' said Thor. 'Not long ago I was in the north and I met your husband, Aurvandil the Brave.'

Groa stiffened. Then she began to shake her head sadly.

'You may think he's dead,' said Thor, 'but I brought him out of Jotunheim. I waded across the streams of venom, Elivagar, carrying him in a basket strapped on to my back.'

'Stuff!' said Groa gruffly, not because she wanted to disbelieve Thor but because she did not dare to believe him.

'Do you need proof?' asked Thor.

'Yes,' said Groa.

'All night you've sung charms over my head,' said Thor, 'and it is almost morning. Come with me.' The Thunder God led the way out of Bilskirnir into the silent courtyard. 'Look!' said Thor, pointing into the sky. 'Have you ever seen that star?'

Groa frowned and shook her head.

Thor smiled faintly. 'One of Aurvandil's toes stuck out of the basket, and froze. So I broke it off and hurled it into heaven. Now and always that star will be known as Aurvandil's Toe.'

Groa's heart was pounding; her eyes shone with tears of joy.

'Now are you satisfied?' said Thor. 'And I'll tell you one thing more. It won't be long at all now before your husband gets home.'

Groa felt as if nothing else in the world had ever mattered; and she felt as if there were no way in which she could properly thank Thor.

'Only finish your charms and spells,' said Thor. 'Then I too will be happy.'

Groa looked at Thor and gaped.

'The charms,' said Thor.

The sybil's head and heart whirled and her blood raced round her body. She was so excited that she could not recall a single charm.

'Think, woman!' said Thor fretfully.

Groa buried her face in her hands but it was no good.

'Think, woman, think!' roared Thor. His eyes blazed and his red beard bristled.

But Groa was able to think only of her husband Aurvandil's homecoming, and of a shining star. Thor sent her packing with a bellow of fury. And that is why the whetstone remained in Thor's head.

For note on this myth see page 212.

20 *Odin and Billing's Daughter*

'CREAKING BOW,' cried the High One, 'a burning flame, a yawning wolf, a croaking raven, a grunting wild boar, a tree with shallow roots, mounting waves, a boiling kettle, a flying arrow, tide on the ebb, new ice, a coiled snake, a bride's pillow talk, a sword with a hairline, a playful bear, the sons of a king, an ailing calf, a stubborn thrall, a witch's flattery, a fresh corpse, a chance encounter with your brother's murderer, a half-gutted house, a racehorse – if he lames one leg he will be useless: no man should be such a fool as to trust these things.'

The High One cried, 'A man should not trust a woman's word and he should never rely on her promises. The hearts of women were turned on a whirling wheel and imbued with caprice.

'To love a fickle woman is like this: setting out over ice with a two year old colt, unshod, restive and unbroken; or sailing a ship without a rudder in a storm; or hunting reindeer over slippery rocks, with a pulled hamstring.

'I will speak clearly,' cried the High One, 'for I know them both: men deceive women. The fairer our words the falser our thoughts. We undermine their commonsense. A man who longs for a woman's love mouths soft words, and brings gifts, and praises her beauty; sophistry works wonders.

'Let no man mock another because of his love. Time and again the wise are fettered by beauty, and ache with love-longing, while fools remain unmoved and free.

'Let no man mock another over what touches many men. Time and again wise men behave like idiots in the name of some grand passion. Each man must be his own best judge; nothing is worse for a man who knows himself than frustrated desire.'

The High One cried, 'I learned this for myself when I sat among the reeds, waiting and waiting for my love. I prized that woman as much as my own life. Much good it did me!

'I first saw Billing's daughter while she slept. She was as dazzling as the sun. I thought the whole earth would become a wilderness unless I

112

could lie with her. "Come back after dark, Odin, if you want to win this woman." That was what she said. "It would be the worse for us if anyone found we were lovers."

'I hurried off, light-headed with desire, wholly taken in by her dulcet words. I was sure she would soon be mine and mine and mine again.

'I came back after nightfall. All the warriors in the stronghold were awake, holding burning torches, waving blazing brands. I had followed a false trail.

'I would not be shaken off. I came back at dawn, and all the warriors were asleep. What did I find? Nothing but a bitch that the fair woman had leashed to her bed.

'Men should know that many a fine woman proves fickle when put to the test. I learned this when I wooed Billing's daughter with fair words. That treacherous lady responded with contempt, foul contempt and nothing else,' cried the High One.

For note on this myth see page 214.

21 *Gylfi and Gefion*

'YOU HAVE TREATED ME like a king,' said Gylfi.
The wizened beggar-woman sat in her cocoon of filthy, reeking rags and listened.

'Our bed was only this bare ground,' said Gylfi, 'and our roof was only this whispering tree and the litter of stars beyond. But all that you had to share – your scraps of food, your store of understanding – you willingly offered.'

The beggar-woman's eyes were deep wells, unfathomable and strangely gleaming.

'You have treated me like a king,' Gylfi said, 'and now I want to tell you that I am the king.'

The beggar-woman looked at Gylfi without changing her expression. She sniffed.

'As you shared with me, I will share with you,' said Gylfi. 'You're welcome to as much of Sweden as you can plough with four oxen in one day and one night.'

Then the king and the beggar-woman went their own ways. Gylfi found and followed a track out of the forest and came back to his court. The beggar-woman, none other than the goddess Gefion, left Midgard and journeyed into Jotunheim.

Gefion walked past cauldrons of mud and boiling springs, she worked her way round the base of a mountain and reached a secluded fertile valley. No man lived there, but four huge oxen were grazing under the hot sun – the four sons of the goddess and a giant.

Gefion took her sons with her back to Midgard and into the country of Sweden. She chose a piece of land, very fine to look at and even better for farming, and yoked the four oxen to a massive plough. Now the coulter bit so deep that it began to loosen the crust of the earth. Now the oxen strained with every sinew and muscle and wrenched the mould away from the molten rock beneath.

Gefion laughed as her four sons dragged off a great piece of land. The oxen slowly made their way westward. They reeked with sweat. The goddess urged them on and they waded into the sea, still hauling the land behind them, until at last they stopped in the middle of a sound.

'Leave the land here,' Gefion said. 'Let it lie here until the end of the world!' She unyoked the oxen from the plough, oxen with eyes like moons not unlike their mother. 'And let this fertile island be known as Zealand,' said the goddess.

So Gefion repaid Gylfi's generosity by looting his land. That which made Denmark larger made Sweden smaller. Water oozed from the earth and fell from the sky into the gaping wound where the land had been ripped up, and it became a lake. Men called it Mälar.

And that is why the headlands of Zealand fit the inlets and the bays and the bights of Lake Mälar.

For note on this myth see page 215.

22 *The Lay of Harbard*

A RANK OF MOUNTAINS stood behind Thor. Some were like upturned ships, some like unfinished pyramids and monstrous cones with their tops sawn off, and none of them were smiling.

Thor strode west over the tundra, and the sun kept pace with him. Then late in the morning he left the wilderness behind and hurried across scrub and undulating land.

So he came to a sound, a swift deep channel. The air was utterly still there. The sun placed a dazzling hand on the water, and the water seemed barely to move as it moved.

On the far bank a figure sprawled in the midday sun, and his flat-bottomed boat lounged beside him.

'Hey!' bawled Thor, and the water quivered. 'You over there. Are you the ferryman?'

The figure stirred and sat up. He cupped his hands. 'Who is that oaf yelling over the water?'

'Ferry me across,' called Thor. 'I'll pay you well from this panier.' Thor eased his thumbs under the shoulder straps. 'It's packed out with fine fare, and I've eaten as much as I can already. I had a glut of herrings and a pool of porridge before I set out.'

The ferryman slowly got to his feet and pulled his hat well down over his head. 'You're pleased with yourself, aren't you? Ah! If only you knew what lies in store for you. When you near home, you'll hear nothing but moans. Your mother is dead.'

'My mother dead!' cried Thor. He screwed up his eyes; he screwed up his whole face. 'What grief could be greater?'

Having alarmed and upset the credulous Thor, the ferryman began to insult him. 'Barefoot,' he called scathingly. 'Beggar's clothes. Not even breeches. I doubt if you even have a place you can call your own.'

'Bring over your boat,' roared Thor. 'No need to be afraid: I'll guide you in. Anyhow whose ferry is that?'

Now the ferryman took his time; he turned his back on Thor to taunt him, and smiled grimly.

'Whose ferry is that?' repeated Thor.

116

'Hildolf, the slaughtering wolf, entrusts it to me. He's a wise man. He lives on Rathsey, the Isle of Counsel. And he has given me my orders: no pilferers, no horse thieves; only worthy men and well known faces. So,' said the ferryman, 'if you want to cross here, tell me your name.'

'I'll tell you,' shouted Thor, 'though I stand alone. I am Odin's son. I am Meili's brother, Magni's father, strongest of the gods. You, ferryman, you're talking to Thor.' The god's words made waves on the sound; they ran straight across the channel and broke at the ferryman's feet. 'And who are you, I'd like to know?' shouted Thor. 'Tell me your name, ferryman.'

'My name is Harbard; I seldom hide it.'

'Why should you hide it? Or am I talking to an outlaw caught up in some feud?'

'What if you are?' retorted the ferryman. 'Unless I'm fated, I can look after myself against the likes of you.'

Thor clenched his right fist, rubbed it against his beard and stared at the cold water. 'You're not worth the trouble of wading across this channel and getting soaked up to the waist. But I'll repay you, you knock-kneed ferryman, when I get across this sound!'

Harbard put his hands on his hips. 'Here I stand and here I'll wait. You've not met my equal since you fought Hrungnir.'

'You want to talk about Hrungnir, do you? That lolloping giant, do you know his head was made of stone? And yet I killed him, I laid him out lifeless. And you, Harbard, what were you doing meanwhile?'

'I spent five winters with Fjolvar on the island of Algron. There was plenty to do. There we fought. We sank our shafts into heroes and virgins.'

Thor rubbed his beard again. 'How did you win them, your women?'

'They welcomed us with good grace; yes, with high spirits. And they were well advised to do so, for they could no more have escaped us than make ropes of sand or dig the bottoms out of valleys.' Harbard opened his arms. 'I was the one they turned to first. I slept with seven sisters, and each one gave me ecstasy. And you, Thor, what were you doing meanwhile?'

'I killed the fierce giant Thiazi and hurled the eyes of Alvaldi's son into scalding heaven. They bear witness to my feats; everyone can see them. And you, Harbard, what were you doing meanwhile?'

'I enticed night riders from their husbands, I wrought love craft with those witches. And that giant Hlebard, he was not made of straw; he gave me a magic branch, and I whipped his wits off him.'

'So,' called Thor, 'that's how you repay a generous gift.'

The grey-bearded ferryman shrugged. 'The oak,' he shouted across the shining water, 'grows strong on shavings from all sides. Each man for himself. And you, Thor, what were you doing meanwhile?'

'I journeyed east to Jotunheim. I slaughtered slovenly giant women as they shambled over the fells. If they were still alive, there would be a terrible throng of giants and no men in Midgard. And you, Harbard, what were you doing meanwhile?'

'I was the cause of war in Valland, the land of slaughter. I set princes at each other's throats. I thwarted peace.'

Thor looked at the ferryman. He listened; his brow was creased in thought.

'After they've fallen in the fight,' shouted Harbard, 'the nobly born journey to Odin. But Thor, he caters for a great gang of thralls.'

'I see how even-handed you'd be in your gifts of men to the gods,' retorted Thor. 'Not that you've any say in the matter.'

'Your limbs are strong but your heart is faint,' jeered the ferryman. 'Such was your fear, you were glad enough once to crawl into a glove, and there you forgot your name. Thunderer? You were so scared Fjalar might hear you that you didn't dare fart or sneeze.'

'You womanish ferryman! I'd swipe you straight down to Hel if I could reach over this sound.'

'Why bother?' said Harbard, with a voice like oil. 'We have no quarrel. And you, Thor, what did you do next?'

'Away in the east, I patrolled the bank of the Iving. Svarang's sons tried their luck there.' Thor suddenly stooped, and in one movement picked up a block of stone and hurled it over the sound. It whirred as it flew. Harbard stepped hurriedly out of the way and the boulder buried itself in the bank beside him. 'Like that!' yelled Thor. 'They threw boulders; much good it did them! Then they begged for a truce. And you, Harbard, what were you doing meanwhile?'

'I was in the east, too, and came to a certain understanding. I turned the head of a linen-white maid, and we met in secret. I aroused that lady, wearing gold ornaments, and then I enjoyed her.'

'A woman well found,' said Thor.

'I could have done with your help,' called Harbard, 'to hold that white maid down.'

'I wish I'd been with you,' shouted Thor eagerly. 'I'd have been only too ready.'

'And I'd have trusted you,' said Harbard evenly, 'if you were not known for breaking promises.'

'No!' called Thor. 'That's not true. I'm no heel-biter, like an old leather shoe in spring.'

'And you, Thor, what were you doing meanwhile?'

'I was on Hlesey, the island of the sea god. I slew the brides of the Berserks. They were depraved serpents.'

'Thor, you brought shame on your head,' said Harbard scathingly, 'you ladykiller!'

'They were more like wolves than women,' protested Thor. 'They attacked my well trimmed ship and threatened us with iron clubs; Thialfi ran away. And you, Harbard, what were you doing meanwhile?'

'I was one of the host that came to Asgard's frontiers to raise our banners and redden our spears.'

'Are you telling me that you meant to fight the gods?'

'I'll give you a little finger-ring and then you won't fret,' said the ferryman, mockingly. 'It will be a peace-maker between us.'

Thor was enraged. He kicked at the bank and a hailstorm of grit and pebbles ripped the silken water. He gripped Mjollnir in his huge fist. 'Where did you dredge up such filthy abuse? I've never heard so foul an insult.'

'I learned it from men, age-old men who live in the hills of home.'

Thor shook his head in anger and envy. 'That's a fine name for barrows: hills of home.'

'That's what I call them.'

'And your sharp tongue will be the end of you if I choose to wade across this river,' shouted Thor. 'You'll howl more loudly than a wolf if I hit you with this hammer.'

Harbard replied all the more swiftly. 'Your wife, Sif, she's doing some entertaining. She has a lover. Keep your strength for him; that would be more to the point.'

'You witless fool!' roared Thor. 'Shut your mouth and keep your stabbing tongue inside it. You're a liar!'

The ferryman paused and with his one eye peered into the shining water that stops for no man. 'No,' he called, 'I'm telling the truth. Anyhow, how long you're taking to get home! You'd be well on your way by now if you'd crossed in this boat.'

'You womanish ferryman! You've kept me waiting for much too long.' Thor paced up and down the bank of the sound, now swinging round and changing direction, now glaring across the water, like a caged animal. The ferryman watched him. 'I never thought a mere ferryman could detain Asathor.'

Thor's eyes were blazing and he gave a great bellow that rang round the sky. 'Here's some advice: row your boat straight over; keep your mouth shut; and set down Magni's father on the far bank.'

'Go away!' retorted Harbard. 'I'm not rowing you across.'

Thor bent over the swift cold water. He saw himself in it, and saw, too, how the ferryman had toyed with him and how, for once, his strength was no use to him. He lifted his head and thrust out his red beard. 'If you won't ferry me over,' he called, 'at least tell me the way round.'

'Few words but many miles,' replied Harbard. 'Over stock and over stone. Take the track on your left until you come to Midgard; and there you'll find your mother, Fjorgyn. She'll show you the way to the trembling rainbow that brings men to Asgard.'

'Can I get home today?' aked Thor.

'Walk fast, don't rest, and you might be back before sunrise.'

'We've talked long enough,' said Thor angrily. 'You do nothing but mock me.' He turned, and then looked back over his shoulder. 'If we ever meet, I'll pay you in full for refusing me this ride.'

Thor strode away, furious and scorned. And as he went, the jeering laugh of the ferryman followed him. And then Harbard's words: 'Get lost! Let every evil being have you!'

The god quickened into the vast grey wasteland. There was a sandstorm in the wilderness. The wind unwound it, a long scarf leading into the lee of the indigo mountains.

For note on this myth see page 216.

23 *The Ballad of Svipdag*

THE GHASTLY ROTTING SMELL rose towards him. The cold began to burn him. The darkness reached up to him and he drew near to the place as dreadful as the worst of fears, the worst of dreams.

Even now, he did not flinch or falter. Svipdag was swift as light. He reached the gates of Niflheim, far under the world, and shouted, 'Groa, wake! Wake, wise mother! I stand at the doors of the dead and call on you. Remember, before you went to your burial mound, remember how you told your son to ask for help.'

Then the seeress Groa rose out of her grave and slowly moved to the gates of Niflheim. 'My only son,' she moaned, 'what death in life afflicts you? What dire fate makes you call on me who have left the quick world and lie in the mould?'

'My father has married a two-faced woman,' Svipdag said. 'She is working against me. She bids me go where no man can safely go, and win the love of Menglad.'

'That road is long,' said Groa, 'and the quest will be long, but love lasts long too. You may achieve your aim if the fates favour you.'

'Then sing strong charms over me, mother. Guard your son if you can. I fear death will ambush me and I am still young.'

'The first charm I'll sing,' Groa replied, 'is well proven. Rani taught it to Rind. Shrug off whatever sickens you; depend on your own strength.

'I'll sing a second time then in case you are tempted to take the wrong path: the bolts of Urd will be railings to keep you on the right road.

'Then third I'll sing in case swollen rivers threaten you: the rivers Horn and Ruth will plunge into Niflheim, and the waters will part before you.

'Then fourth I'll sing in case enemies attack you on the gallows way: your wish will be their desire, and they'll long only for peace.

'Then fifth I'll sing in case you're fettered and have no freedom

121

of movement: I sing a loosening spell over your thighs – and a lock will spring apart, releasing your limbs; chains will fall from your ankles.

'Then sixth I'll sing in case storms at sea go on the rampage in the way no man can: neither wind nor wave will harm you, and you'll have a fair passage.

'Then seventh I'll sing in case you freeze in the high rocky mountains: the fatal frost will get no grip on your flesh, and your body will be unharmed.

'Then eighth I'll sing in case you have taken some dismal track in the darkness: no curse from a dead Christian woman will ever harm you.

'Then ninth I'll sing in case you have to debate with some brute of a giant: your head shall be well stocked with wits and your mouth with wise words.

'Now take the road with all its hidden dangers, and let no evil work against your love! Carry your mother's spells with you and keep them in your heart; you'll prosper for as long as my words live in you.'

Then Svipdag turned away from his dead mother, Groa, and the stone gates of Niflheim. He made his way back up to Midgard and began his search for Menglad through the nine worlds. The road was long and his quest for Menglad seemed longer.

One day, in Jotunheim, Svipdag came to a massive stronghold, girdled by flame and guarded by a giant. 'Who are you?' shouted Svipdag, 'standing there at the gate?'

'What do you want?' retorted the giant. 'What are you looking for? And why are you on the road at all, wanderer?' The giant looked no less unfriendly than he sounded. He dismissed Svipdag with a nod, and stuck a thumb over his shoulder. 'That's your way, anyhow: a dew-path through the forest. There's no welcome for weaklings here.'

'Who are you,' repeated Svipdag, 'standing there at the gate, turning away travellers?'

'Nobody is going to welcome you with outstretched arms,' replied the giant. 'You'd do best to go home. My name is Fjolsvid, and I'm known for my wisdom. But I don't throw food around. You'll never get a foothold in this hall – you'll leave as you've come, ravenous as a wolf.'

Svipdag shook his head. 'Few men turn their backs when they mean to set eyes on their loved one. The gates of this golden hall are gleaming; I mean to make my home here.'

'Who is your father, then,' asked Fjolsvid, 'and what is your ancestry?'

'My name is Vindkald,' said Svipdag. 'I'm the son of Varkald whose father was Fjolkald; Wind Cold, Cold of the Early Spring, Great Cold: those are our names. Now tell me this, Fjolsvid, and tell me truly: Who sits in the high seat of this fine hall? Who is its owner?'

'Her name is Menglad of the necklaces, and her father was Svafrthorin's son,' said the giant. 'She sits in the high seat of this handsome hall. She is its owner.'

Svipdag said, 'Now tell me this, Fjolsvid, and tell me truly: what's the gate called? It's even more unyielding than anything in Asgard.'

'It's called Clanging Thrymgjol,' said the giant, 'and it was made by the three sons of the sun-blinded dwarf Solblindi. Whoever touches the latch is at once trapped by it.'

Svipdag said, 'Now tell me this, Fjolsvid. What's the name of the building? It's even more massive than anything in Asgard.'

'Its name is Gastropnir the Guest Crusher,' the giant said and he smiled grimly. I made it myself a long while ago from the limbs of the clay giant Leirbrimir. And I braced it so firmly inside and out that it will stand for as long as the world lasts.'

'Now tell me this, Fjolsvid,' said Svipdag. 'What is the tree called that spreads its limbs over all the worlds?'

'It's called Mimir's tree, Yggdrasill,' the giant replied. 'No man alive has seen all its roots; and few can guess what will fell it, for neither axe nor fire will be its downfall.'

'Tell me this, then, Fjolsvid,' Svipdag said: 'What issues from the seed of this mighty tree that neither axe nor fire will fell?'

'Women in childbirth cook the fruit,' said the giant. 'Then the hidden child is delivered safely. That's why people esteem it.'

'What's the cock called,' Svipdag said, 'that sits on the topmost bough, adorned with gleaming gold?'

'He's called the tree snake Vidofnir,' answered Fjolsvid. 'He illumines Yggdrasill's limbs like lightning. And he brings nothing but sorrow to Surt and his wife Sinmora.'

'Tell me this, then, Fjolsvid: What are the hounds called that prowl and snarl in front of this stronghold?'

'To tell the truth,' said the giant, 'they are Gif and Geri. They're huge already and will grow more huge before Ragnarok.'

'Can no one hope to get inside this stronghold,' Svipdag asked, 'while these ravenous hounds are asleep?'

'They never sleep at the same time,' said the giant. 'That is why they were made hall wardens. One sleeps by night, the other by day, and so no one can ever pass unseen into the stronghold.'

'Is there no meat a man can throw to them,' said Svipdag, 'and dart in while they are wolfing it down?'

'To tell the truth,' said Fjolsvid, 'the cock Vidofnir has two wings. That alone is the meat a man can throw to them and dart in while they are wolfing it down.'

'What's the weapon with which to dispatch Vidofnir to the House of Hel?' Svipdag asked.

'That's the sword Laevateinn, the Wounding Wand,' said the giant. 'Loki made it, he forged it with runes at the gates of Niflheim. It lies in Laegjarn's chest, guarded by nine locks, and Sinmora watches over it.'

'Can a man hope to steal that sword and get away unscathed?' asked Svipdag.

'A man can hope to steal that sword,' Fjolsvid replied, 'if he takes what few can win as a gift for Sinmora.'

'What is the treasure a man should take to delight that gaunt giantess?' Svipdag demanded.

'In your pouch,' said the giant, 'take Vidofnir's tail feather. Give it to Sinmora and she'll give you Laevateinn in return.'

'What's the name of this hall, girdled with flickering, magic flames?' asked Svipdag.

'It's called Lyr, the Holder of Heat,' Fjolsvid replied. 'It will always quiver and shimmer like a spear point. All men know of this noble hall and no hall more noble than this.'

'Which of the gods fashioned this great hall that I see within the stronghold?' said Svipdag.

'It was Loki,' said the giant, 'the Fear of the Folk. And he was helped by the dwarfs Uni and Iri, Bari and Jari, Var and Vegdrasil, Dori and Ori and Delling.'

Then Svipdag asked, 'What's the mountain called on which that lovely woman is reclining?'

'It's called Lyfjaberg, the Hill of Healing,' replied Fjolsvid, 'and it will always be a source of comfort to the sick and the suffering. Every woman who climbs it will be cured, even if she has long been confined to her bed.'

'Who are the maidens smiling and sitting at Menglad's knees?' asked Svipdag.

'One is called Hlif the Helper,' said the giant. 'Then there are

Hlifthrasa and Thjodvara; and shining Bjort and Bleik the white, Blid and Frid, kindly Eir and the gold-giving Aurboda.'

'Now tell me this, Fjolsvid,' said Svipdag. 'Do they help all those who make offerings, and truly need succour?'

'They soon help all those who make offerings on the high altars,' said the giant. 'And if they see someone is in danger, they will guard him.'

Svipdag said, 'Now tell me this, Fjolsvid, and tell me truly: Is there any man who can hope to sleep in the arms of fair Menglad?'

'No man but one,' said the giant, 'can hope to sleep in the arms of fair Menglad. And that man is Svipdag. That woman who shines like the sun is destined to be his bride.'

'Throw back the gates!' cried the wanderer. 'Open a wide gateway! I am none other than Svipdag!' He looked at Fjolsvid, elated. 'Hurry to Menglad and ask her to grant me my heart's desire.'

The giant made his way up the green slope behind the stronghold and reached Menglad and her maidservants.

'Listen!' he said. 'A man has arrived at the stronghold whom you must come and see for yourself! The hounds are fawning on him, and the great gates burst open of their own accord. I think this man is Svipdag.'

Menglad looked at Fjolsvid and her heart beat as if it would burst out of her. She said in a low voice, 'If you're lying when you say that this hero has come to my hall at last. . . .' Her voice hardened. 'It will not be long before greedy ravens peck out your eyes while you swing from the gallows tree.'

Menglad and her maidens and the giant Fjolsvid picked their way down the slope, and crossed the stronghold to the main gateway. Menglad at once faced the wanderer. Anxiously she asked, 'Where have you come from? How did you get here? What do your kinsmen call you? I must know your name, your ancestry, before I can be sure I am to be your bride.'

'I am Svipdag, the son of sun-bright Solbjart; and I've followed wind-cold ways to this place. No man can deny Urd, even though her gifts are unearned.'

Menglad opened her arms. 'Svipdag,' she said. 'You are welcome here. I've waited so long for you. The kiss of welcome is yours, Svipdag.' Then she moved slowly towards the traveller, and she asked, 'Is there any greater sweetness than the long awaited meeting between lover and loved one?'

Svipdag stretched out his arms towards Menglad.

Menglad said: 'Day after day I've sat on the Hill of Healing, waiting for you. And now I have what I've always dreamed of.'

Menglad and Svipdag stepped towards each other and touched. And Menglad said: 'We've yearned alike; I longed for you and you have longed for my love. But now, and from now on, we know we will live to the end of our lives together.'

For note on this myth see page 218.

24 *Thor and Geirrod*

'LEND ME YOUR FALCON SKIN,' Loki said.

Frigg smiled and nodded; then her maidservant Fulla fetched the feather coat and draped it over Loki's shoulders.

'That's the trouble,' said Loki, leering at Frigg and then at Fulla. 'These things so easily won, barely worth winning . . .' With that he tied on the skin, and flew round Fensalir and out of the door.

The Sky Traveller was bored with the string of days in Asgard that unwound without a knot or a twist in them. He headed for Jotunheim and, some time after he had crossed the Iving came to a circle of green fields that he had never seen before. They were enclosed by a jumble of silver and grey rock that stretched for as far as the eye could see. A hall stood there and Loki swooped and settled on a window ledge.

The Sky Traveller peered in and saw a giant and his two daughters feasting in that hall.

The giant, Geirrod, peered out and saw a handsome hawk sitting on the window ledge. 'Catch that bird,' said the giant. 'Bring it to me.'

Loki's eyes gleamed and when one of Geirrod's servants came out of the hall, he hopped on to the top of the wall just out of his reach.

Geirrod's servant got a foothold on the window ledge and stretched out a hand to snare the hawk. But the Sky Traveller had no intention of allowing himself to be caught. He hopped up the side of the roof until he stood on the top, near the chimney hole, and he gave a mocking screech. He saw no point in flying off until he had forced the giant servant to climb on to the steep roof where there were no handholds, and risk his life.

Once again the servant reached out and Loki thought it was time to take to the air. He spread his wings, he stood poised. But then, to his dismay, Loki found he was unable to move; his two feet were fixed to the thatch like branches to the trunk of a tree, and Loki knew what kind of a giant it was that he had to deal with. So the servant grabbed the hawk and brought him in to his master, Geirrod.

'I'll put jesses on him,' Geirrod boomed. 'I'll feed him in his fetters, offer him mere morsels until he's trained to my hand.'

The servant put the hawk into the giant's cupped hands and Geirrod grasped it and looked at it. Loki's eyes were red and green and subtle.

'This is no hawk,' said Geirrod to his daughters, Gjalp and Greip. 'This is some being in disguise. Look at his eyes.' The giant squeezed the bird in his horny hand. 'Who are you?' he demanded.

Loki said nothing.

Geirrod squeezed again until Loki felt that he had been moulded into one solid mass. He gasped and screeched; but still he said nothing.

'Hunger opens the mouth,' said Geirrod, getting up from his seat and striding across the hall. He unlocked a huge chest, thrust the hawk into it, slammed down the lid and locked it again.

For three months Loki sat in darkness. He had nothing to eat; he fouled his own nest; he breathed stale air; he began to feel extremely sorry for himself. And he became so weak from hunger that he could not call out loudly enough to make himself heard; or else, if they did hear him, Geirrod and his daughters chose to ignore him. At the end of three months Geirrod opened the chest and pulled out the hawk. 'Long enough?' was all he said.

The hawk blinked and looked around.

'Not long enough,' said Geirrod.

'Loki,' said the hawk.

'Ah!' exclaimed Geirrod. He took an even firmer grip on his victim. 'Loki,' he repeated, and smiled.

The Sky Traveller looked longingly towards the hall door. But the giant had much too firm a hold on him for any chance of escape.

'Well, Loki,' said the giant, 'do you want to live any longer?'

Loki listened.

'We can make this bargain,' said Geirrod. 'If you swear on oath that you will bring Thor to this hall without his hammer or his belt of strength, I'll spare your life.'

When Loki said nothing, Geirrod began the terrible squeezing again and it was plain that he did not mean to stop. So Loki saw that he had no choice but to agree. He swore to bring Thor to Geirrod's hall. Then Geirrod let Loki eat as much as he wanted. The Sky Traveller scowled at Geirrod and Gjalp and Greip, spread his wings and flew home to Asgard.

Thor and Loki had a great liking for each other's company, and often travelled together through the nine worlds. Once they were walking through the rocky uplands to the east of Asgard and, trusting as he was,

Thor suspected nothing when Loki said they need travel only a little further, across green meadows springy underfoot, to visit the giant Geirrod.

Thor said he had never heard of Geirrod.

'He's rather ugly,' said Loki, 'but he has two attractive daughters. He'd like to meet you and you'd like to meet them.'

Thor puckered his mouth, wishing he had brought his hammer Mjollnir and his girdle of strength in case things did not turn out too well.

'What's more,' said Loki, 'we can stay with Grid tonight – her door is always open.'

Thor liked the sound of that.

'Odin went in through it; Vidar came out through it,' said Loki gleefully, raising his eyebrows.

Thor kept walking and before nightfall the two of them crossed the river Iving and Grid welcomed them into her hall.

Not long after supper Loki spread out some straw and fell asleep. In the flickering firelight his expression seemed to change from moment to moment, light and dark, gay and grim.

'Now that Loki is asleep,' said Grid, 'let me tell you the truth about Geirrod.'

Thor looked at the giantess drunkenly.

'Listen!' said Grid. 'Geirrod has little love for the gods, and even less for the god who killed Hrungnir.'

'But that was me!' exclaimed Thor.

'That's what I am saying,' said Grid sharply. 'Listen! Geirrod is as cunning as a fox; he'll be a worthy enemy, even for you. He will let you walk into his hall and arrange for you to be carried out of it.'

Thor wished the ale mist would clear from his head. He kept screwing up his eyes, then opening them wide and rolling them round and round.

'Go if you must,' said Grid, 'but go well armed. I'll lend you my own weapons.' Then the giantess gave Thor her belt of strength, her iron gloves and unbreakable staff.

Thor thanked her and fell asleep.

The next morning Thor and Loki left Grid's hall and continued their journey. Loki looked at Thor's weapons and wondered what Grid had said to him after he had fallen asleep; Thor looked at Loki and wondered how much he knew about Geirrod.

After a while the two gods came to the Vimur – a wide torrent of water and menstrual blood. The face of the river was broken by worn rocks and grazed by more rock just under the surface; it frothed and hissed as it hurried downstream.

Thor secured the belt of strength and told Loki to hang on to it. Then he grasped Grid's staff and, putting his weight on it, began to wade across the river. The pebbles were slippery underfoot, dogfish tickled his ankles, and Thor was soon in up to his waist; Loki's head was only just above the surface.

By the time the two gods were midstream, Loki had his arms round Thor's neck. The river was breaking over Thor's shoulders and seemed to be rising all the time. Thor cursed and shouted at the river, 'You cannot stop me on my way to the giants. However high you rise, I'll rise higher. I'll rise as high as heaven!'

Thor paused to regain his breath and looked upstream into a rocky ravine. And there he saw the cause of their hardship: Geirrod's daughter, Gjalp, was standing astride the torrent and blood was streaming from her, increasing the depth of the river.

'Aha!' shouted Thor. He stooped, ducked and gouged a rock from the river bed. 'A river must be dammed at its source,' he called, and with huge strength he hurled the hunk of rock at Gjalp. He aimed well. Gjalp was maimed. She howled and dragged herself back to her father's hall.

At that moment, the power of the torrent was so great that Thor was swept off his feet, with Loki still clinging to his neck. As he was carried downstream he grabbed hold of a rowan tree growing in the river, and it held firm in the river bed. Thor recovered his footing, and from there he was able to make his way into the shallows and so, at last, on to the far bank.

'That rowan tree saved our lives,' said Thor.

After a while the two gods went on their way and, late in the afternoon, they reached Geirrod's hall. Geirrod himself was nowhere about but their arrival was clearly expected for a giant servant welcomed them and offered to show them where they would be sleeping.

Thor and Loki readily accepted. They were tired, and caked with mud and blood after their journey.

Then the servant led the gods through the outhouses to a gloomy, rank goat shed. It was furnished with a heap of rotten straw and a single chair. Thor bristled at such an insult; nevertheless he said nothing. He thought he would bide his time until he came face to face with Geirrod himself.

Loki took himself off to wash in the stream that ran past Geirrod's hall, and Thor sat down in the chair. He clenched his fist round Grid's staff, then he yawned. His fatigue got the better of his anger and he began to drowse.

When Thor closed his eyes, it was not long before he imagined he was crossing the river Vimur again – losing his foothold, flailing in the bloody water, floating . . . Thor opened his eyes and at once saw the reason for his dream: he was indeed floating once more. He was rising in his chair towards the rafters of the goat shed, and was close to being driven against them, head first.

Thor gripped Grid's staff with both hands. He raised it and rammed it against the roof tree, and pushed with all his strength. He thrust so hard that whatever was beneath him, hoisting him towards the roof, could not resist him and gave way. Thor fell back to the ground with a great crash and screams shook the shed.

Gjalp and Greip, Geirrod's two daughters, had been hiding under the chair when Thor first sat in it, and tried to crush him to death. They themselves suffered the fate they had planned for the Thunder God. Thor's massive weight was more than their bone-chambers could withstand. Their rib-cages were smashed, their backs were broken, and they died in agony.

It was not long before Loki returned from the stream and, shortly after, the giant servant stood outside the shed and shouted that Geirrod was waiting for Thor in the hall. 'He has it in mind to challenge you to a game or two,' he said.

Thor needed no further warning. He put on Grid's belt of strength and iron gauntlets and then he and Loki made their way back through the outhouses to Geirrod's hall. Thor was surprised to see that in place of the usual single fires there was a string of huge furnaces right down the length of the hall. The turf walls glowed and, lofty as it was, the room was rather too warm for comfort.

Geirrod was waiting for his guests at the far end of the hall. As soon as one of his servants had closed the door behind the gods, Geirrod stepped forward with his hand outstretched.

This was not to greet Thor; it was to pick up a pair of tongs. Geirrod gripped a large ball of red-hot iron between the tongs. 'Welcome!' he shouted, and aimed the ball straight at Thor.

Thor saw it coming. He dropped his staff, raised both hands and caught the red-hot ball in his iron gloves. He did not move. His eyes flamed, his red beard bristled. Everyone in the hall scrambled under the tables, and Geirrod himself quickly stepped back behind one of the hall supports – an iron pillar.

Then Thor raised his right hand; the ball had begun to smoke. He took one step forward and put all his strength into hurling it down the hall.

The ball punched a hole through the iron support; then it passed through the giant Geirrod's midriff; it punctured the end wall and lodged in the earth slope outside.

Geirrod fell backwards. He hissed as if all the venom bottled inside him were escaping. Then suddenly he gave a violent jerk, gurgled and was dead.

Then Thor picked up Grid's staff and began to lay about him. While Loki took the chance of slipping out of the hall unnoticed, the Thunder God smashed the skulls of all the dolts who had waited on Geirrod and his daughters.

That was that. Thor strode out of the silent hall and looked at the jumble of rocks around him. He thought he remembered words about green meadows springy underfoot, and talk of two attractive daughters. Thor shook his head and vowed to settle the score with two-faced Loki.

For note on this myth see page 219.

25 *The Lay of Loddfafnir*

I N A FARMHOUSE IN MIDGARD, a gathering of men and women whiled away a winter evening; they talked and drank, they sewed and gossiped and sang. Then one of their number got up from his place and stepped across to the flickering fire.

'It's time I took the chanter's stool,' Loddfafnir said. 'I've stood and stared into the Well of Urd, stared in silence, wondered and pondered. For a long while I listened at the door of the High One's hall, and inside the High One's hall. This is what I heard.

'"Listen, Loddfafnir, and listen carefully! My advice will help you if you heed it; you will prosper if you set proper store by it: never get up at night except to guard your house or relieve yourself in the outhouse.

'"Listen, Loddfafnir, and listen carefully! My advice will help you if you heed it; you will prosper if you set proper store by it: never succumb to a witch's sweet words and soft snaring embraces. She'll cast a spell and you'll lose all delight in meetings and friendship with other men; you'll hate the sight of meat; every sweetness will be sour and you'll take to your bed, bowed down with sorrow.

'"Listen, Loddfafnir, and listen carefully! My advice will help you if you heed it: never try to seduce another man's wife, or hope to come to secret understandings with her.

'"Listen, Loddfafnir, and listen carefully! If you have to cross mountains or fjords, make quite sure you take enough food.

'"Listen, Loddfafnir, and listen carefully! Never trust an evil man when you're out of luck; the evil man receives good and pays out with evil. I saw a man mortally wounded by an evil woman's words. Her flickering tongue was the cause of his death, and yet it spoke not one true word.

'"Listen, Loddfafnir, and listen carefully! If you want a friend whom you can wholly trust, foster his friendship; brambles and waving grass quickly grow on a little-trodden road.

'"Listen, Loddfafnir, and listen carefully! Find a wise man for your friend, and take note of his charms for healing.

'"Listen, Loddfafnir, and listen carefully! Never be the first to strain and break the bonds of a friendship. If you cannot tell another man your thoughts, anxiety will begin to eat at your heart.

'"Listen, Loddfafnir, and listen carefully! Never waste time on a witless ape. An evil man never gives as much as he gets, whereas a good man will win you great respect by singing your praises. When one man can open his heart to another, that is true friendship; nothing is worse than a liar and no true friend tells you only what you want to hear.

'"Listen, Loddfafnir, and listen carefully! Three angry words are three too many if spoken to a bad man; and the better man often comes off worse when a bad man's sword starts talking.

'"Listen, Loddfafnir, and listen carefully! Only make those shoes and spear shafts you mean to use yourself. If a shoe fits badly or a shaft snaps, men will abuse you.

'"Listen, Loddfafnir, and listen carefully! If you know of some evil, ensure everyone knows all about it, and do not make peace with your enemies.

'"Listen, Loddfafnir, and listen carefully! To do evil brings no lasting pleasure; to do good will make you glad.

'"Listen, Loddfafnir, and listen carefully! Don't raise your eyes when battle is raging and the sons of men are filled with frenzy, otherwise warriors may use spells to snare you.

'"Listen, Loddfafnir, and listen carefully! If you want to win a woman's love and enjoy her favours, make her a fair promise and then stick to it. Nobody loathes what rewards he gets.

'"Listen, Loddfafnir, and listen carefully! I tell you to be cautious, but not fearful; above all, beware of ale, another man's wife, and a thief's sharp wits.

'"Listen, Loddfafnir, and listen carefully! Never mock a guest or deride a traveller. As often as not a man who sits in his own house knows next to nothing about a guest. There's no one so perfect that he has no shortcomings, no one so wicked that he counts for nothing.

'"Listen, Loddfafnir, and listen carefully! Don't despise the grey-haired singer, for the old are often wise. Though they hang with the hides and flap with the pelts and rock with the guts in the wind, shrivelled skins frequently offer good advice.

'"Listen, Loddfafnir, and listen carefully! Don't abuse your guest or show him the door. Be generous to a needy man. But the beam that is raised to admit every guest would have to be a strong one; put a ring over it, or your own open house will bring you to a bad end.

'"Listen, Loddfafnir, and listen carefully! When you're drinking ale, offset it with the power of earth. As earth cures ale, fire cures sicknesses and oak cures constipation; use the ear of corn against witchcraft, rye against rupture, the moon against hatred, grass against the scab and runes against a sword wound; earth absorbs floods of water.

'"Now the High One has spoken in the hall – words for the good of the sons of men, accursed words for the sons of giants. Hail to the speaker and him who listens! May whoever learns them prosper because of them! Hail to those who listen!"'

For note on this myth see page 221.

26 *Otter's Ransom*

WINTER HAD LOST ITS HEART. Every day the stallions Arvak and Alsvid rose earlier to haul the Sun's chariot across the sky, and quietly the snow pulled back from the valleys and plains of Midgard. Small choirs of birds sang and Odin, Loki and Honir were eager to leave Asgard and resume their exploration of the worlds.

Early one morning the three gods crossed Bifrost. Talking and laughing they spring-heeled into Midgard, and Odin and Loki had to stretch their legs to keep up with swift Honir.

Suddenly a late snowstorm assaulted the travellers. They shrugged their way through thick wet flakes that tangled and danced and spun and flew in every direction till that wild onslaught ended as abruptly as it had begun; the sun boomed through layers of shapeless cloud, filling it with fierce yellow light; and then there was only the orb of the sun, the expanding acres of pale blue sky, and the blue and green levels of open Midgard.

The three gods followed the course of a river towards its head. And in the afternoon, they walked up under a waterfall. They strode into the thunder, through the spray-diamonds, and stared into the maelstrom.

Then Odin spotted an otter stretched out on the scraggy bank not fifty paces from them; he pointed it out to Loki and Honir. The otter's eyes were shut. Feeling blessed and rather drowsy in the afternoon sun, it had just begun to eat a salmon it had caught in the waterfall.

Loki pursed his lips. He bent down and picked up a fist-sized stone, took aim, and threw it as hard as he could at the otter. The stone hit the animal on the head and killed it outright.

'Well, then,' shouted Loki, struggling back to Odin and Honir with the salmon under one arm and the limp otter under the other, 'what do you say to that? Two for the price of one?'

The three companions were all equally delighted: Loki at his prowess, and Odin and Honir at the prospect of a good meal that evening.

They climbed up the steep bank beside the waterfall and continued on their way up the narrowing river valley.

The sun had already been drawn out of sight, and it was half-way to dark when the gods saw a farm only a little way ahead of them. Smoke lifted from its chimney. They quickened their step and gave thanks for their good fortune.

'Can you give us lodgings for the night?' Odin asked the farmer Hreidmar. 'We've no wish for a dew-bed.'

'How many are you?' said Hreidmar.

'There are two others outside,' Odin replied. 'And we can pay for our beds with food. We were in luck today and there's enough for everyone.'

'For my sons as well?' said Hreidmar. 'For Fafnir and Regin? And for my daughters Lyngheid and Lofnheid?'

'Enough for everyone,' said Odin airily.

Then Hreidmar nodded without much enthusiasm, and Odin went to the door and called to Loki and Honir.

'Here we are,' said Honir.

'And here's our supper,' said Loki cheerfully. 'I bagged them both with one stone.'

When Hreidmar saw the otter draped under his nose, he stiffened. For a moment his eyes glazed; then he turned and walked out of the room.

'What's wrong with him?' said Loki.

Odin shrugged. 'A cool welcome is better than a cold night,' he said.

'I'm not so sure,' said Honir.

'No,' Odin replied. 'You never are!'

Hreidmar walked down the low passage, punching the turf walls, and found Fafnir and Regin. 'What do you think?' he said. 'Your brother Otter is dead.'

'Dead?' exclaimed the brothers, leaping up.

'Dead. And what else do you think? His murderers are our guests for the night.'

Fafnir and Regin were outraged and swore to avenge Otter's death.

'There are three of them and three of us,' said Hreidmar, 'so we'll have to surprise them. Each of us must take one when I give the nod. One has rather a fine spear and might be better off without it; and one has strange shoes and could be better off barefoot; I see nothing harmful about the third. I'll use my magic – I'll chant spells to weaken them. I'll sing a charm to bind them.'

Fafnir and Regin did just as their father said. The three of them leaped on to their visitors, and the farmer-magician Hreidmar weakened their resistance so that Odin lost his spear Gungnir, and Loki was relieved of his sky-shoes. When the three gods lay on the ground, bound hand and foot, Hreidmar shouted, 'My son, you've killed my son. I'll kill you all for vengeance. You've killed my son.'

'What does he mean?' asked Odin.

'Otter was our brother,' Fafnir said.

'The finest of fishermen,' said Regin.

'He had the likeness of an otter by day,' Fafnir said. 'All day he lived in the river and beside the river.'

'And brought his prey to our father.'

'A supply of fresh fish.'

'Our brother.'

'We didn't know this,' said Odin. 'If we had, Loki would never have killed him.'

'Dead is dead,' said Hreidmar.

'We didn't know this,' Odin said again. 'Do you think we'd have come straight to his father's farm? You must at least give us a chance to pay a ransom before killing us.'

Hreidmar looked down at his three visitors and said nothing.

'I speak for the three of us,' Odin said. 'We'll pay as much as you demand.'

Hreidmar thought for a while. 'That would be fair,' he said, 'if you were to keep to your word. You must swear an oath – and if you break it, you will all pay with your heads.'

Then the three companions swore that they would raise as much as Hreidmar asked.

'All right,' said the magician, turning to Fafnir and Regin. 'Where are Lyngheid and Lofnheid? Have them flay Otter and bring me his skin again.'

Fafnir and Regin obeyed their father, and then Hreidmar laid out Otter's handsome skin beside the fire. 'First you must fill this with red gold,' he told the gods, 'and then you must cover it with red gold into the bargain. It must be wholly covered. That is the ransom for the death of my son.'

'So be it,' said Odin. And he rolled over until he was close enough to Loki to whisper in his ear.

Loki listened carefully and then he said, 'Let me go for the gold. Let me go, and hold the other two as hostages.'

So Hreidmar untied Loki's bonds and, with a snatch of a look and a jeering laugh that left Hreidmar and his sons and even Honir uneasy, Loki threw open the door and ran out into the night.

Loki had left his sky-shoes in the care of the magician and, in any event, he was in no great hurry. He knew Hreidmar had nothing to gain by killing Odin and Honir and everything to win by waiting for his return with the red gold; and he was not especially averse to the thought of mighty Odin and long-legged Honir lying for a while, bound hand and foot. He dawdled all the way across Midgard to the island of Hlesey.

There, Loki visited Aegir and Ran in their hall on the sea bed. 'The gods are in danger,' he told Ran breathlessly. 'Odin himself lies bound, Odin and Honir, and only your net can save them.'

The wife of the sea god opened her cold pale eyes very wide.

'Lend me your drowning net. I can use it, and not to snare men but to save gods.'

When Loki had talked Ran into parting with her net, he left the hall beneath the waves quickly in case she changed her mind, and headed for the world of the dark elves.

Loki picked his way down a chain of dripping tunnels and through a maze of twilit chambers, until he came to a massive cavern. Its roof was supported by columns of rock thicker than tree trunks, and its corners were still and dark. A little light, however, filtered into the middle of the cavern from a vertical shaft in the roof, and showed Loki what he had come to see: a large silent pool, filled with water that seemed to spring from nowhere and flow nowhere.

Loki spread out Ran's finely meshed net and cast it into the pool. He dragged it and pulled it up and there, furiously lashing and writhing, was a large pike snared in the net.

Avoiding its nasty teeth and the equally nasty look in its yellow eyes, Loki took hold of it. 'First,' he said, as he gave the pike a horrible shaking, 'you'll change shape.'

'Change shape,' echoed the cavern.

Then there was no pike but the dwarf Andvari in Ran's dripping net. Loki disentangled him, keeping a firm hold all the while on the back of his neck.

'What do you want?' whined Andvari.

'You want,' said the cavern.

'What I want is all your gold. Otherwise I'll wring you out like a piece of washing. All your gold.'

'All your gold,' boomed the cavern.

Andvari shuddered. He led Loki out of that echoing chamber and down a twisting passage into his smithy. It was hot and smoky but well fitted out, and well-stocked with gold that gleamed in the firelight. The dwarf spread out his hands and shrugged.

'Gather it up,' said Loki, kicking a gold nugget.

Andvari scrambled around, cursing and moaning. He made a pile of discs and chips and splinters and small bars of red gold, of objects already made and objects half made. Loki looked at the stack and was well satisfied. 'Is that all?' he said.

Andvari said nothing. He stowed the gold into two old sacks; it filled them both. Then, grunting, he dragged them across the smithy and stood with them in front of Loki.

'What about that ring?' said Loki, pointing at the dwarf's closed right hand. 'I saw you hide it.'

Andvari shook his head.

'Put it in the sack,' said Loki.

'Let me keep it,' begged Andvari. 'Just this ring.'

'Put it in the sack,' said Loki.

'Let me keep this, just this,' pleaded the dwarf. 'Then at least I'll be able to make more gold again.'

'I have no need of more,' said Loki, 'and I'm going to strip you to the bone.' He stepped forward and, knocking aside one sack, forced open Andvari's fist and seized the little twisted ring. It was marvellously wrought and Loki slipped it on to his own little finger. 'What is not freely given must be taken by force,' he said.

'Nothing was freely given,' Andvari replied.

Loki shouldered the sacks and turned towards the door of the smithy.

'Take that ring!' yelled the dwarf. 'My curse on that ring and that gold! It will destroy whoever owns it.'

Loki turned round and faced Andvari. 'So much the better,' he said.

'No one will win joy with my wealth,' shouted Andvari.

'If,' said Loki, 'if I repeat your words to those about to get this gold, then, Andvari, your curse will come to pass.' And with that, Loki turned round again and, with oaths and spells in his ears, made his way out of the world of the dark elves and into Midgard.

'You took your time,' said Odin.

Honir said nothing; he looked rather fearful.

'Hard won and well won,' said Loki. He dumped the sacks of red gold in front of his companions. 'And what do you say to this?' he whispered, showing Odin the twisted finger-ring which he had wrenched from Andvari.

Odin blinked, and marvelled at its subtle beauty. 'Give it to me,' he said.

'At last,' said Hreidmar as he walked into the room, followed by his two sons and two daughters. He nodded, and Fafnir and Regin cut Odin and Honir free from their bonds.

Slowly and stiffly the two gods stood up. They flexed their muscles, they rubbed their hands together, they looked at their chafed wrists and ankles.

'Well then?' said Hreidmar.

'You must stuff the skin yourself,' said Loki, 'or you'll never be satisfied.' He emptied one sack on to the ground and the magician stowed piece after piece inside Otter's skin. He filled it so that it was plump and taut, bursting from top to tail.

'Now we'll cover it completely,' Loki said, opening the second sack and pouring another mound of metal over the marl floor. While Honir held Otter's skin upright, snout down, Odin and Loki heaped the gold around it. They built Otter a barrow of gold.

'So,' said Odin, with the satisfaction of a job well done, 'come and look for yourself, Hreidmar! We've covered the skin completely.'

The magician walked round and round the stack. He walked round it again. He examined the gold inch by inch. 'Here!' he said. 'Here's a whisker! This must be covered and hidden. Otherwise, I'll hold that you've broken your oath – and that will be the end of our understanding.'

Loki looked at Odin and Odin looked at the twisted ring on his little finger. He sniffed and drew it off and placed it over the single whisker showing. 'Now,' said Odin loudly, 'we've paid Otter's ransom in full.'

'You have indeed,' said Hreidmar.

Still rather unsteady on his feet, Odin lurched across the room to where his spear Gungnir was propped up in the corner. And Loki fell on his sky-shoes and at once put them on. A sense of their own strength surged within them. They looked at Hreidmar and Fafnir and Regin with no great liking.

'Listen carefully!' said Loki. 'That ring and all that gold was made by the dwarf Andvari. I only wrested it from him with his curse.' Loki paused. 'And what he said, I say; what he said will hold.' Loki's voice was low and compelling. 'Take that ring! My curse on that ring and that gold! It will destroy whosoever owns it.'

Odin looked at Loki. His eye glittered and Loki smiled crookedly. Then Honir took one step and was at their side. The three companions stepped out of the farmhouse into the welcoming spring air.

For note on this myth see page 222.

27 The Lay of Alvis

ALVIS TRAMPED ALL THE WAY from the world of the dark elves to Asgard. He hurried towards Bilskirnir and in that hall he saw the god he was looking for, but he did not recognise him.

'I've come for my bride,' the dwarf said bluntly. 'It's taken long enough to get here, I must say, and now it's high time that Thrud graced her new home. Everyone will say I can't wait for my wedding night, but I don't mean to hang around here any longer than I have to.'

'Who are you?' asked Thor. 'Or should I say, what are you? Why is your nose so pale? Do you sleep in a grave mound and keep corpses company?' Thor considered Alvis. 'You look like a kind of monster. You certainly won't be the one to marry Thrud.'

The dwarf drew himself up to his full height, such as it was. 'I am Alvis,' he said, 'and there's nothing I do not know. I live way down under a hill, my home is a cavern hewn out of rock.' Then the dwarf testily brushed aside this talk with a sweep of his hand. 'I've come to claim Thrud – the agreed price for my work and for many weapons. Let the gods not break their oath!'

'I'll break it,' said Thor indignantly. 'I know nothing of this promise.' He stalked down the hall and then called out, 'A father has the last word as to whom his daughter marries. It's up to him and him alone.'

'So who are you then, hero?' demanded Alvis. 'And what kind of right do you think you have over my radiant bride? You're nothing but some vagabond, seldom noticed, little known.' The corners of Alvis's mouth twitched. 'Which woman had to be bought with rings before she would bear you?'

'I,' said the god very slowly, and his eyes flashed so that Alvis began to quail, 'am Thor the Hurler; I am the wide wanderer; and I am Odin's son. You'll never win and marry my daughter if I can help it.'

'Ah!' said Alvis, and he smiled a pallid smile. 'Well, I'll soon win your good will and your consent. I long for your snow-white daughter and I'll struggle for her.'

'Wise guest,' said Thor, 'I won't be able to stand in the way of your love if you can answer whatever I ask you about all the worlds. Tell me, Alvis! You're the dwarf who knows everything about our fates and fortunes: what is the name for the land, that stretches all around us, in each and every world?'

'Men call it Earth,' the dwarf replied. 'The Aesir say Field and the Vanir say the Ways. The giants name it Evergreen and the elves Grower. The most holy gods call it Clay.'

'Tell me, Alvis! You're the dwarf who knows everything about our fates and fortunes: what is the name for the sky, child of the ocean, that we can all see, in each and every world?'

'Men call it Heaven,' the dwarf replied. 'The gods say the Height and the Vanir say Wind Weaver. The giants name it High Home, the elves Fair Roof and the dwarfs Dripping Hall.'

'Tell me, Alvis! You're the dwarf who knows everything about our fates and fortunes: what is the name for the moon, that we can all see, in each and every world?'

'Men call it Moon,' the dwarf replied, 'but the gods say Mock Sun. It's known in Hel as Whirling Wheel. The giants name it Rapid Traveller, the dwarfs Gleamer and the elves Time Teller.'

'Tell me, Alvis! You're the dwarf who knows everything about our fates and fortunes: what is the name for the sun, that we can all see, in each and every world?'

'Men call it Sun,' the dwarf replied. 'The gods say Orb and the dwarfs Dvalin's Delight. The giants name it Ever Bright, the elves Fair Wheel and the sons of god All Glowing.'

'Tell me, Alvis! You're the dwarf who knows everything about our fates and fortunes: what is the name for the clouds, that hold the rain, in each and every world?'

'Men call them Clouds,' the dwarf replied. 'The gods say Chance of Showers and the Vanir say Wind Kites. The giants name them Hope of Rain, the elves Weather Might, and in Hel they're known as Helmets of Secrets.'

'Tell me, Alvis! You're the dwarf who knows everything about our fates and fortunes: what is the name for the wind, that ranges far and wide, in each and every world?'

'Men call it Wind,' the dwarf replied. 'The gods say Waverer and the most holy gods call it Neigher. The giants name it Wailer, the elves Roaring Traveller, and in Hel it's known as Blustering Blast.'

'Tell me, Alvis! You're the dwarf who knows everything about our fates and fortunes: what is the name for the stillness, the settling peace, in each and every world?'

'Men call it Calm,' the dwarf replied. 'The gods say the Quiet and the Vanir say Winds' Hush. The giants name it the Sultry, the elves Day's Lull and the dwarfs Day's Refuge.'

'Tell me, Alvis! You're the dwarf who knows everything about our fates and fortunes: what is the name for the sea, on which men sail, in each and every world?'

'Men call it Sea,' the dwarf replied. 'The gods say Smooth-lying and the Vanir say Waves. The giants name it Eel Home, the elves Drink Stuff and the dwarfs call it the Deep.'

'Tell me, Alvis! You're the dwarf who knows everything about our fates and fortunes: what is the name for fire, that burns for men, in each and every world?'

'Men call it Fire,' the dwarf replied. 'The gods say Flame and the Vanir say Wave. The giants name it Hungry Biter, and the dwarfs Burner. In Hel it's known as the Hasty.'

'Tell me, Alvis! You're the dwarf who knows everything about our fates and fortunes: what is the name for the wood, that grows for men, in each and every world?'

'Men call it Wood,' the dwarf replied. 'The gods say Mane of the Field and in Hel it's known as Seaweed of the Hills. The giants name it Fuel and the elves Fair-limbed. The Vanir call it Wand.'

'Tell me, Alvis! You're the dwarf who knows everything about our fates and fortunes: what is the name for the night, daughter of Narvi, in each and every world?'

'Men call it Night,' the dwarf replied. 'The gods say Darkness and the most holy gods say Hood. The giants name it Lightless, the elves Sleep's Soothing and the dwarfs the Weaver of Dreams.'

'Tell me, Alvis! You're the dwarf who knows everything about our fates and fortunes: what is the name for the seed, sown by men, in each and every world?'

'Men call it Barley,' the dwarf replied. 'The gods say Grain and the Vanir say Growth. The giants name it Edible, the elves Drink Grist, and in Hel it's known as Slender Stem.'

'Tell me, Alvis! You're the dwarf who knows everything about our fates and fortunes: what is the name for ale, that men quaff, in each and every world?'

'Men call it Ale,' the dwarf replied. 'The gods say Beer and the Vanir say Foaming. The giants name it Cloudless Swill, and in Hel it's known as Mead. Suttung's sons call it Feast Draught.'

Thor said, 'I've never known one person to be the mine of so much ancient wisdom.' He smiled at his guest, a long slow smile, and he slowly nodded his head. 'But your own tongue has trapped you, Alvis. The sun's rays arrest you.'

The dwarf whirled round but it was already too late.

'The sun's rays arrest you,' gloated Thor, 'and they turn you into stone. And now the sun shines in my hall once again.'

For note on this myth see page 224.

T HE GOD MOANED. He twisted and writhed as he tried to escape the dark shapes. He panted and moaned again, and then he woke. For a long while the fairest of the gods lay in the half light, his brow gleaming as white as the whitest flower, his hair shining, and he tried to snare his dream – to name each form and dismiss it. But the shapes skulked in the shadows, shapeless now that he was awake. And in time his fear lapsed into a dull foreboding; he closed his eyes and began to drift.

No sooner was he asleep than his ghastly skull-guests crept forward yet again, monstrous forms intent on snuffing out the light of him. He threshed and kicked. He called out and his own shout woke him. Once more he felt fearful and exposed and doomed.

When the gods and goddesses heard about Balder's dreams they anxiously gathered to discuss their meaning. They said that he was the most merciful, the most gentle and loved of them all, the least deserving of such unwelcome night visitors; they said nothing tainted had ever crossed the threshold of Breidablik before. But all they said only disturbed them more. They could not unravel Balder's dreams.

'I will go myself,' said Allfather, Balder's father, 'and return with a meaning.' The magician, old as time, stood up and hurried out of the council. He saddled Sleipnir, galloped over the quivering rainbow, and took the long, long track that led north from Midgard down into the gloom and the swirling mists of Niflheim.

Hel's hound heard Odin coming. The hair on Garm's throat and chest was caked with blood and he bayed from his cliff cave at the entrance to the underworld. The Master of Runes took no notice. He galloped so hard that the frozen ground thrummed under Sleipnir's eight hooves, and he did not let up until he had reached Hel's forbidding hall.

Here Odin dismounted. He peered into the hall – it was packed out with the dead, and gleaming with gold rings and gold ornaments – and then led Sleipnir round to the east door near which a seeress was buried. Odin stood beside her mound and fixed his one glittering eye upon it. Then he began to use charms and, in the gloom, the pale spectre of the seeress rose out of the earth and loomed over him.

'Who,' she moaned, 'who is the stranger who forces me up and unearths me to sorrows? Snow has settled on me, rain has lashed me, dew has seeped through me; I have long been dead.'

'My name is Vegtam the Wanderer,' Odin said, 'and I am Valtam's son. Give me news of Hel; I have travelled already through the other worlds. Why are gold rings strewn along the benches in Hel's hall and why is the whole place decorated with gold? Who are you expecting?'

'The shining mead,' said the seeress, 'is brewed for Balder; a shield covers the cauldron. For all their glory, the gods will be filled with despair. I was unwilling to speak and I will say no more now.'

'Seeress, you must stay,' Odin said. 'You must answer all that I ask. Who will slay Balder and drain the life-blood of Odin's son?'

'Blind Hod will carry a fatal branch. He will slay Balder and drain the life-blood of Odin's son. I was unwilling to speak and I will say no more now.'

'Seeress, you must stay,' Odin said. 'You must answer all that I ask. Who will take vengeance on Hod? Who will carry Balder's slayer to the pyre?'

'Rind will lie with Odin,' said the seeress, 'and their son will be Vali, born in Vestrsalir, the Western Hall. He will take vengeance when he is only one night old. He will not wash his hands nor comb his hair before he has carried Balder's slayer to the pyre. I was unwilling to speak and I will say no more now.'

'Seeress, you must stay,' Odin said. 'You must answer all that I ask. Who are the maidens who will keen then, and toss their scarves up against the sky?'

'You are not Vegtam,' said the seeress, 'as I believed you to be. You are Odin, the magician, old as time.'

'And you are no seeress,' Odin said, 'nor are you wise. You are the mother of three monsters.'

'Ride home, Odin, and boast about your skills,' said the seeress. Her voice was rising and gloating. 'No one will raise me again until Loki breaks free from his fetters and all the forces of darkness gather before Ragnarok.'

The spectre, pale and gleaming, began to ooze and to sink back into her grave.

Then Odin turned away. He mounted Sleipnir with a heavy heart.

For note on this myth see page 224.

29 *The Death of Balder*

THE GODS AND GODDESSES gathered in the shadow of Balder's terrible dreams, dreams that threatened to pitch him into the darkness for ever. Not one of them doubted his life was in danger and for a long time they discussed how to protect him.

The gods and goddesses thought of all the ways in which one can die; they named each earth-thing, sea-thing and sky-thing that can cause sudden death. Then Balder's mother, Frigg, began to travel through the nine worlds and get each and every substance to swear an oath that it would not harm Balder.

Fire swore an oath. Water swore an oath. Iron and every other kind of metal swore an oath. The stones swore oaths. Nothing could stay Frigg from her mission or resist her sweet troubled persuasion. Earth swore an oath. The trees swore oaths. Each kind of illness swore an oath. Balder's mother was untiring and painstaking. All the animals swore an oath and so did every sidling snake.

Then the gods and goddesses met again and Frigg satisfied them that she had done as they asked, and that nothing in creation would harm Balder.

'We should put it to the test,' they said. And one picked up a pebble and lobbed it so that it landed right on Balder's head.

Whatever power that small stone had, it withheld it. Balder did not even know that the pebble had struck him. 'I could not feel it at all,' he said.

Then all the gods and goddesses laughed. They left Gladsheim and streamed out into the sunlight. The hall's gold roof and gold walls were glowing and the green plain of Idavoll teemed with activity – the gods' servants coming and going, troops of light elves hurrying about their business, visitors to Asgard staring in wonder about them, and animals of many kinds grazing or dozing, all of them glad to be alive.

The foremost gods met in Gladsheim and the goddesses in Vingolf. They ruled over Asgard; they discussed the feats and the fates of heroic men in Midgard. And after their councils, they often met together and were joined by a jostling throng – gossiping, sociable, eager for amusement. Sometimes they drank, sometimes they sang, they made trials of their strength and played games of all kinds.

It was not long before the gods thought they should check Balder's safety again; they could not resist the sport. One tossed a pebble at him and it struck him on the cheekbone; another aimed a stick at him and hit him on the chest.

'I could not feel them at all,' said Balder.

Then the gods laughed and tried other tests. One thing led to another and soon they became very bold. They made Balder stand against a wall as a target. Some threw darts with wicked points at him, and the darts bounced off him and fell at his feet. Some brought in stones and hurled them at him. The rest struck at him with axes and slashed at him with swords and the tempered metal would not scathe Balder, it would not even graze him. The fairest and most gentle of the gods became the butt of the most violent assaults and they did not harm him. Everyone present enjoyed this new game hugely and they all rejoiced that it was impossible to hurt him.

All except Loki: the Sly One watched with distaste and impatience. Trouble and suffering were meat and drink to him, and it sickened him to see that Balder was immune from every kind of attack. This grudge grew in him day by day and began to consume him. He refused to take part in the games and yet he was unable to keep away.

One afternoon Loki was loafing as usual against the door of Gladsheim, watching the assembly, when an idea occurred to him. He half closed his eyes; he licked his twisted lips and smiled. Unnoticed, he stepped out of the hubbub and quickly walked off in the direction of Fensalir.

Loki paused. He had a careful look round; there was nobody about. Then he whispered the charm; the Shape Changer turned himself into an old woman.

As Loki hoped, Frigg was in her hall and alone. Loki hobbled across the floor; she sniffed, wiped her dripping nose with the back of her hand and rubbed it against her grubby dark dress. 'Where am I?' she demanded.

Frigg rose, greeted the old woman, and named herself.

'It's a long way from home,' observed the old woman. 'And I'm not sure it's been worth coming.'

Frigg listened patiently.

'I passed a place some way back. What a noise! I couldn't get anyone

151

to listen. And the people there were all stoning one man. Poor man! He had a white face, so white . . . shining hair. One against all, yes; I didn't know that sort of thing went on in Asgard.'

Frigg smiled faintly and thought it wise to wait until the old woman had had her say.

'I didn't stay long; I never did like stonings. Who would have thought it? So far to have come, and then it's much the same. He hadn't got long, poor man. He'll be dead by now, yes.' As the old woman rambled on, it seemed she had quite forgotten she was in company. But now she shook her head fiercely and glared at Frigg. 'What was going on then? Do you know why they were stoning him?'

Frigg told the old woman that what she had seen was not a stoning but a host of gods and goddesses sporting with her own son. She explained that Balder had not been hurt by a single stone and was just as ready to take part as anyone else.

'What kind of magic is that then?' asked the old woman. She had the makings of a moustache and it was twitching in rather a disturbing way.

'Nothing will hurt Balder,' replied Frigg. 'No metal will harm him, no wood will wound him. I've taken an oath from everything.'

'Everything?' said the old woman. 'Even a pinch of salt, I suppose?'

Frigg began to feel irritated with this wearisome crone; she shrugged as if she were trying to get rid of her.

'Everything?' The old woman sniffed. 'You really mean that everything has sworn you an oath that it will not injure Balder?'

'Everything,' said Frigg dismissively, 'except the little bush that grows west of Valhalla, the mistletoe. That's so young I didn't bother with it.'

The old woman grunted. 'Well you've given me the time of day,' she said. 'You've given me the time of day, yes; now I'll be getting along.'

Frigg inclined her head.

The old woman turned and painfully made her way to the doors of Fensalir. And Frigg was not in the least sorry to see her go.

As soon as he was quite certain he was alone, the Shape Changer muttered the magic words. Then, crowing, he resumed his old form – Loki again.

Jauntily the Trickster walked across the plain of Idavoll – deserted now except for the animals that stood in motionless groups, as if they were waiting, or had never moved. The air was thickening, the distance and middle distance were blurred and bluish; it was almost night.

Loki hurried past Gladsheim. He hurried towards Valhalla and

152

smiled to himself as he heard the Einherjar shouting. He hurried on west in the fading light, whistling and looking sharply to left and right and under his feet. Then he entered a small grove. And there, rooted neither in earth nor water, but growing out of the trunk of an oak, the Sly One found what he had come for – the spray of mistletoe.

Its berries gleamed like clusters of pale eyes. Its leaves were green and yellow-green, its stem and small branches and twigs were green. Unmoving and otherworldly it seemed in broad daylight, and even more strange now in the half light.

Loki grabbed at the little bush and wrenched at it until it came away from the oak. Then he left the grove and took the path to Gladsheim, picking at the spray as he hurried along. He chose the straightest branch, almost as long as his forearm, and stripped it down, leaving a small trail of droppings behind him. Loki sharpened one end of it; he stropped it against his belt, and stepped into the warm light of the hall.

The gathering in Gladsheim was so caught up in the game they were playing that no one was aware Loki had gone and no one noticed he had come back again. The Sly One looked around. He smiled when he saw that Frigg had joined the company; his lips tightened and his eyes narrowed as he watched blind Hod, Balder's brother, standing a little aside as usual – pathetic in his slow fumbling movements; and when Loki saw that many of the gods were once again hurling darts at long-suffering Balder, he doubled up. For a moment his whole body was convulsed, as if in laughter or terrible pain.

A servant hurried up and offered Loki wine. Loki drained the cup at one draught and then sauntered across the spacious hall, behind the semicircle of the gods and their followers. He sidled up to Hod and poked him in the ribs.

'That can only be Loki,' said Hod.

'None other,' said a voice in his ear.

'Well?' said Hod.

'Why don't you join in? Why aren't you throwing darts at your brother?'

'Because I can't see where he is,' said Hod.

Loki sucked his cheeks.

'Another thing,' said Hod. 'I have no weapon.'

'This is not as it should be,' said Loki with measured indignation. 'They do wrong to ignore you – and you his brother.'

Hod's expression did not alter. He had long since learned to accept his fate. 'Nothing comes,' he said, 'of rankling resentment.'

153

Hod's words were drowned in a roar of laughter.

'What was that?' he asked.

'Only more of the same,' said Loki. 'A dart well aimed. But now it's your turn, Hod. You should pay your respects to Balder like everybody else.'

'I have no weapon,' Hod repeated.

'Take this twig then,' said Loki, and he put the sharpened mistletoe between Hod's hands. 'I'll show you where he's standing. I'll stand behind you and guide your hand.'

Loki's eyes were on fire now. His whole body was on fire. His face was ravaged by wolfish evil and hunger.

Hod grasped the mistletoe and lifted his right arm. Guided by Loki, he aimed the dart at his brother Balder.

The mistletoe flew through the hall and it struck Balder. It pierced him and passed right through him. The god fell on his face. He was dead.

There was no sound in Gladsheim, no sound, only the roaring of silence. The gods could not speak. They looked at the fairest and most wise of them all, shining and lifeless, and they could not even move from where they stood to lift him.

The gods stared at each other and then they turned to stare at Hod and Loki. They had no doubt. They were all of one mind about who had caused Balder's death and yet none of them were able to take vengeance. The ground of Gladsheim was hallowed and no one was ready to shed blood in the sanctuary.

Hod could not see the fearsome gaze of that gathering, Loki could not withstand it. He loped towards the doors of Gladsheim and slunk away into the darkness.

Then the terrible silence was broken. One goddess began to weep, seized by wild grief. And the weeping of one unlocked the floodgates of them all. When they tried to speak, they found they could not tell their grief and their words were choked with tears.

Odin himself was there and, of all the gods and goddesses, he was the most deeply afflicted. He best understood that this was the greatest evil ever sustained by gods and men, and foresaw what loss and sorrow would follow in the wake of his son's death.

Frigg was the first to speak. 'Does anyone . . .' she asked. 'Does anyone here want to win all my love and favour?'

The mourning company turned to face her.

'Is there anyone here who will ride the long road to Hel and try to find Balder?'

Then the goddesses buried their faces in their hands and sobbed again.

'Is there anyone here,' said Frigg, her voice rising, 'who will offer Hel a ransom, offer her a ransom if she'll allow my son Balder to come home to Asgard again?'

Then Hermod stepped forward, Odin's son whom everyone admired for his boldness. 'I will,' he said. 'I am ready to go.'

Gladsheim began to breathe and sound again. Odin gave servants orders. They hurried out of the hall and soon returned with Sleipnir, Odin's own horse.

Allfather took the reins and handed them to Hermod. Then, in Gladsheim, Hermod mounted Sleipnir. He looked down at the upturned faces of the gods and goddesses and at the fair fallen body of Balder. He raised his hand and spurred the steed; Sleipnir's hooves clattered against the marble floor. Hermod galloped out into the darkness and on towards the endless night.

The gods and goddesses did not sleep; they kept a silent vigil in Gladsheim. Ranged around Balder's body, so white that it was gleaming, each of them was prey to his own thoughts and hopes and fears – what chance Hermod had of bringing Balder back from the dead, how to avenge Balder's death on his own unhappy brother Hod, what kind of punishment would begin to suffice for Loki, and what meaning the death of one must have for them all.

Day began to dawn: a lightening in the east at first mysterious, then quickly gathering speed and spreading in every direction.

Then with aching hearts, four of the gods lifted Balder's body on to their shoulders, and all the others formed a long cortège. They carried him down to the sea and laid his corpse near Ringhorn, his own great boat with its curved prow.

The gods wanted to build Balder's pyre in the waist of the boat, up against the mast. They took hold of the stern and tried to launch the boat, but their grief had so exhausted them that they could not summon up the strength to shift it on its rollers.

Then the gods sent a messenger speeding to Jotunheim to ask for the help of the giantess Hyrrokin. A great crowd out of Asgard sat near the water, watching the pulse of the waves. They were pensive and subdued, none of them so strong that he could escape the flux of his own feelings and comfort the others.

In a while Hyrrokin came. She was huge and grim, riding a wolf with vipers for reins. As soon as she leaped off her steed, Odin summoned four Berserks and told them to watch over the wolf (and the vipers) and ensure they caused no harm.

The very sight of the four men in their animal skins angered the wolf; its eyes flickered and it snarled.

The Berserks seized the viper-reins but they were unable to hold the wolf fast. First it dragged them one way, then another, slithering helplessly through the sand, as it tried to break free. Then the Berserks became as mad as wolves themselves and in fury they rained blows on the wolf with their club-like fists. They struck it down and left it for dead in the sand.

Hyrrokin, meanwhile, stalked up to Ringhorn. She looked at the boat, so large and yet so sweeping and graceful, and gripped the prow. Then she dug in her heels and with a horrible grunt she pulled – pulled so hard that Ringhorn raced screaming down the rollers and crashed into the water. The pine rollers burst into flames and the nine worlds trembled.

'Enough!' shouted Thor. His fingers closed round his hammer and he felt his old strength surging back into him.

Hyrrokin looked at Thor scornfully.

'Enough!' repeated Thor. 'I'll teach you respect.'

But Odin and several other gods hurried to Thor's side and restrained him. They took his arm and reminded him, 'She is here at our bidding.'

'I'll crack her skull,' muttered Thor.

'It would be wrong to injure her,' said the gods. 'Leave her. Ignore her.'

And slowly Thor's volcanic anger subsided inside him. He kicked at the sand, causing a sandstorm, and walked up and down.

Then the four gods who had carried Balder's body down to the sea gently raised it again and waded out to Ringhorn, rocking on the water. They set down his spotless body on a high bench, covered in crimson cloth.

Balder's wife, Nanna, was watching. And when she saw Balder lying there lifeless, her body shook; she could not control it. She was tearless, in too much pain for tears now. Then Nanna's heart broke. The daughter of Nep died there, and she was carried out to Ringhorn and laid beside her dead husband.

The cortège had swollen to a vast gathering. Odin was there; his ravens, Thought and Memory, perched on his shoulders. Frigg accompanied him, and so did the Valkyries: Shaker and Mist, Axe Time and Raging, Warrior and Might, Shrieking, Host Fetter and Screaming,

Spear Bearer, Shield Bearer, Wrecker of Plans – all those beautiful maidens, choosers of the slain, stood grouped around the Father of Battle.

Freyr had come to the cremation in his chariot drawn by Gullinbursti, the gold-bristled boar fashioned for him by the dwarfs Brokk and Eitri. Heimdall had ridden out of Asgard on his mount Gold Tuft. And Freyja sat in her chariot drawn by cats.

The elves were there. The dwarfs were there. And hundreds of frost giants and rock giants stood there too, a great gang who had followed Hyrrokin out of Jotunheim. That was a vast concourse, a mingling of mourners and the merely curious on the foreshore, scuffing the strip of sand that never wholly belongs to earth or to sea. The seabirds rose and wheeled and dipped, screaming, the sea sobbed, and everyone there watched the ritual on Ringhorn.

A pyre was built round the body of Balder and his wife Nanna, dry faggots that needed nothing more than a spark to leap into their own life and consume the lifeless bodies that lay upon them, releasing their spirits to travel on.

Then many treasures were laid within Ringhorn – buckles and brooches and rings, clasps and pins – and not only treasures but knives and buckets and scissors and spindles and spades and all the fabric of life.

Balder's horse, meanwhile, was galloped along the foreshore and worked into a steaming sweat. Then a servant plunged a short dagger into its throat. It gave a violent jerk and, without a sound, crumpled amongst the wrack. No sooner was it dead than its body was hacked up, and the pieces were thrown into Ringhorn.

Now Odin strode through the shallows and gripped the gunwale. He climbed into the boat and stood over the body of his dead son. For some time he gazed at him. Slowly he took off his arm-ring Draupnir, the gold ring that dropped eight rings of equal value on every ninth night, and slipped it on to Balder's arm. Then Odin bent down and put his mouth to Balder's ear. Again he gazed at his son; then he left Ringhorn.

At a sign from Odin a servant stepped forward with a lighted brand. He set fire to the pyre and at once a steady plume of smoke, twisting and spiralling, rose into the calm air.

Thor raised his hammer. Slowly and solemnly he intoned the magic words to hallow the cremation.

Then a dwarf called Lit, who had lost all interest in the proceedings, came running along the water's edge. He passed right in front of Thor and Thor was so enraged that he put out a foot and tripped him. Before Lit had time to pick himself up, Thor gave him a terrible kick. The dwarf flew through the air and landed right on the licking and curdling pyre. In this way, he was burned to death beside Balder.

The painter was released and with it the pent emotions of the mourners. They wept as the boat began to drift out, rocking, across the water. They wept and they talked about Balder – the most beautiful, the most gentle, the most wise of them all.

Ringhorn rode across the water. Sea winds caught at her and tugged her away. First she was more boat than flame, but soon more flame than boat. She was a quivering shape, a farewell on the horizon, moving on under a great cloud of her own making.

For nine nights Hermod rode through a valley so deep and dark that he was unable to see anything. The ground fell away from him and the cold fingers of the underworld began to reach up towards him and search him. The god crossed many rivers, all of which spring from the seething cauldron of Hvergelmir: cool Svol and defiant Gunnthra, Fjorm and bubbling Fimbulthul, fearsome Slid and storming Hrid, Sylg, Ylg, broad Vid and Leipt which streaked past like lightning. At last Hermod came to the icy river Gjoll, a swirling torrent of water. Sleipnir needed no spurring. He galloped across the bridge there; it was thatched with strips of gold.

On the far side, Hermod was stopped by the maiden Modgud, warden of the bridge. She raised one pale arm and it gleamed with an unearthly pallor. 'Before you go further,' she said, 'tell me your name and your lineage.'

Hermod kept quiet.

'Five troops of dead men came this way yesterday,' said Modgud. 'They rode over this bridge. But you make as much noise as they all made together.'

Still Hermod said nothing.

'I can't say you look like a man who has died,' said Modgud. 'Who are you?'

'I am Hermod,' said the god, 'and I am Odin's son. I must ride to Hel in search of my brother, dead Balder. Have you seen him yourself on his way there?'

'He has crossed this river,' Modgud replied. 'He rode over this bridge. But the way to Hel is no short way; far as you have come, it is still a little further northwards and downwards.'

Hermod thanked Modgud and she stepped aside. Then Sleipnir saw the way before him: horse and rider galloped onward. So at last Hermod came to the massive gates and towering walls that Hel had set up in front of her hall Eljudnir.

Sleipnir stopped in his tracks and whinnied.

Hermod dismounted and looked around in the dismal light. The gates were locked; impassable, it seemed, for all those not fated to pass beyond on their way to dreadful Nastrond, the shore of corpses. Hermod tightened his stirrups. He swung himself into the saddle and spurred Sleipnir fiercely.

Odin's steed galloped at the gates. For a moment he seemed to pause, then he gave a great thrust with his back legs and leaped clear of the iron gates.

Hermod boldly took Sleipnir right up to Eljudnir's doors. There he dismounted once more and walked straight into the cavernous hall. Faces without number turned towards him – the faces of the newly dead, faces green and rotting, faces less flesh than bone; faces pitiful, unanswered, resigned, many scowling or leering or treacherous or murderous and in agony, all of them with eyes only for Hermod.

But Hermod saw only the fair figure sitting in the high seat: his brother Balder.

For Balder's sake and the sake of the gods, resolute Hermod stayed all night in the hall. He sat by the door and kept his own counsel, silent in that company of the dead who could not speak unless he spoke to them; he waited for Hel to rise from Sick Bed and draw back its hangings, Glimmering Misfortune.

Hel's face and body were those of a living woman; but her thighs and legs were those of a corpse, mottled and mouldering. She crept towards the god, looking gloomy and grim.

Hermod greeted Hel and told her of the grief of the gods. He said all Asgard was caught in a tearfall and a storm of sorrow. He wove his words with care and love and asked Hel if she would agree to let Balder ride home with him.

Hel thought for a while and her expression did not change. 'I'm not so sure,' she said at last, 'that Balder is as much loved as people say.'

She waited for Hermod to reply and Hermod said nothing.

'However,' said Hel, 'it can be put to the test.' She spoke as slowly as Ganglati and Ganglot, her aged servants, moved – so slowly that her words were only like punctuations between her silences. 'If everything in the nine worlds, dead and alive, weeps for Balder,' Hel declared, 'let him return to Asgard. But if anything demurs, if even one thing will not weep, Balder must remain in Niflheim.' And with these words Hel slowly turned away from Hermod.

Then Balder stood up and Nanna rose from the shades and stood beside him. They walked the length of the hall; they passed between the benches of corpses and Balder's face was white and shining. Balder and Nanna came up to Hermod and greeted him and led him out of Eljudnir. Then Balder took off the arm-ring Draupnir that Odin had fixed on him when he was lying lifeless on Ringhorn, and he put it into Hermod's hands. He said, 'Give this to my father in remembrance of me.' And Nanna offered Hermod linen for a head-dress and other gifts. 'These are for Frigg,' she said. 'And this is for Fulla.' She handed Hermod a gold ring.

Hermod took leave of Balder and Nanna. He mounted Sleipnir and rode without rest until he reached Asgard. And there, in Gladsheim, he told the gods and goddesses all he had seen and all that had been said to him.

The Aesir sent out messengers to every corner of the nine worlds. And all that they asked was that dead Balder should be wept out of Hel. As each substance had sworn an oath before that it would not harm Balder, each substance now wept. Fire wept, iron and every other metal wept, the stones wept, earth wept, the trees wept, every kind of illness wept, all the animals wept, all the birds wept, every kind of poisonous plant wept and so did every sidling snake – just as these things weep when they are covered with rime and begin to thaw again.

The gods' messengers were making their way back to Asgard and they all felt they had overlooked nothing. Then they came across a giantess sitting in a cave.

'What is your name?' asked one.

'Thokk,' said the giantess.

Then the messengers explained their mission and asked Thokk to weep as all things had wept, weep and weep Balder out of Hel.

The giantess glowered at the messengers and then she answered sourly, 'Thokk will weep dry tears over Balder's funeral. I never cared for the Old Man's son – alive or dead, I have no use for him. Let Hel hold what she has.'

Despite the messengers' prayers and entreaties, Thokk refused to say another word. She would not recant, she would not weep.

Then the messengers left her; they mournfully crossed Bifrost. And what they had to say was clear from the manner of their coming.

The gods and goddesses ached; they felt old and confused and unable and weary. And not one of them doubted that Thokk, the giantess in the cave, was also Loki.

For note on this myth see page 225.

 # 30 *Loki's Flyting*

O N ONE OCCASION some while after Balder's death, when they could think about him quietly and talk about him calmly for all their foreboding, many of the gods went over to the island of Hlesey for a feast.

Aegir received them in his gleaming hall under the waves. And since Thor and Tyr had secured Hymir's mighty cauldron for him, he had no choice but to keep his promise, brew a welter of ale and entertain his guests.

Thor himself was away on another foray into Jotunheim, but Odin and Frigg led the way; Thor's wife, Sif, and Bragi and his wife Idun, accompanied them. So did Tyr who had left one hand in the mouth of the wolf Fenrir and to him the gods renewed their thanks for the part he had played in wresting the cauldron five miles deep from his father Hymir. Njord and his wife Skadi made the journey; so did Freyr and Freyja, with Freyr's two servants Byggvir and Beyla. Odin's son Vidar, went with them. And Loki was there.

This was not all. Many other gods and a throng of elves gathered in the hall that was lit with great nuggets of shining gold. The guests sat down at the benches and Aegir's two serving-men, Fimafeng the Swift Handler and Eldir the Man of Fire, moved amongst them. The cups filled themselves with ale, and the hall was filled with the peaceful hum of good talk.

When Loki heard one god after another praise the diligence of Aegir's two servants, he began to bridle. The pleasure and good will in that place became too much for him; he seethed like boiling water. Then suddenly Loki leaped up; he lunged at Fimafeng with his knife and killed him.

There was uproar along the benches. The gods stood up, shook their shields and howled at Loki. They drove him out of the hall and he escaped into the darkness of the forest on the island of Hlesey. Aegir and his wife Ran, the gods and the elves resumed their places. They began to drink once more.

It was not long before Loki returned from the darkness to the feasting hall. He ambushed Aegir's second servant outside the door. 'Don't move, Eldir,' he said. 'Not one step further until you've told me this. What's all that hubbub? When they're not slopping their ale and slurping, what are the great gods talking about?'

'The great gods are comparing their weapons,' said Eldir, 'and their prowess in battle. You won't find a single god in there, not even an elf, with a good word to say for you.'

Loki's mouth twisted into a hideous smile. 'Never mind,' he said. 'I'm going back in. I don't mean to miss this feast. I'll fill their hearts with hatred and grief, and mix venom with their ale.'

'They'll rub your face in your own filth,' said Eldir.

'Have a care, Eldir, before you start to trade insults with me. Whatever you dredge up, I'll repay you twice over.' Loki scornfully elbowed Eldir out of the way and stepped into the hall. When the feasters saw who had come in, they all stopped drinking and stopped talking.

Loki faced the barrier of silence. He sidled to the middle of the great hall. 'Here's the Sky Traveller and he's rather thirsty,' he announced drily. 'It's a long journey to Aegir's hall. Would one of the gods care to bring me a cup of shining ale?' Loki stood motionless; his head swivelled as he surveyed the gathering ranged all around him. 'Why are you all so silent, you dismal gang of gods? Haven't you one word between you? Either make room and give me a place at this feast, or else tell me I'm unwelcome.'

Bragi was never at a loss for words. He called out, 'The gods will no longer make room and give you a place amongst them. You're not the kind of company they want at a feast.'

Loki ignored Bragi altogether and addressed himself to the High One. 'Remember, Odin, how – long ago – we mixed our blood in brotherhood. You swore then that you would only drink if a drink were brought to us both.'

'Move up, then, Vidar,' said Odin, turning to his son. 'Make room for the wolf's father at this feast. We don't want any more of Loki's trouble-making here in Aegir's hall.'

Vidar got up, poured out a cup of ale and handed it to Loki. Then Loki looked around him and anyone who was close enough to him could see his spiteful expression. 'Greetings, gods! Goddesses, greetings!' called Loki. 'I greet all this holy gathering – all but one: Bragi slumped on the bench over there.'

Bragi shook his head. 'If only you'll keep your rancour to yourself and spare yourself the fury of the gods, I'll give you a horse out of my own hoard; I'll give you a sword and, what's more, I'll give you a ring.'

'Bragi the bragger!' said Loki. 'You've never had a horse or a ring to your name, and you never will have. Of all the gods and elves in this hall, you're the greatest coward. When arrows are loosed, you barely dare peep from behind your shield.'

'If I were outside,' said Bragi evenly, 'and not sitting here in Aegir's hall, I'd twist your head off your miserable body. That would be a fair price for your lies.'

'If only your actions matched up to your big mouth,' Loki retorted. 'Look at Bragi sitting on the bench, as sweet and soft as any bride! If you feel so angry, why don't you get up and fight? Heroes don't waste words mapping things out.'

Then Idun turned to face her husband. 'Bragi, I beg you, think of us and our children and all the gods. Leave Loki alone. Don't exchange any more insults here in Aegir's hall.'

'Enough, Idun!' shouted Loki. 'I know no woman as wanton as you. What an appetite! You even wound your white arms about your brother's murderer.'

Despite Loki's withering abuse, Idun did not lose her composure. 'I will not exchange insults with Loki here in Aegir's hall. All this ale has made Bragi talkative, and I've told him to keep his temper.'

Then the goddess Gefion added, 'Why do these two gods bandy gibes and sneers? Everyone knows how Loki revels in foul mockery and hates the gods in Asgard.'

'Enough, Gefion,' shouted Loki. 'I know a thing or two about you. I even know who seduced you – that boy offered you a sparkling necklace and you, you straddled him.'

'Loki, you're mad to incense Gefion,' Odin called out. 'You've lost your senses. She can see all that is to come as clearly as I can.'

'Enough, Odin!' shouted Loki. 'You never could be even-handed: you've often let the weaker man snatch victory in battle.'

'I may have let the weaker man snatch victory in battle,' Odin replied. 'You lived under the earth for eight winters in the shape of a woman, a milkmaid. Yes, and you've borne babies and been milked by them – a woman through and through.'

'They say that on Samsey you once worked charms and spells like a witch,' replied Loki. 'They say you moved amongst men in the shape of a witch – a woman through and through.'

Now Odin's wife, Frigg, tried to restore peace. 'You would both do better to keep these things to yourselves,' she said. 'There's nothing to be gained from raking up what's best forgotten.'

'Enough, Frigg!' shouted Loki. 'You're Fjorgyn's daughter and you were born a whore. You may be Odin's wife but you've shared your bed with his brothers, Vili and Ve, into the bargain.'

'If I had a son,' said Frigg, 'a son such as Balder sitting beside me in Aegir's hall, you'd not get away without a fight.'

'Ah! Frigg,' said Loki scathingly, 'I can see you'd like to know more about my skills. It was I who fixed things so that you'll never again welcome Balder home.'

Freyja rounded on Loki, her eyes blazing. 'Loki, you're mad to boast about your terrible crime. There's nothing Frigg does not know, even though she may remain silent.'

'Enough, Freyja!' shouted Loki. 'I know you through and through and you're not wholly spotless. You've slept with every single god and elf gathered in this hall.'

'Your mouth is full of lies,' said Freyja, 'and you're spelling out your own doom. You'll leave here wishing you'd never bothered to come.'

'Enough, Freyja!' shouted Loki. 'You're a foul witch with a string of evil works to your name. The bright gods caught you in bed with your own brother, and then, Freyja, you farted.'

Njord raised his voice in defence of the goddesses and against Loki.

'A woman lies with her husband or lover or both. Does it really matter much in the end? It's far worse to clap eyes on this womanish god who has borne babies.'

'Enough, Njord!' shouted Loki. 'You were sent from the east and given to the gods as a hostage. Hymir's daughters squatted over you and pissed straight into your mouth.'

'The journey was long,' said Njord, 'but it was a great honour to be given to the gods as a hostage. And I fathered a son who is well loved and highest of those on high.'

'That's too much, Njord,' said Loki. 'I'll cap your absurd boast and share your secret. You spawned your fair son on your own sister – so at least you knew what to expect!'

Then Tyr spoke up in support of Njord's son. 'Freyr,' he called out, 'is the noblest of all the brave gods. He doesn't trifle with virgins or seduce other men's wives, and he frees bound men from their fetters.'

'Enough, Tyr!' shouted Loki. 'You've never been much of a hand at bringing two parties to an understanding.' He smiled wickedly. 'Need I remind you how you lost your right one when Fenrir snapped it off?'

'I lost a hand, but you lost Hrodvitnir, the Mighty Wolf; we were both hapless. And now, in his fetters, Fenrir must chafe and wait until the worlds' end.'

'Enough, Tyr!' shouted Loki again. 'Your good wife was lucky enough to be the mother of my son. And were you paid one penny, you poor fool, by way of recompense?'

'The wolf,' cried Freyr, 'will lie in chains at the mouth of the river until the gods meet their doom. And unless you bite on your tongue, you lie-smith, you'll soon be chained up too.'

'You're the one who bought Gymir's daughter with gold,' retorted Loki, 'and sold your sword into the bargain. You poor fool, when the sons of Muspell ride through Mirkwood, you'll have to await them empty-handed.'

Freyr's servant Byggvir was enraged at the way in which Loki had insulted his master. 'If I were as nobly born as Freyr,' he said, 'and sat in so high a seat, I'd grab this ghastly crow, and beat his bones into pulp.'

'Who's that little creature,' asked Loki, 'grovelling and yapping and snapping? You're always whispering in Freyr's ear or quibbling by the quern.'

'I am Barley Byggvir,' said Freyr's servant, 'and I'm quick to get my way, as gods and men allow. To see Allfather's sons all gathered to drink ale fills me with delight.'

'Enough, Byggvir!' shouted Loki. 'You've never been able to give men their due portion of meat. And when heroes made ready to fight, no one could find you. You were hiding under the straw strewn on the floor.'

'You're drunk, Loki,' called Heimdall. 'Your jabs and gibes are insane. Loki, why not leave off now? No one in his cups cares about curbing his tongue.'

'Enough, Heimdall!' shouted Loki. 'It was settled long ago that your life should be menial. You can never sleep or even sit down; day and night you stand awake, the watchman of the gods.'

'You're as quick as they come, Loki,' said Skadi, 'but you won't be at large, twirling your tail, much longer. The gods will bind you to a boulder with gut ripped out of your ice-cold son.'

'Even if the gods bind me to a boulder with gut ripped out of my ice-cold son, I led the way when we killed and captured your father, the giant Thiazi,' jeered Loki.

'If you led the way when the gods captured and killed Thiazi,' Skadi said, 'my hall and my temples will always echo with curses on your name.'

Loki's mouth twisted and his eyes shone orange and green. 'You spoke so much more sweetly to Laufey's son when you invited him into your bed. That's well worth a mention, since we're both giving our weaknesses an airing.'

Thor's wife, Sif, stood up. She left her place at the bench and stepped towards Loki. Gently she took the cup out of his clenched right fist and filled it again with ale. 'Greetings, Loki!' she said in her sweet, clear voice. 'Take this crystal cup brimming with fine ale. At least allow you find me, alone amongst us all, wholly guiltless.'

Loki took the cup, raised and drained it in one movement. 'You'd certainly stand alone if you were as chaste with all men as you are with most. But I think I know one who inveigled you out of your husband's arms, and set you on fire: his name was crafty Loki.'

Freyr's second servant, Beyla, raised her voice in Aegir's hall. 'The mountains are quaking. That can mean only one thing: Thor is on his way here from Bilskirnir. He'll silence the one in this hall who slanders and sneers at gods and men alike.'

'Enough, Beyla!' shouted Loki. 'You are Byggvir's wife and you're poisonous through and through. It's a scandal that you mix with the gods at all – caked with your own excrement.'

Loki was so carried away by his flight of words that he did not see that Thor had walked into Aegir's hall. The God of Thunder waited until Loki had had his say and then stepped forward and crashed his fist on to a trestle table so that the crystal cups leaped into the air. 'Hold your tongue, you scum,' he roared, 'or my hammer Mjollnir will shut your mouth! I'll swipe your shoulder-stone off your neck and that will be the end of you.'

'Look everyone!' cried Loki, unabashed. 'Here's the Son of Earth! What a blustering bully you are, Thor. But you'll be less fierce when you grapple with Fenrir and see him gulp down Odin, the Father of Victory.'

'Hold your tongue, you scum,' roared Thor, 'or my hammer Mjollnir will shut your mouth! I'll pick you up and hurl you into the east and no one will have to set eyes on you again.'

'If I were you, Thor,' said Loki, 'I wouldn't say too much about your own journey east. You cowered in the thumb of a glove, you noble god! You quite forgot your name was Thor.'

'Hold your tongue, you scum,' roared Thor, 'or my hammer Mjollnir will shut your mouth! I'll raise my right hand and what smashed Hrungnir will smash your bones too.'

'For all your threats with your hammer,' said Loki, 'I fancy I have a long life before me. Do you remember the Giant Skrymir's bag and how unyielding those straps were? You were unable to get at the provisions and felt quite faint with hunger.'

'Hold your tongue, you scum,' roared Thor, 'or my hammer Mjollnir will shut your mouth! What smashed Hrungnir will dispatch you to Hel, right down to the doors of the dead.' The god of thunder gripped Mjollnir menacingly.

Loki raised one hand and shook his head. 'I've shown the gods and the sons of gods the sharp edge of my thoughts. But because of you and you alone, I think I'll take my leave now. I know all about your strength.'

Loki paused and looked defiantly around him and then addressed himself to his host. 'You've brewed fine ale, Aegir, but you'll never hold another feast such as this.' Loki's voice was rising. 'Flickering flames will gorge on this hall and gut it and destroy everything you own; your body will be flayed by fire.'

Loki turned and was gone and his terrible words still echoed round the walls. For a long time the gods and goddesses and elves stared into their ale, shaken and grieving. In silence they sat, and in silence they rose and left Aegir's hall.

For note on this myth see page 231.

31 *The Binding of Loki*

LOKI KNEW THAT HIS DAYS IN ASGARD had come to an end. He knew how soon anguish can give way to anger and was sure the gods would avenge Balder's death and detention in Hel.

He ran away. He made for a deserted part of Midgard, a remote place in the mountains at the head of a steep valley that fell into the sea. He found a hollow near Franang's Falls and, using the rock and rubble lying all around, built a low house that no man was likely to see until he had stumbled into it. It had four doors so that Loki could keep watch in every direction.

Even so, he felt unsafe. When a gull circled and shrieked, or scree shifted on the mountain, or wind whistled in his walls, the Trickster leaped up in alarm, certain he had been tracked down. It did not matter that days passed without a single visitor: Loki's anxiety grew greater day by day; he could not escape his own canker.

He thought he might be better off if he were out of the house and in disguise. At dawn the Shape Changer often turned himself into a salmon and leaped into the seething cauldron at the base of Franang's Falls. The cross currents whirled around him, the thunder roared above him; still the salmon felt unsafe.

In Loki's mind it was not a question of whether but of when the gods would catch up with him. But fearful as he was, hunted and in hiding, he was more fearful of vengeance, and vowed to remain at large for as long as he had the wits to do so.

Early one evening, Loki sat beside his fire and began to play with some lengths of linen twine. He arranged them and rearranged them; he laid them out across each other and tied them and made them into a net with so fine a mesh that not even a small fish could hope to slip through it. For a long time he stared at his fine device.

Suddenly he heard the sound of voices down in the valley; he saw a group of gods making their way towards him. Loki jumped up, threw the net into the fire and hurried out of the door overlooking Franang's

169

Falls. He ran down the slope, turned himself into a salmon once more and slid into the boiling icy water.

There was nothing that escaped Odin's eye when he sat in Hlidskjalf. He saw the comings and goings of every living creature in the nine worlds; and when he saw Loki's efforts to escape his fate, he sent a party of gods from Asgard to capture him.

The first to step across the threshold of Loki's house was Kvasir, the wisest of them all. In the half light, he peered around without a word. He looked at the rough table and bench, the bare walls, the almost lifeless fire. Kvasir bent down and stared at the pattern of gleaming white ash; he carefully examined it and understood what he saw. 'This,' he said to his companions, 'is some device for catching fish. Let us catch a fish.'

The gods sat down in Loki's house and gave over the rest of the evening to making a wide net with which to drag the pool at the base of the Falls and the river that hurried down the valley to the sea. They copied the subtle pattern Kvasir had found in the embers and, before they slept, they had finished their work and were well content with it.

At dawn the gods walked down under Franang's Falls. The roar of water slamming against water was deafening. The air was misty with whirling and drifting spray; the gods stared around them and the whole world looked oyster and ivory and grey. Then Thor took one end of the net and, motioning to the others to stay where they were, waded across the water. So the gods began to drag the river and the salmon swam downstream in front of them. After a time, wily Loki found a safe place where the water sluiced between two slimy boulders and he nestled there so that the net only scraped his back and did not snare him. When the gods brought up the net, there was nothing in it. They were all sure, though, that they had felt something alive in the water. They decided to try again, and this time they used stones to weight the bottom of the drag-net so that nothing could swim under it.

Now, the gods made their way back to the base of Franang's Falls – Thor on one side and all the rest on the other – and dropped the net into the water. Once more Loki swam ahead of them as they dragged the river, but this time there was no safety on the river bed. He had no choice but to hurry on downstream. When Loki saw that the gods meant to drag the tumbling river right down to the shallows where it opened on to the sea, he turned round to face the net. He arched his back, and with all his strength, sprang into the air and right over it.

The gods shouted and pointed at the salmon shining in the sunlight. They hurried back up to Franang's Falls and there they argued about how to catch it. Each god had his own idea but, in the end, they bowed to Kvasir: he said they should split into two groups – one on either bank – all except Thor who was to wade in midstream just behind the net.

Now the gods began to drag the river for a third time. As before, Loki swam downstream some way in front of them. He knew that only two choices were open to him: to squirm and jump across the long stretch of shallows into the sea or to turn and leap over the drag-net again. He thought the gods might catch him before he reached the safety of deep water and so he turned, arched his back into a rainbow, and sprang into the air. The salmon flashed in the sunlight and jumped clear of the net.

Then Thor groped and clutched at it and the salmon slithered through his hands. Thor held on and tightened his grip; he squeezed and stayed the slippery salmon by its tail. It writhed and it twisted but it could not escape. Loki was caught at last and he knew it.

After Balder's death, not one of the gods would stain Gladsheim by spilling Loki's blood. But there was nothing holy about the barren ground of Midgard, and they were all eager to take vengeance on him.

While Thor and one group of gods led Loki into a twilit cave, a dismal cavern belonging to bats and ticking with the drips of water from stalactites, the other party went off in pursuit of Loki's two sons, Vali and Narvi. They changed Vali into a wolf and at once he leaped at his brother and sunk his teeth into his throat. He ripped Narvi's body apart before bounding away, howling, toward Jotunheim.

The gods took over where Vali had left off. They drew out Narvi's entrails and made their way to the cave. Loki's faithful wife, Sigyn, went with them, sorrowing over the fate of her two sons, the fate of her husband.

Loki was thrown to the ground. He lay still; he looked at nobody and said nothing. Then the gods took three slabs of rock, stood them on end and bored a hole through each of them. They stretched Loki over them, unwound Narvi's entrails and bound him with the gut of his own son as no one had ever been bound before. They trussed Loki's shoulders to one slab, twisting the gut round his body under his armpits; they strapped Loki's loins to one slab, winding the gut round and round his hips; they clamped Loki's kneecaps to one slab, tying the gut round his legs. And no sooner was Loki bound than the entrails of his son became as hard as iron.

Then Skadi carried a vile snake into the cave. She fastened it to a stalactite high up in the darkness so that its venom would drip straight on to Loki's face. For all his wiles and wit, there was nothing Loki could do. He lay still; he looked at nobody and said nothing. Then the gods left Loki there; no longer flushed but heavy-hearted and sorrowing they left him to his fate, and to faithful Sigyn.

Sigyn and Loki wait in the damp twilit cave, listening to the eerie echoes of each drip, the sound of the silence, the sound of their own breathing. Sigyn holds a wooden bowl over Loki's face and slowly it fills with the snake's venom. When it is brimming, Sigyn carries the bowl away and empties it into a rock basin – a fermenting pool of poison.

Loki is left unguarded; he screws up his eyes. The snake does not wait. Its venom splashes on to Loki's face and in torment he shudders and writhes. He cannot escape and the whole earth quakes.

Loki lies bound. That is how things are and how things will remain until Ragnarok.

For note on this myth see page 233.

32 *Ragnarok*

AN AXE-AGE, A SWORD-AGE, shields will be gashed: there will be a wind-age and a wolf-age before the world is wrecked.

First of all Midgard will be wrenched and racked by wars for three winters. Fathers will slaughter sons; brothers will be drenched in one another's blood. Mothers will desert their menfolk and seduce their own sons; brothers will bed with sisters.

Then Fimbulvetr, the winter of winters, will grip and throttle Midgard. Driving snow clouds will converge from north and south and east and west. There will be bitter frosts, biting winds; the shining sun will be helpless. Three such winters will follow each other with no summers between them.

So the end will begin. Then the children of the old giantess in Iron Wood will have their say: the wolf Skoll will seize the sun between his jaws and swallow her – he will spatter Asgard with gore; and his brother Hati will catch the moon and mangle him. The stars will vanish from the sky.

The earth will start to shudder then. Great trees will sway and topple, mountains will shake and rock and come crashing down, and every bond and fetter will burst. Fenrir will run free.

Eggther, watchman of the giants, will sit on his grave mound and strum his harp, smiling grimly. Nothing escapes the red cock Fjalar; he will crow to the giants from bird-wood. At the same time the cock who wakes the warriors every day in Valhalla, golden combed Gullinkambi, will crow to the gods. A third cock, rust red, will raise the dead in Hel.

The sea will rear up and waves will pummel the shore because Jormungand, the Midgard Serpent, is twisting and writhing in fury, working his way on to dry land. And in those high seas Naglfar will break loose – the ship made from dead men's nails. The bows and the waist and the stern and the hold will be packed with giants and Hrym will stand at the helm, heading towards the plain Vigrid. Loki too, free from his fetters, will take to the water; he will set sail towards Vigrid from the north and his deadweight will be all that ghastly crew in Hel.

Then the brothers Fenrir and Jormungand will move forward side by side. Fenrir's slavering mouth will gape wide open, so wide that his lower jaw scrapes against the ground and his upper jaw presses against the sky; it would gape still wider if there were more room. Flames will dance in Fenrir's eyes and leap from his nostrils. With each breath, meanwhile, Jormungand will spew venom; all the earth and the sky will be splashed and stained with his poison.

The world will be in uproar, the air quaking with booms and blares and their echoes. Then the sons of Muspell will advance from the south and tear apart the sky itself as they, too, close in on Vigrid. Surt will lead them, his sword blazing like the sun itself. And as they cross Bifrost, the rainbow bridge will crack and break behind them. So all the giants and all the inmates of Hel, and Fenrir and Jormungand, and Surt and the blazing sons of Muspell will gather on Vigrid; they will all but fill that plain that stretches one hundred and twenty leagues in every direction.

The gods, meanwhile, will not be idle. Heimdall will leave his hall, Himinbjorg, and raise the great horn Gjall to his mouth. He will sound such a blast that it will be heard throughout the nine worlds. All the gods will wake and at once meet in council. Then Odin will mount Sleipnir and gallop to Mimir's spring and take advice from Mimir there.

Yggdrasill itself will moan, the ash that always was and waves over all that is. Its leaves will tremble, its limbs shiver and shake even as two humans take refuge deep within it. Everything in heaven and in earth and Hel will quiver.

Then all the Aesir and all the Einherjar in Valhalla will arm themselves. They will don their helmets and their coats of mail, and grasp their swords and spears and shields. Eight hundred fighting men will forge through each of that hall's five hundred and forty doors. That vast host will march towards Vigrid and Odin will ride at their head, wearing a golden helmet and a shining corslet, brandishing Gungnir.

Odin will make straight for the wolf Fenrir; and Thor, right beside him, will be unable to help because Jormungand will at once attack him. Freyr will fight the fire giant Surt. And when Surt whirls his flaming blade, Freyr will rue the day that he gave his own good sword to his servant Skirnir. It will be a long struggle, though, before Freyr succumbs. The hound Garm from Gnipahellir will leap at the throat of one-handed Tyr and they will kill one another. The age-old enemies Loki and Heimdall will meet once more and each will be the cause of the other's death.

Thor, Son of Earth, and gaping Jormungand have met before too; they are well matched. At Vigrid the god will kill the serpent but he will only be able to stagger back nine steps before he falls dead himself, poisoned by the venom Jormungand spews over him.

Odin and Fenrir were the first to engage and their fight will be fearsome. In the end, though, the wolf will seize Allfather between his jaws and swallow him. That will be the death of Odin.

At once his son Vidar will stride forward and press one foot on Fenrir's bottom jaw – and the shoe he will wear then has been a long time in the making; it consists of all the strips and bits of leather pared off the heels and toes of new shoes since time began, all the leftovers thrown away as gifts for the god. Then Vidar will take hold of Fenrir's other jaw and tear the wolf apart, so avenging his father.

Then Surt will fling fire in every direction. Asgard and Midgard and Jotunheim and Niflheim will become furnaces – places of raging flame, swirling smoke, ashes, only ashes. The nine worlds will burn and the gods will die. The Einherjar will die, men and women and children in Midgard will die, elves and dwarfs will die, giants will die, monsters and creatures of the underworld will die, birds and animals will die. The sun will be dark and there will be no stars in the sky. The earth will sink into the sea.

The earth will rise again out of the water, fair and green. The eagle will fly over cataracts, swoop into the thunder and catch fish under crags. Corn will ripen in fields that were never sown.

Vidar and Vali will still be alive; they will survive the fire and the flood and make their way back to Idavoll, the shining plain where palaces once stood. Modi and Magni, sons of Thor, will join them there, and they will inherit their father's hammer, Mjollnir. And Balder and Hod will come back from the world of the dead; it will not be long before they, too, tread the new green grass on Idavoll. Honir will be there as well, and he will hold the wand and foretell what is to come. The sons of Vili and Ve will make up the new number, the gods in heaven, home of the winds.

They will sit down in the sunlight and begin to talk. Turn by turn, they will call up such memories, memories such as are known to them alone. They will talk over many things that happened in the past, and the evil of Jormungand and the wolf Fenrir. And then, amongst the waving grass, they will find golden chessboards, treasures owned once by the Aesir, and gaze at them in wonder.

Many courts will rise once more, some good, some evil. The best place of all will be Gimli in heaven, a building fairer than the sun, roofed with gold. That is where the rulers will live, at peace with themselves and each other. Then there will be Brimir on Okolnir, where the ground is always warm underfoot; there will always be plenty of good drink there for those who have a taste for it. And there will be Sindri, a fine hall that stands in the dark mountains of Nidafjoll, made wholly of red gold. Good men will live in these places.

But there will be another hall on Nastrond, the shore of corpses. That place in the underworld will be as vile as it is vast; all its doors will face north. Its walls and roof will be made of wattled snakes, their heads facing inward, blowing so much poison that it runs in rivers through the hall. Oath breakers and murderers and philanderers will wade through those rivers. Nidhogg, too, will outlive the fire and the flood and under Yggdrasill he will suck blood from the bodies of the dead.

The two humans who hid themselves deep within Yggdrasill – some say Hoddmimir's Wood – will be called Lif and Lifthrasir. Surt's fire will not scorch them; it will not even touch them, and their food will be the morning dew. Through the branches, through the leaves, they will see light come back, for before the sun is caught and eaten by the wolf Skoll, she will give birth to a daughter no less fair than herself, who will follow the same sky-path and light the world.

Lif and Lifthrasir will have children. Their children will bear children. There will be life and new life, life everywhere on earth. That was the end; and this is the beginning.

For note on this myth see page 234.

176

And now, if you have anything more to ask, I
can't think how you can manage it, for I've never
heard anyone tell more of the story of the world.
Make what use of it you can.

Snorri Sturluson
Prose Edda

NOTES

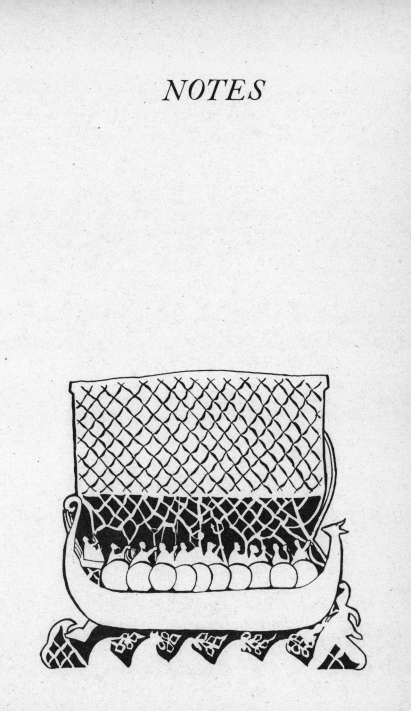

Snorri Sturluson provides a detailed and strikingly vivid account of the creation in the *Prose Edda*. His most important source is *Voluspa* (Sibyl's Prophecy), most inspiring of the eddaic poems, an account of both the creation and of how the world will end, that was composed in the late tenth or early eleventh century. At times, Snorri's description differs from *Voluspa* – as in the creation of the first man and first woman – and it is rich in details that do not appear either in that poem or in his two other surviving sources for this myth, *Grimnismal* and *Vafthrudnismal*, so he was clearly also drawing on some other source or sources that have not survived. I have followed Snorri closely but, in the interests both of consistency and the structure of my retelling, I have placed the making of Asgard after the setting of Night and Day, Moon and Sun in the sky, and the creation of the dwarfs.

In effect, the Norse account of the creation is three myths in one: the world is fashioned from Ymir's body; the cow Audumla releases the first man by licking ice; and Bergelmir and his wife escape the flood and go on to found a race of giants.

The concept of a world flood, often to purge creation of its wickedness and usher in a new age of innocence, is fundamental to the human imagination and shared by many mythologies. It is, for example, found in Babylonian, Indian and Russian myths; it features in Indonesian and Melanesian and New Guinean mythology and in the myths of the Mojave Apache Indians in North America and the Sherente in South America. Some scholars have taken the Norse myth to have been influenced by (or even to be a direct imitation of) the biblical flood, but the two accounts have nothing much in common and the floods differ in cause, function and particular. It is more to the point to see the Norse account as one of a group of Indo-European myths ultimately deriving from a common source.

On the other hand, there has been a wide measure of agreement about the provenance of the first and second elements in the myth. There are parallel Indian and Iranian myths in each instance and, in the case of Audumla, there is a striking parallel with the Egyptian goddess Hathor, the cow who was mother of all the deities. Audumla can similarly be seen as mother both of the gods and the frost giants. She licked Buri out of the ice and she gave suck to Ymir.

Ymir himself was both father and mother of the frost giants. His name probably derives from the Sanskrit *yama* (twin or hermaphrodite) and the Iranian parallel is particularly significant because the world is actually made, as in the Norse myth, from the body of the first bisexual being. His head (like Ymir's head) is the sky, and his feet are the earth, his tears are the ocean and his hair turns into every kind of plant. This idea is shared by many Indo-European mythologies (including the first recorded creation myth, the Babylonian), while Jacob Grimm shows in his *Teutonic Mythology* that the giant Banio, from whose body Buddha made the world, occupies much the same role in Cochin-Chinese tradition, and notes that 'similar macrocosms are met with in Japan and Ceylon'.

These parallels are such that it is certain that these two elements in the Norse creation myth were oriental in origin. What is not so certain is *when* they were incorporated with the Norse tradition. They may have resulted from contact along trade routes in the first few centuries after the birth of Christ. But a more exciting theory dates the contact to between one and two thousand years before Christ. Teutonic tribesmen moving west into Europe from the Russian steppelands in the Age of Migrations, and then north into Scandinavia, may have brought with them the fundamentals of the Norse creation myth (just as other Indo-Europeans carried the same elements east to India, China and Japan and south to Iran and the Near East). But whatever its origin, the Norse creation myth was decisively shaped and coloured by the country in which it was ultimately transmitted and recorded. Iceland is an island of extreme opposites: seething volcanoes and sweeping glaciers, summers where the light never fails and winters of unending darkness. The character of Muspell and Niflheim, of the Elivagar and the freezing mist are instantly recognisable to anyone familiar with Iceland. The poets who gave the myth its final shape drew heavily on what they were able to see with their own eyes. In considering the nature of creation, those poets must have seen that life was insupportable at either extreme and logically concluded that where those opposites met and fused, life began.

A familiar sight in Iceland, outside the few towns, is a lone-standing farmhouse with a solitary tree growing right up against it. These trees must be a twentieth-century echo of the traditional guardian tree, object of veneration outside (or sometimes inside, surging up through the roof) farmstead and shrine alike in pre-Christian Northern Europe. The first and greatest of such trees was Yggdrasill, the ash that appears to have had no beginning and will survive Ragnarok, and that guarded the world itself. The concept of a tree that embraced and linked all creation is a familiar one in many European and Asian mythologies and the myth of Yggdrasill may well be no less old than the myths of the bisexual progenitor and the divine cow. It is fully discussed in the introduction (see also *Myth* and *Note 4*).

I referred above to the divergence between Snorri's and *Voluspa*'s accounts of the creation of man. For reasons explained elsewhere, I have followed Snorri wherever it seemed reasonable to do so and supplied important alternative versions in the notes. *Voluspa* substitutes Odin, Honir and Lodur for the three sons of Bor. In Henry Adams Bellows' translation:

> Soul gave Odin, sense gave Honir,
> Heat gave Lodur and goodly hue.

It is probable that Lodur and Loki are one and the same in which case this is the first of three occasions (see *Myths 8* and *26*) in which these three gods are associated.

After describing the creation of the dwarfs, Snorri Sturluson lists their names. I did not want to encumber my retelling with them, but record them here: Nyi, Nidi, Nordri, Sudri, Austri, Vestri, Althjof, Dvalin, Bifur, Bafur, Bombor, Nori, Oinn, Mjodvitnir, Vig, Gandalf, Vindalf, Thorin, Fili, Kili, Fundin, Vali, Thror, Thrain, Thekk, Lit, Vit, Nyr, Nyrad, Rekk, Radsvid, Draupnir, Dolgthvari, Haur, Hugstari, Hledjolf, Gloin, Dori, Ori, Duf, Andvari, Heptifili, Har, Sviar, Skirfir, Virfir, Skavid, Ai, Alf, Ingi, Eikinskjaldi, Fal, Frosti, Fid and, last of the least, Ginnar! Snorri's list largely coincides with *Voluspa* (though in many cases the spelling differs) which, however, also names these dwarfs: Sviur, Frar, Hornbori, Frag, Loni, Aurvang and Jari. Very few of these dwarfs are mentioned elsewhere in the myths and, conversely, several dwarfs who do feature significantly elsewhere (e.g. Brokk and Eitri and Alvis) do not appear in this list!

After he has settled the Aesir in Asgard, Snorri Sturluson names the principal gods and goddesses, their characteristics and halls. I have not included this information as part of the creation myth, but it emerges in many of the myths and is discussed in the introduction and pertinent notes.

2 THE WAR OF THE AESIR AND VANIR

The only rounded account of the first of all wars occurs in Snorri Sturluson's *Ynglinga Saga* (Chapter IV), and I have taken that as the basis for my version. But Snorri also alludes to the war in 'Skaldskaparmal' in the *Prose Edda*; he says that the gods put the seal on their truce by spitting into a communal crock and made out of the divine spittle a man called Kvasir. In this respect, Snorri contradicts himself, for *Ynglinga Saga* describes Kvasir as the wisest of the Vanir and involved in the exchange of leaders with the Aesir.

The description in the *Prose Edda* appears to represent an older tradition, and goes on to tell how Kvasir's blood was brewed into divine mead – the mead of poetry (*Myth 6*). So Mimir's head seems to serve precisely the same purpose in one version of the myth as does Kvasir's body in another; it embodies the source of inspiration. I have therefore rather reluctantly laid aside the older tradition in the *Prose Edda* (to which I return in *Myth 6*), since it has nothing to say of the war itself, and followed *Ynglinga Saga* in the interests of presenting as complete a version of the myth as possible.

Ynglinga Saga is silent, however, about the causes of the war. And here I have had recourse to the third and remaining source, *Voluspa* (stanzas 21–4). The substance of these stanzas forms the basis of the first four paragraphs of my retelling.

The myth of divine conflict has parallels in many other traditions. This myth could represent the folk memory of hostility between the adherents of two different cults – cults which were ultimately fused. The Vanir, who must have been the original gods, are fertility gods and the Aesir are primarily gods of war (see introduction). What is certain is that in both *Ynglinga Saga* and the *Prose Edda* the Aesir gain control of the embodiment of inspiration; that in *Ynglinga Saga* and *Voluspa* the Aesir learn the magic that was known before only to the Vanir; and that, following the war, all the gods are referred to as Aesir. In other words, the Aesir succeed and embrace the Vanir.

The name of indestructible Gullveig is associated with gold and has been interpreted as 'the madness and corruption caused by this precious metal'. Gullveig's second name is Heid (*heidr*) which means 'the bright one' or 'the shining one'. Gullveig can, therefore, clearly be equated with Freyja, foremost of the Vanir, whose connexion with gold is apparent in a number of the myths (see especially *Myth 13*) and who was also both a seeress and mistress of witchcraft. Gullveig-Freyja was the immediate cause of the divine war and, in accompanying her father and brother in the exchange of leaders, she was making her second journey to Asgard.

Odin set Mimir's head to guard the well that lay under the root of Yggdrasill in Jotunheim (*Myth 4*), and both *Voluspa* and Snorri refer to how Odin gave one eye for a draught from that well which contained wisdom and understanding. The power of the severed head is a familiar motif in both primitive and civilised societies. Earlier this century, headhunters in the Philippines needed heads to guarantee the success of their rice crop; in *The Golden Bough*, J. G. Frazer noted that after the death of the King of the Abeokuta in West Africa, the chiefs decapitated him and his head became the fetish of the new sovereign; in *The Tain*, we read how Irish warriors carried off the heads of their enemies, tied to their saddles; the English folktale 'Three Heads in a Well' (likewise Perrault's 'Diamonds and Toads' and similar stories found in Norway, Sweden, Denmark and Germany) illustrates the power of the severed head to reward good and punish evil; and, of course, Keats made powerful use of the motif in *Isabella*.

3 THE BUILDING OF ASGARD'S WALL

The only complete version of this myth appears in Snorri Sturluson's *Prose Edda*. A couple of stanzas in *Voluspa* allude to a debate among the gods about who was responsible for promising Freyja to a giant and tell how the gods violated their oaths when Thor, swollen with rage, struck out at the giant; Snorri quotes them, but only as a kind of imprimatur for his version (and some scholars think he interpreted them wrongly and that they refer to another event altogether); at all events, neither they nor a glancing reference to Loki's mothering of Sleipnir in *Hyndluljoth* add to Snorri's account.

Snorri writes elsewhere in the *Prose Edda* of the time after the creation called the Golden Age, a time when gold was the metal used for every kind of making, and a time of peace and contentment 'before it was spoiled by the arrival of the women who came from Giantland'. The building of Asgard's wall is, then, the first of the myths devoted to the enmity of gods and giants – the theme that dominates the entire cycle and only resolves itself at Ragnarok. The gods were far from unblemished and the giants were not totally destructive (several gods even married giantesses) but in the end the antagonism of gods and giants can only be seen as the conflict of good and evil. The gods embody aspects of natural and social order; the giants subvert that order and seek to overthrow it.

The nature of their conflict shows clearly in the giant mason's price for building the wall. The idea of a bargain such as that struck between gods and mason is the stuff of folklore (and parallels have been cited in which the builder is troll or devil and the penalty is sun or moon or soul), but the mason demands not just the sun and moon but, first of all, Freyja. Most beautiful and sexually attractive of the goddesses, Freyja was one of the Vanir – the foremost goddess of fertility. The giant's intention was, therefore, to bring an end to the natural revolution of the seasons and deprive the gods of the possibility of regeneration – and, moreover, by taking away the sun and moon, to consign them to eternal freezing darkness into the bargain.

This is also the first myth in which Loki comes into play; he is fully considered in the introduction. Snorri Sturluson says that Loki is called 'the mischief-monger of the Aesir and the father-of-lies and the disgrace-of-gods-and-men'. It is entirely in keeping with his character in the majority of the myths, dynamic and ambivalent, that he should let the gods in for trouble, talking them into a contract about which they have doubts, and then get them out of it again.

Loki's ability to change shape is displayed in a number of myths where he assumes the form of flea, fly, bird and salmon. But he is not only a shape changer; like Odin, he can change sex, and even bear a child. In the 'Death of Balder' (*Myth 29*), Loki takes the form of an old woman and in this myth he changes himself into a mare. Bisexuality was not a characteristic that appealed to the early Icelanders, and homosexuality was a crime punishable by outlawry. It seems likely that Loki's sexual antics, even if acceptable in a god, would have aroused more distaste than amusement in the minds of believers.

The fruit of Loki's and Svadilfari's union is the grey Sleipnir. He has no peer and is Odin's own horse – a symbol of fertility and of death (bones of horses have often been found in Viking burials). Sleipnir was able to journey to the world of the dead; he carried both Odin and Hermod there (*Myths 28* and *29*). His eight legs may suggest phenomenal speed; but they may also suggest, as H. R. Ellis Davidson has suggested, the eight legs of four mourners, bodies and heads hidden, carrying a coffin.

A few other points need brief mention. Allusions to Mjollnir and the Necklace of the Brisings anticipate their making in *Myths 10* and *13* respectively. The myths were not composed at one time and there are inevitably a number of internal inconsistencies. The war between the Aesir and the Vanir that led to the breaking of the original wall round Asgard is the subject of *Myth 2*. And, lastly, Hraesvelg, the Corpse Eater, is a giant in eagle's guise who, according to *Vafthrudnismal*, sits at the end of heaven, overlooking Hel, and makes the wind by flapping his wings.

4 LORD OF THE GALLOWS

Several myths in the cycle concern Odin's relentless quest for wisdom and the way he displays and uses that wisdom. Odin learns from wise giants, especially Vafthrudnir (*Myth 15*); he learns from *volvas* or seeresses whom he raises from the dead (*Myth 28*), and from hanged men; and in this myth Odin makes the supreme sacrifice. He dies so as to win the occult wisdom possessed only by the dead, and rises again to use that wisdom in the world of the living.

The principal sources are those two parts of *Havamal* or 'Words of the High One' that describe how Odin won the runes and characterise their power. *Havamal*, which is one of the poems in the *Codex Regius* of the *Elder Edda*, is not of one piece – it also includes a sustained collection of proverbs and advice on right living, some of it addressed to one Lodd-fafnir (*Myth 23*) and the stories of Odin and Billing's daughter (*Myth 20*) and of how Odin secured the mead of poetry (*Myth 6*).

I have thought it appropriate to preface the material based on *Havamal* with a description of Yggdrasill and of Odin's sacrifice of one eye at the spring of Mimir to win understanding. The sources for this description are stanzas in *Grimnismal* and paragraphs in the *Prose Edda* by Snorri Sturluson.

The powerful conception of the world tree at the heart of the universe recurs in many mythologies and is fully discussed in the introduction. *Ygg* means 'the terrible one' and *drasill* means 'horse', and it is now generally accepted that this compound noun must mean 'Odin's horse'. The image of Odin 'riding' the ash is appropriate, for Old Norse poets often spoke of a gallows tree as a horse.

It is known that the worship of Odin (and other, related Germanic war gods) included human sacrifice. The eleventh-century historian Adam of Bremen records that he saw many human bodies hanging in the sacrificial grove at Uppsala near the temple that housed idols of Odin, Thor and Freyr, while evidence in the sagas establishes that sacrificial victims were pierced with a spear and dedicated to Odin. Two of the god's names are, indeed, 'God of the Hanged' and 'God of the Spear'. So Odin himself dies on Yggdrasill in precisely the manner of his own sacrificial victims.

The parallels between Odin's death and Christ's crucifixion are striking: both die voluntarily; Odin is pierced with a spear and so is Christ; Odin alludes to the lack of a reviving drink and Christ is given vinegar; Odin screeches or shrieks before he dies, and Christ cries out 'in a loud voice'. But although it is possible that the poet who composed this part of *Havamal* had heard the story of the crucifixion and been influenced by it, scholars have demonstrated how, in the words of E. O. G. Turville-Petre, 'nearly every element in the Norse myth can be explained as part of pagan tradition, and even of the cult of Odin'. Those interested in a detailed comparison can do no better than to turn to his *Myth and Religion of the North* (pp. 42–50).

What did Odin learn by dying on Yggdrasill? Firstly, he learned nine songs from the son of the giant Bolthor, who was also the father of Bestla. Since Bestla was Odin's mother, this means that he learned the songs from his mother's brother – his maternal uncle. In pre-Christian Germanic society there was an especially close bond between a man and his sister's son; the older man was a kind of godfather, responsible for the moral upbringing, and on occasion the guardianship, of the younger. Anglo-Saxon poets frequently referred to this *swustersunu* relationship. These nine songs apparently enabled Odin to secure the mead from Suttung's daughter (*Myth 6*) and the cauldron Odrorir is mentioned in that myth.

Secondly, Odin learned eighteen runes, which gave him, amongst other things, the power to heal, to blunt or break metal, to anticipate and thwart evil intentions, to quench flames and calm stormy water, to seduce, to send witches into a spin, and to speak to hanged men. We do not, of course, discover what the runes themselves were but are simply told of their application: it is not so difficult, reading this myth, to visualise many-faced Odin as many Norsemen visualised him – a terrifying master of magic. Why eighteen runes? I can only point out that this is twice times nine, and that nine was the most significant number in Norse mythology (see Introduction, p. xxiv).

Two further points should be made. First, wise Mimir was one of the two gods sent by the Aesir to the Vanir as hostages (*Myth 2*). The Vanir, though, lopped off Mimir's head and returned it to the Aesir. Odin pickled it, and placed it beside the spring that welled under the root of Yggdrasill in Jotunheim, and took advice from it. Second, the Norse names for the three Norns are *Urd* (Fate), *Skuld* (Being) and *Verðandi* (Necessity). These supernatural ladies stood next in rank to the Aesir themselves and were thought to weave the destinies not only of men but of gods, giants, dwarfs and every living being. In the myths (unlike one or two of their grisly appearances in the sagas), they remain little more than embodiments of concepts; they are, in effect, the North European equivalents of the three *Parcae* or fates of Greek and Roman mythology: Clotho (who held the distaff), Lachesis (spinner of the thread of life), and Atropos (who snipped the thread to end a life).

5 THE SONG OF RIG

The only source for this myth is the poem *Rigsthula*. Although it comprises part of the *Elder Edda*, this poem appears in neither of the two principal codices (*Regius* and *Arnamagnaean*) and survives only as an interpolation in a manuscript of Snorri Sturluson's *Prose Edda* (*Codex Wormianus*). It is also the last entry in this manuscript, the final sheets of which are missing; that explains why the poem is fragmentary.

It is not easy to date or place the poem. But since Dan and Danp appear in genealogies of Danish kings, *Rigsthula* was possibly composed in Denmark, and perhaps for a specific king, to establish the divine descent of the Danish kings; the poem breaks off at the critical moment. It is unlikely to have been composed in Iceland, home of many of the eddaic poems, because that island had no tradition of kingship and was a republic from the first. It is also unlikely that a poem associating kings with heathen gods would have been composed after the arrival of Christianity in Denmark in 960. So maybe an attribution to Denmark in the first half of the tenth century makes the best sense.

The scribe who added *Rigsthula* to the *Codex Wormianus* prefaced it with a couple of sentences in which he identifies Rig with Heimdall. The only other place in which Heimdall is taken to be the progenitor of the races of men is the formal opening of *Voluspa* where the *volva* asks for the attention of 'Heimdall's sons, both high and low'.

It is generally agreed that whoever composed this poem borrowed the word *Rig*, meaning 'King', from the Irish. But the connexion with the Celtic world is deeper than that. In Irish mythology there is a tradition that a god of the sea, Manannán, does the rounds, fathering children in one house after another. Now Heimdall is a complex figure with a number of facets to his character; what is pertinent here is that he is said to have been the son of nine mothers – nine daughters (perhaps the waves) of the sea god Aegir. (Given that Heimdall also either assumed the form of a ram or was strongly associated with the ram, tenuous but fascinating support for the question of his parentage was supplied by a Welsh antiquarian, quoted by Georges Dumézil, who wrote in 1909 that breaking waves were called sheep of the mermaid but that the ninth was called the ram!) It is impossible to establish the relationship of *Rigsthula* and its Irish parallel: the *Rigsthula* poet may have been directly influenced, and may even have lived in the western part of the British Isles; but it is thought to be more likely that both myths shared a common Celto-Germanic root and developed independently. In either case, though, it does seem clear that the scribe had good reasons for identifying Rig with Heimdall. One wishes only that more were known about this god so that we could say *why* he (and not Odin, as one might expect) was recognised as the father of men.

This myth rather resembles a folk tale in its threefold variations and its repetition in both descriptive passages and dialogue. It provides a detailed and colourful picture of the three classes – serf, peasant and warrior – into which society was divided throughout the Viking world. This is true not least in the entertaining lists of names. To have provided them only in the original would have been tooth-cracking, and to have provided them only in translation would have been to sacrifice sound effect and wit. I have attempted a combination. My 'placing' of Heimdall at the start of the retelling and the reiterated paragraph about day and night and the turning of the seasons are based on material drawn from the *Prose Edda*; otherwise I have followed *Rigsthula* strictly.

Jarl's youngest son is called Kon the Young; the Old Norse *konungr* may also be translated 'king'. Both he and his father, like Odin, learn the runes and their meanings. The poem says that Kon was even more wise than his father. And so he was: like Sigurd, he could understand the speech of birds. He listens to a crow and the crow knows what's what. It chides and chivvies Kon, extolling the demanding and ruthless qualities required of a Viking, the harsh values of Viking society.

6 THE MEAD OF POETRY

The remark attributed to George I – 'I hate all Boets and Bainters' – is ludicrous not only for its content but also for its failure to master the language to express that content. In the beginning was the word, and primitive societies venerated poets second only to their leaders. A poet had the power to name and so to control; he was, literally, the living memory of a group or tribe who would perpetuate their history in song; his inspiration was god given and he was in effect a medium.

Most mythologies number a myth specifically associated with poetry and Norse mythology is no exception. Just as 'Lord of the Gallows' (*Myth 4*) reveals Odin as God of the Hanged and God of the Spear, able to commune with the dead and acquire occult wisdom, this myth displays another of his masks: god of poetry and inspiration. One may wonder in passing about Bragi who is also described by Snorri Sturluson as the god of poetry. He was one of Odin's sons and there are reasons to suppose that he may have been a relatively late invention, maybe no more than an embodiment of this aspect of multi-faceted Odin.

Much the most detailed account of how Odin secured the mead of poetry is provided by Snorri Sturluson in the section of the *Prose Edda* called 'Skaldskaparmal' (Poetic Diction), and I have followed it in my retelling. Snorri's purpose was to explain various kennings for poetry (see Introduction, p. xxxiii) used by scaldic poets, such as 'Kvasir's blood', 'dwarfs' drink', 'dwarfs' ship', 'Suttung's mead', 'Hnitbjorg's sea', and so on. The myth also crops up three times in *Havamal*: in one brief allusion, Odin says that by hanging on Yggdrasill he learned nine magic songs from the son of Bolthor that enabled him to win the mead; in another, he says he tasted the mead 'in the house of wise Fjalar' (presumably the dwarf who features in Snorri's version) and that it made him drunk; and in stanzas 103–110 he describes how he seduced Gunnlod and deprived her of the mead. The main differences between this and Snorri's account are that the *Havamal* poet says that the auger Rati was used to get out of the mountain, not into it, and that when the frost giants came to Asgard to enquire about Bolverk, Odin himself swore on his ring that Bolverk was not there (the giants apparently had not realised that Odin and Bolverk were one and the same); Gunnlod was left to her grief and the poet asks who will ever be able to trust Odin again. There are two points to make: the fragments in *Havamal* and the dateable scaldic kennings establish that the myth was already popular in different versions in the tenth century; secondly, Snorri must have drawn not only on *Havamal* but also on some other version or versions now lost.

The myth-makers visualised the inspiration of poetry in quite specific, tangible terms: it was mead, and the mead was brewed from Kvasir's blood mixed with honey. The creation of the sage Kvasir from spittle as a truce token is outlined in *Note 2*. Spittle, like yeast, causes fermentation; and appropriately enough, the name Kvasir derives from *kvas*, a strong beer – the modern English 'quash' and 'squash' derive from the same word. In *Myth and Religion of the North*, E. O. G. Turville-Petre says that there is an Indian parallel to the creation of the mead of poetry from Kvasir's blood in which the four parts of a slain monster represent four kinds of drunkenness; and in another Indian myth, soma, an intoxicating drink that stimulates the voice and gives immortality, is stolen by an eagle from an iron fortress. Such similarities plainly cannot be accidental. Like elements in several other myths, the concept of divine and coveted liquor must have been carried to Europe just as it was carried to India in the Age of Migrations, and embodied in a story that was shaped and reshaped by generation after generation for between one and two thousand years before it was fixed in its final form by Snorri Sturluson.

The name of Bolverk (Evil-Doer) assumed by Odin in Jotunheim and his ruthless treatment of the nine human serfs that he meets there represent another of Odin's masks – the God of War. This is the shape in which most Norsemen would probably first have thought of him: evil, untrustworthy, setting man against man, delighting even in setting friend against friend. This episode, generally thought to be Asiatic in origin, is of a piece with Odin's requirement of Freyja (*Myth 13*) that she must promote war and stir up such hatred between two kings, each supported by twenty vassal kings, that they will meet only on the battlefield. The faces of Odin are discussed in more detail in the introduction.

7 LOKI'S CHILDREN AND THE BINDING OF FENRIR

Snorri Sturluson's version in the *Prose Edda* is the only account that has survived, and masterly it is. It shows him at his best, terse and vivid and witty. Snorri prefaces the myth with a description of Loki's three children and I have elected to do the same; I have also developed his mention that the gods anticipated trouble 'from prophecy' by introducing the three Norns.

Tyr was the original Germanic god of war, the precursor of Odin. By the time the Norse myths were recorded, his importance in the hierarchy had diminished, and he appears only in this myth and *Myths 17*, *30* and *32*. But Tyr's early significance, taken together with mythological parallels and archaeological discoveries relating to a one-handed god, suggest that this myth is immensely old, and was known in Northern Europe for between one and two thousand years before Snorri Sturluson included it in his *Prose Edda*.

Tyr appears also to have been a god of justice. His name derives from Tiw or Tîwaz, and Tacitus and other Roman writers described him as the recipient of human sacrifice and equated him with Mars. That, incidentally, is why the Roman *Dies Martalis* came to be known as *Tysdagr* (O.N.) and *Tiwesdaeg* (O.E.) or, in plain modern English, Tuesday. Parallels to Tyr have been found in the one-handed Nuadu in Irish mythology and in Mitra, just god of the day, in Indian mythology. The etymology of the name Tîwaz is particularly interesting. E.O.G. Turville-Petre writes

> It has been equated with the Latin *deus*, Old Irish *dia*, Sanscrit *deva–*, which is also seen in the O.N. plural *tívar* (gods). In this case Tyr means no other than 'god'. Some, however, relate it more closely with names of gods deriving from the same root, Greek *Zeus*, Sanscrit *Dyaus*. In this case, Tyr is stamped as an exceedingly ancient god of the sky and the day. In either case he must once have occupied a high position in the hierarchy, although he is not clearly described in our records.

As the bravest of the gods, it is fitting that it should be Tyr who makes possible the binding of Fenrir; in Old Norse, a wrist was called a 'wolf-joint'. It is also poetically just that the gods should have had to sacrifice Tyr's right hand, perhaps once regarded as their most powerful asset, in order to contain their greatest enemy.

Monstrous as the giants may be, there is a reassuring sameness about them; one feels that, once Thor has got a firm hold of his hammer Mjollnir, they will never actually get the better of the gods. But Fenrir, Jormungand and Hel are a different matter: they are Loki's offspring, extensions of the enemy within, the only enemy that can affect and corrupt and finally destroy the spirit of the gods.

Hel presides over the realm of the dead in Niflheim, and there receives both those who die from illness and old age and the wicked. Jormungand is not the only serpent in Norse mythology but he is much the most fearsome. He is so vast that he actually encircles Midgard; all humankind is caught within his coil as he lies on the ocean bed, biting on his own tail. One is irresistibly reminded of the ribbon ornamentation, often developed into almost inextricable knots, that is such a common feature of Viking jewellery.

For the Norseman, the wolf was a real and frightening creature. He was with the eagle and the raven one of the three traditional beasts of battle in northern literature. Whoever lost in the fight, the wolf was always the winner. As the *Beowulf* poet says:

> *... craving for carrion,*
> *the dark raven shall have its say*
> *and tell the eagle how it fared at the feast*
> *when, competing with the wolf, it laid bare the bones of corpses.*

In Norse mythology, two wolves pursue the sun and moon and will swallow them before Ragnarok; and the wolf-hound Garm (often equated with Fenrir) bays in his cave at the entrance to Niflheim, and will kill Tyr at Ragnarok. But Fenrir himself is the master-wolf who so threatened the gods that he had to be bound no matter what the cost; even so his jaws pressed against earth and sky and he is to devour Odin at Ragnarok. No other monster so embodied destruction (and maybe self-destruction).

Skirnir, Freyr's messenger, reappears in 'Skirnir's Song' (*Myth 11*). The ribbon Gleipnir that he brings back is only the first example of how the ambivalent, greedy dwarfs assisted the gods (see *Myth 10*) against the forces of evil. Snorri's description of how one can prove what went into the making of Gleipnir is a delightful piece of tongue-in-cheek, 'negative' logic! In Jean I. Young's translation:

Now, although you may not have known this before, you can easily prove that you are not being told a falsehood, since you will have observed that a woman has no beard, a cat makes no noise when running, a mountain has no roots and, upon my word, everything I have told you is just as true, although there are some things that can't be put to the test.

8 THE THEFT OF IDUN'S APPLES

The only detailed version of this myth, as of so many others, is provided by Snorri Sturluson in his *Prose Edda*, but it had already been in circulation for at least three hundred years in much the same form that Snorri recorded it. One of the court poets of Harold Fairhair (*c*. 860–933), the first king of all Norway, was Thiodolf of Hvin and he devoted one quarter of his 'shield' poem *Haustlong* (a poem which described figures represented on a shield) to this myth and one quarter to Thor's duel with Hrungnir (*Myth 19*); the remaining two quarters are missing. Snorri Sturluson faithfully followed Thiodolf's twelve allusive and elliptical stanzas but also supplied other details; he described how Loki enticed Idun out of Midgard, said that Thiazi was away from Thrymheim when Loki arrived there, and specified that Loki turned Idun into a nut. Snorri's fidelity to Thiodolf and all we can understand of his method from other myths suggest that he did not simply invent these elements but drew on another source or sources now lost. I have followed Snorri closely but fleshed out the descriptions of Midgard and Thrymheim, put specific threats into Odin's mouth when he confronted Loki, and in a couple of paragraphs tried to suggest aspects of old age.

This is the only surviving myth about Idun, named by Snorri as one of the chief goddesses, and one only wishes that there were more myths relating to her and the other goddesses. It is probable that Idun was originally one of the Vanir, a goddess of fertility, youth and death. Thus, in the eddaic poem *Lokasenna*, Loki accuses her of being so wanton (a quality she shares with Freyja) that she made love to her brother's murderer, and in 'Skirnir's Journey' (*Myth 11*) her golden apples are shown also to be connected with Freyr, chief of the fertility gods. It must be significant, too, that Idun is turned by Loki into a nut; H. R. Ellis Davidson mentions that fruit and nuts have been found amongst Scandinavian grave goods (to ensure life after death) and that Irish sagas use nuts as symbols of eternal youth.

There are no grounds for thinking that Idun is a late northern echo of the three Hesperides who guarded the golden apples, or that this myth is directly influenced by Greek mythology. Even if one allows that the old Norse *epli* does mean apples in this context (it can in fact mean any kind of rounded fruit), the nearest parallel to this myth is, rather, the Irish story of the Sons of Tuireann. In all likelihood, the Greek, Irish and Norse myths developed independently from a common source, and Idun and her apples of youth were an early and integral part of Scandinavian tradition.

This myth is one of two, or possibly three, occasions in which Odin, Loki and Honir act in concert (see *Note 1* and *Myth 26*). Loki is now no longer merely *agent provocateur* but acts directly contrary to the interests of the gods. Here, too, we meet Loki as a shape changer again; he dons Freyja's falcon skin (see also *Myths 14* and *24*) in order to get to Jotunheim. Loki's debonair use of the falcon skin should not obscure its true purpose which must have been to carry the goddess's spirit, in her role as shamaness, to the underworld. Freyja is fully discussed in the introduction.

9 THE MARRIAGE OF NJORD AND SKADI

After telling how Thiazi stole Idun's apples, and died after pursuing Loki to Asgard, Snorri Sturluson goes straight on to describe how Skadi tried to avenge her father's death. His *Prose Edda* is the only source for this myth but the allusion of an eleventh-century scaldic poet to Skadi's unsuccessful marriage establishes that it was known for at least two hundred years before it was recorded.

Since Snorri describes Skadi as the 'Snow-shoe goddess', it seems logical to identify her as the embodiment of all that a northern winter could mean: snow, freezing cold, darkness, lack of growth, and death. Her name could derive either from the Old Norse *skaði* or the Old English *sceadu*; the former means harm or injury and the latter shadow or a dark shape. Skadi's devotion to skiing and hunting remind one of the god Ull, known for precisely the same activities, but there does not appear to have been any connexion between them.

The way in which Skadi is allowed to choose her future husband only by his feet is odd; it sounds like an episode from a folktale but there are no known folk parallels to it. Njord, it may be remembered, came to Asgard with his son Freyr and daughter Freyja when peace was established between the Aesir and Vanir. He had fathered Freyr and Freyja on his own sister; the Aesir, however, did not permit incest and his luckless sister/lover makes no further appearance in the myths. Although Njord's specific association is with seafaring and fishing (the name of his hall Noatun means shipyard) his domain was more extensive; he endowed those who worshipped him with land and wealth and was, like his children, an important fertility god.

The myth of a marriage between Njord and Skadi therefore commemorates some kind of union between a god of life and a figure of death. It brings together opposites – sea level and the high mountains, summer and winter, life and death. But why does their marriage break down? The explanation may simply be that because Njord and Skadi represent extreme opposites, each denies the very existence of the other.

Odin's transformation of Thiazi's eyes into two stars has its counterpart in Thor's transformation of Aurvandil's frozen toe into a star (*Myth 19*). Both remind one of the creation myth in which Odin, Vili and Ve made the stars out of embers from Muspell.

Loki makes Skadi laugh by tying his testicles to a goat, and she forgives him – for a time. But Skadi has the last, savage laugh: when Loki is bound, it is she who fixes a snake above his head, to drip poison on to him.

10 THE TREASURES OF THE GODS

In the part of the *Prose Edda* called 'Skaldskaparmal' (Poetic Diction), Snorri Sturluson glossed a number of kennings or condensed metaphors by retelling the myths and heroic legends underlying them. As one might expect, there were a large number of kennings for gold. It was called 'Otter's ransom' for the reasons described in *Myth 26*; it was called 'Fafnir's lair' and 'the metal of Gnita Heath' and 'Grani's burden', and these kennings prompted Snorri to tell how Sigurd killed the dragon Fafnir on Gnita Heath and loaded his gold hoard on to his horse Grani; it was called 'Sif's hair', and this enabled Snorri to recount the present myth. It does not survive in any other version, although there is a reference in the tenth-century *Grimnismal* to how the sons of Ivaldi built Skidbladnir.

This is one of the most popular of the Norse myths, and deservedly so, for it is a fine wide-ranging story, with sharp characterisation, wit, and an element of suspense. It also holds an important place in the cycle (though it is not thought to be particularly ancient in anything like its surviving form) because it embodies associations, such as Thor and the hammer, that had existed for as long as the gods had been known in Scandinavia.

There is not very much to say about Draupnir. It does not appear to represent a specific aspect of Odin's character and none of Odin's names relate to it. The ring was, however, a symbol of a close bond and Draupnir may suggest that there was no limit to the number of people – especially warriors and poets – who could hope for Odin's protection. The placing of Draupnir on Balder's pyre (*Myth 29*) cannot be without significance. Did it invest Balder with the power of self-renewal? Does it anticipate the time after Ragnarok when Odin will be dead and Balder alive again?

Gungnir is a recognition of the terrible face of Odin – god of war and giver of victory. *Myth 2* tells how the first war in the world was fought after Odin had thrown his spear into the host of the Vanir, and this action was imitated by Norsemen anxious for Odin's support in battle. In the *Eyrbyggja Saga*, one reads:

> It was an ideal place to make a stand because of the stones lying everywhere; and there they braced themselves for the fight. As Snorri and his men were coming up the scree, Steinthor cast a spear over them for good luck, according to the ancient custom.

The spear Gungnir also symbolises the human sacrifice entailed in the worship of Odin (see *Note 4*). Two of Odin's names were 'God of the Spear' and 'God of the Hanged', and both his sacrificial victims, about to be hanged, and warriors dying in their beds, dreaming of Valhalla, were marked with a spear. In so doing, they were identifying themselves with the god who hung on Yggdrasill, his side gashed by a spear.

In the same way, the ship Skidbladnir reflects Freyr as a fertility god. From very early times in the north, ships have been associated with fertility and the cycle of birth, life and death: Bronze Age carvings have been found in Scandinavia depicting ship and horse, tamers of sea and earth, in conjunction with the sun wheel, the prime source of life; and, of course, ship burials (whether in an old tub or in a ship as elaborate and richly laden as the Gokstad and Sutton Hoo ships) symbolised the journeys made by their passengers beyond death in this world to life in another. But why was it possible to dismantle Skidbladnir and pack it into a pouch? H. R. Ellis Davidson has suggested that

> . . . a cult ship was at the base of this tradition, the kind of ship used in processions and folded up when not in use. There is abundant evidence for ships carried in processions and kept in churches in Scandinavia from the Middle Ages down to modern times, some of those from Denmark being used for ceremonies of blessing the fields, and it may be that here we have the tradition of Freyr's sacred boat surviving in a Christian setting.

As for Gullinbursti both Freyr and his sister Freyja are associated with boars and yet the boar is, above all, connected with protection in battle. The *Beowulf* poet is explicit:

> The boar-crest, brightly gleaming,
> stood over their helmets: superbly tempered,
> plated with glowing gold, it guarded the lives
> of those grim warriors.

Archaeological discoveries have corroborated this description. The Benty Grange helmet, found in Derbyshire and dating from the seventh century, is crowned by a splendid boar studded with silver bristles, while the nose guard is inlaid with a cross for good measure! The lesson seems to be that one should not try to define the principal gods of fertility or war too narrowly, and that their roles overlapped in many respects. The Vanir were sometimes invoked on the field of battle; the Aesir were sometimes invoked in the name of fertility.

Thor's hammer, Mjollnir, is the perfect embodiment of this precept. It was the symbol of Thor's strength, but that does not mean its function was simply to keep the giants out of Asgard. When Thor threw his hammer, it was a thunderbolt; and no matter how often he threw it, it always returned (like a boomerang) to his hand. It was accompanied by divine fire and necessary rain. The word *vigja*, meaning 'to consecrate' or 'to hallow' is often used in connexion with Mjollnir. We know from 'The Lay of Thrym' (*Myth 14*) that it was brought into the hall to hallow the bride, and in this context it probably symbolised a phallus. We know, too, from sagas, that the hammer was used to hallow the new-born child and from 'The Death of Balder' that it was used to hallow the dead. Since Thor also raised Mjollnir over his dead goats to bring them back to life (*Myth 16*), it could be argued that the hammer's function at a funeral was not only to consecrate but in some way to ensure resurrection. In sum, it is reasonable to say that Mjollnir is an agent of destruction *and* fertility *and* resurrection: it embodies Thor's own position not simply as war god but as the widely respected caretaker of freemen on middle earth.

Not very much is known about Sif. Thor was her second husband and the identity of the first is unknown; her son by her first marriage was Ull; and in *Lokasenna*, Loki boasts that he has made love to her. Much her most striking feature is her golden hair, surely representing ripe corn. In all likelihood, Sif was a fertility goddess whose importance had diminished by the time this myth was recorded. Her marriage to

Thor, though, is another significant pointer to the way in which Thor was regarded by the Norsemen.

Loki's ability to change shape is rehearsed in *Note 3* and the dwarfs are discussed in the Introduction.

11 SKIRNIR'S JOURNEY

This myth comprises part of the *Elder Edda*. It appears in full in the *Codex Regius* (where it is called *For Scirnis*: Skirnir's Journey) and in part in the *Arnamagnaean Codex* (where it is called *Skirnismal*), and is thought to date in its present form from the first part of the tenth century. Snorri Sturluson offers a paraphrase of the former in his *Prose Edda* and quotes its last stanza. There is no reason to suppose that he was drawing on any other sources.

Freyr was, with Odin and Thor, one of the three principal male deities. He was the foremost fertility god (see Introduction), Lord of the sun, the rain, and harvests. He is often described as *skirr* (shining) which is also the root of the name Skirnir. Freyr's messenger is, therefore, no more than an extension of this aspect of his master.

The giantess Gerd's name is thought to derive from *gerð*, meaning field. *Skirnismal* describes how her arms so glittered that they filled the sky and sea with dazzling light and also refers to the 'frost cup' she offers Skirnir. She must be the embodiment, then, of a frozen field, a field covered with snow and ice where nothing grows.

Skirnir's initial overtures leave Gerd unmoved. But as a result of his fierce threats, which could perhaps be taken to mean the full force of the sun, she melts and yields and agrees to meet Freyr in a grove called Barri. This name is usually taken to derive from *barr*, meaning barley, in which case the union of Freyr and Gerd represents the fruitful meeting of sunlight and the frozen earth. This seasonal fertility myth is in some respects similar to that in which Freyr's father, Njord, marries another giantess, Skadi (*Myth 9*).

There are two elements in the poem that appear to connect Gerd with Idun. When Skirnir first arrives at Gerd's hall, she fears that her visitor is her brother's slayer; in *Lokasenna*, Loki taunts Idun with making love to her brother's slayer. Secondly, Skirnir offers Gerd eleven golden apples which must surely be the same apples looked after by Idun; it is as if they are to be joint custodians of the youth of the gods. Without more evidence we can only conjecture, but it does seem possible that early in time Idun and Gerd were identical and only later developed into two separate figures. In *Note 8*, I mentioned the Celtic parallel to the myth of Idun and her apples; the concept of riding through magic flames, as Skirnir has to do to reach Gerd's hall, also has Celtic parallels and may be Celtic in origin.

Freyr sees Gerd from Hlidskjalf, Odin's high seat in silver-roofed Valaskjalf from which he and Frigg can look down on all that happens in the nine worlds. The concept of a seat in the sky is not unique to Norse mythology. In his *Teutonic Mythology*, Jacob Grimm notes that 'The sitting on the right hand is in the Bible, but not the looking down . . . Zeus also sits on Ida, and looks at mortal men; he rules from Ida's top . . .' and he goes on to tell of a widely circulated folktale in which a man, admitted to heaven, 'ended by climbing into the "chair of the Lord, from which one can look down and see all that is done on the whole earth".'

When Skirnir offers the ring Draupnir to Gerd (and it is not clear how he has come by it), he anticipates *Myth 29* by saying that it burned with Balder on the pyre. The question of unavoidable chronological inconsistency is discussed in the introduction.

For Scirnis is, I think, a poem of considerable passion – in its expression of Freyr's love anguish and in Skirnir's torrent of terrifying threats. At one level it is a moving love poem, not least in the authentic cry with which it ends, and at another a celebration of the sunshine and growth for which Norsemen must have so longed after being hidebound and cooped up all winter.

12 THE LAY OF GRIMNIR

The Norse myths, like all mythologies, were originally transmitted orally. The agent of this transmission, relaying material from community to community and generation to generation, was the storytelling poet, and part of his stock in trade consisted of mnemonic poems. These 'memory bank' poems, often little more than lists of names and events many of which must have prompted memories of separate stories attaching to them, are common to all oral cultures and sometimes survive that culture's transition to a literary tradition. The source of this myth, *Grimnismal*, which appears in both the *Codex Regius* and the *Arnamagnaean Codex*, and which cannot date in its present form to earlier than the first half of the tenth century (the prose interpolations are much later – see below), belongs to this mnemonic tradition; it must have occupied very much the same position in Old Norse poetry as the triads in early Welsh and *Widsith* in early Anglo-Saxon poetry.

But *Grimnismal* was not only an *aide-mémoire*, a poem for poets. Since its formidable amount of mythical knowledge is contained within a narrative framework, it was evidently composed for recital. As time passed, the details of this framework (perhaps once supplied impromptu before and after the poem was delivered) must have begun to be forgotten, for a twelfth- or thirteenth-century scribe went to the trouble of topping and tailing the poem with narrative prose passages. But we do know this scribe did not invent the narrative framework because the bare bones of the dramatic situation – Odin roasted on a spit by Geirrod and pitied by Geirrod's son, Agnar – exist within the original stanzas.

There are four other poems in the *Elder Edda* in which the mnemonic element is paramount: *Voluspa*, *Vafthrudnismal* and *Hyndluljoth* and *Alvissmal*. The latter is a glossary of scaldic synonyms (*Myth 27*) and *Hyndluljoth* is a historico-genealogical poem (*Myth 18*), but the two former are, like *Grimnismal*, dictionaries of mythical knowledge. For this reason, they were invaluable to Snorri Sturluson who made very extensive use of them in his *Prose Edda*. A list of all the material that Snorri derived from *Grimnismal* would be little shorter than the poem itself. He quotes more than twenty of its fifty-four stanzas verbatim and owes to it, for example, much of his accounts of the Creation and Ragnarok, his descriptions of Yggdrasill and Valhalla (*Grimnismal* provides the only detailed account of Valhalla in Old Norse poetry) and his list of Odin's names. There are also a number of allusions in the poem to individuals and events, such as Odin's deception of the giant Sokkmimir, that are not mentioned anywhere else; they are reminders that what has survived is only a very small proportion of all that once existed.

The question of how to render more than two hundred and twenty names without making this myth unreadable was a difficult one. I have outlined my general policy and the exceptions to it (which apply especially in the case of this myth) in the introduction.

13 THE NECKLACE OF THE BRISINGS

Much the earliest reference to the Brisings' necklace occurs in the scaldic poem *Husdrapa* by the tenth-century poet Ulf Uggason; and the author of the *Laxdaela Saga* describes (Chapter 29) how Ulf first recited that poem just over one thousand years ago, in the winter of 978, at a wedding feast. It was a verbal complement to the carvings of mythical scenes on the wainscoting and roof timbers of the hall in which the feast was being celebrated.

Little survives of this poem – only part of a prayer calling for the audience's attention, three stanzas concerning Thor's struggle with the Midgard Serpent while out fishing with Hymir (*Note 17*), five stanzas listing the gods (and some of their attributes) who attended Balder's funeral, and just one stanza about the Brisings' necklace. This has been translated by Lee M. Hollander:

> *Quick in counsel, Bifrost's*
> *keeper strives with the wondrous*
> *subtle son of Laufey*
> *at Singastein, for the necklace:*
> *wins the son of eight and*
> *one mothers the brisings' —*
> *neckring: known I make it*
> *now to you in the poem.*

Husdrapa was known to Snorri Sturluson. He quotes this verse in 'Skaldskaparmal' in the *Prose Edda*, and adds that Heimdall was the son of nine mothers. Elsewhere, he comments that Heimdall was a frequenter 'of Singastein, where he contended with Loki for the necklace of the Brisings.... Ulf Uggason composed a long passage in the *Husdrapa* on that legend, and there it is written that they were 'in the form of seals.' And that, unfortunately, is all we know of this early form of the myth. It is not sufficient material on which to base a retelling.

There is, however, a second version of the theft of the Brisings' necklace. This is *Sorla Thattr*, a short story in the *Flateyjarbok* (*c.* 1400 AD) in which the gods appear as humans (Odin is king of a people called the Aesir who live in Asia and whose chief city is Asgard) but nevertheless retain so many of their familiar characteristics that the author was evidently drawing on earlier sources. The only translation I know of is by Eiríkr Magnússon and William Morris in *Three Northern Love Stories* (Longmans, Green & Co., London, 1895). Rather than omit the myth of the acquisition and theft of the Brisings' necklace from the cycle altogether, I have taken this late version as the basis for my retelling. I have elevated Odin, Freyja and Loki to the status of deities once more and discarded the anachronistic Christian element from Odin's stipulations at the end of the story. For after requiring Freyja to stir up war in which all those who are killed 'stand up and fight again', the author of *Sorla Thattr* adds, in Magnússon's and Morris's words:

always unless some christened man be so bold of heart, and the fate and fortune of his lord be so great, that he shall dare go into that battle, and smite with weapons these men: and so first shall their toil come to an end, to whatsoever lord it shall befall to loose them from the pine and trouble of their fell deeds.

Christianity has always worked as much on the principle of appropria-
tion as of suppression!

In this story, the behaviour of every protagonist is unredeemably
self-centred. It would be inadequate to read it as a simple moral tale
about the price of greed but it is not easy (and possibly fruitless, given
the lack of earlier source material) to analyse the meaning of this myth.
Who were the Brisings? And what was the necklace of the Brisings
(*brisingamen*)? These are unsettled questions. It is uncertain whether
Brising is the name of some tribe or family or whether the word derives
from the Old Norse *brisingr*, meaning fire – used to describe the
brilliance of the ornament. The Old Norse word *men*, moreover, can
mean either necklace or belt; but a passing reference to the 'Brosinga
mene' in the Anglo-Saxon *Beowulf* quite clearly refers to a necklace.
The two must in some way be connected and 'necklace' is therefore the
likely translation.

In the *Gods and Myths of Northern Europe*, H. R. Ellis Davidson
writes: 'A necklace is something which is associated with the mother
goddess from very early times. Figurines wearing necklaces found in
the Mediterranean area date back as far as 3000 BC, and small female
figures wearing them have survived from the Bronze Age in Denmark
and are thought to represent a fertility deity.' And, in a footnote, she
adds, 'Students of Freud will recognise the significance of a necklace for
a fertility goddess. It illustrates the familiar tendency to represent the
sexual parts of the body by others higher up, and by ornaments worn on
these.' Perhaps we can reasonably postulate, then, that *Sorla Thattr*
describes Freyja's acquisition – her sexual acquisition – of the most
salient symbol of her fertility. She is the goddess of love; and she is the
goddess of lust.

Sorla Thattr displays Freyja, furthermore, as mistress of war and
death. One stanza in *Grimnismal* says that Freyja's hall is situated in
Folkvang (Field of Folk) and that each day she divides the dead with
Odin. Although the author of *Sorla Thattr* may not have understood it
as such, Odin's final demand that Freyja should stir up war between
kings and use her magic to resurrect them may well have been to the
goddess's liking. In her command of magic, her relationship to the slain
and her promiscuity, Freyja has much in common with Odin. That the
author of *Sorla Thattr* should hint at a liaison between them is just what
one might expect. No other source, however, develops or corroborates
this but it has often been argued that Freyja's 'lost' husband Od is none
other than Odin himself.

Odin is shown in *Sorla Thattr* as the fierce and uncompromising god
of war. Sigfod, Father of Battle; Herteit, Glad of War; Bolverk, Worker

of Evil: of Odin's many names, these are most pertinent to this myth. His injunction to Freyja at the end of the story reminds one of the words, describing war and Odin's part in it, that Saxo Grammaticus puts into the mouth of the warrior Biarki.

> War springs from the nobly born; famous pedigrees are the makers of war. For the perilous deeds which chiefs attempt are not to be done by the ventures of common men ... No dim and lowly race, no low-born dead, no base souls are Pluto's prey, but he weaves the dooms of the mighty, and fills Phlegethon with noble shapes.

Finally, Dvalin may have enjoyed Freyja but he was destined to come to a nasty end. As we learn indirectly in *Myth 27*, Dvalin was arrested by the rising sun and turned into stone. The other three dwarfs are not heard of again.

14 THE LAY OF THRYM

The only source of this myth is the poem *Thrymskvitha* which forms part of the *Codex Regius* of the *Elder Edda*. It is rather surprising that Snorri Sturluson, who knew and mined the eddaic poems so extensively, and described every other known contest between Thor and a giant (those that appear in the eddaic poems and those that do not), should have omitted this one alone from his *Prose Edda*; and it is all the more surprising when one considers how much both the tone and situation of *Thrymskvitha* would have been to his liking. Estimates as to the date of the poem's composition vary from the tenth to the thirteenth century. If one were to accept the later date, Snorri's disregard for *Thrymskvitha* could be most satisfactorily explained by the fact that he composed the poem himself!

Thrymskvitha is a burlesque. There is no point in looking for a deep meaning; its purpose was to entertain. And to understand how much it must have delighted its original audience, remember Thor's place in the pantheon – virile, bearded and muscular; the powerful guardian of gods and men alike; somewhat thick-skulled and susceptible to ridicule; the most hot-tempered of the gods (especially with the giants); an extremely unlikely candidate to appear in drag! The whole poem consists of no more than thirty-two quatrains with a one line envoi; it is rapid, unfailingly sharp in its characterisation, and packed out with telling detail (the constituents, for instance, of Thrym's lavish and hollow life, and the pieces of Thor's bridal costume); and its tone is beautifully judged, always understated and always deadpan. From a literary point of view, *Thrymskvitha* seems to be more consistently satisfying than anything else in the *Elder Edda*, and to stand comparison with the best ballads in any language.

Most of the noteworthy mythical elements in the poem have already been mentioned elsewhere. The function of Mjollnir both as protector of Asgard and phallic hallower is fully discussed in *Note 10*. Although there is no other mention of a hammer consecrating a marriage in Old Norse literature, it is clear from *Thrymskvitha* that Thor fully expected it to be brought into the hall to hallow the bride; he would never have consented to wear disguise otherwise.

Freyja's falcon skin is discussed in the introduction; this is one of the three occasions on which Loki wore it. Freyja's association with fertility and sexual love are her most outstanding features, and her attractiveness to the giants is well documented; not only Thrym but the giant who built Asgard's wall (*Myth 3*) and Hrungnir (*Myth 19*) lusted after her. Her most precious possession, the Necklace of the Brisings, shattered in this myth, is the subject of *Myth 13*. It is far from clear why it should have been Heimdall who came to Freyja's rescue by suggesting that Thor be disguised as a bride, but we do know that the earliest allusion to the Brisings' Necklace (see *Note 13*) refers to Heimdall's struggle with Loki for its possession; so there, too, he is Freyja's champion. One line in *Thrymskvitha* suggests that Heimdall was, like Freyja, one of the Vanir and could read the future. He is further discussed in *Note 5*, but it seems clear that there is some connexion between Heimdall and Freyja that has been obscured by time.

Finally, Thrym alludes to Var. She is named by Snorri as one of the principal goddesses. 'She listens,' he wrote, 'to the vows and compacts made by men and women with each other; for this reason such agreements are called *varar* (promises). She also takes vengeance on those who break their vows.'

15 THE LAY OF VAFTHRUDNIR

Vafthrudnismal, the unique source for this myth, appears in full in the *Codex Regius* and shorn of its first twenty stanzas, because a leaf is missing, in the *Arnamagnaean Codex*. There is general agreement that it was composed in the middle of the tenth century, and there is nothing to suggest that it underwent changes between that time and the time it was written down in the *Elder Edda*. The nature and function of the mnemonic poem, of which this is an example, are discussed in *Note 12*.

Vafthrudnismal was scarcely less useful to Snorri Sturluson than *Grimnismal*; he quotes eight stanzas verbatim and paraphrases many others. There are elements in the poem that do not crop up elsewhere in Old Norse literature: notably, the poet offers an alternative account to that given in *Voluspa* of how the first man and woman were created; he describes the eternal round of fighting and feasting that will occupy the Einherjar in Valhalla until Ragnarok; and he alludes to the survival after Ragnarok of two humans, Lif and Lifthrasir, who will hide themselves in Hoddmimir's Wood. The question asked in relation to *Grimnismal* (*Note 12*) demands to be asked again: if these are the sole surviving references to such significant matters, how much that is equally important has not survived at all?

Some giants were immensely wise. Odin says that he learned nine magic songs from the son of the giant Bolthor by hanging on Yggdrasill and that they enabled him to capture the mead of poetry. But where did Vafthrudnir gain his wisdom? He tells Odin that he is able to read the runes because he has been to Niflheim, the misty world of the dead. The acquisition of wisdom seemingly requires great sacrifice, and it is possible to understand from Vafthrudnir's reply that, like Odin in 'Lord of the Gallows' (*Myth 4*), he died in order to win wisdom, and rose again.

Whether this is so or not, Vafthrudnir's wisdom is not enough to save his head. Odin is not only Sangetall (the One Who Guesses Right) but also a practised deceiver and his final question is of course unanswerable. This question also adds to the chronological inconsistencies in the myths which are discussed in the introduction. And what *did* Odin whisper in Balder's ear? In *Voluspa*, the *volva* tells Odin she sees the earth rising green from the waves after Odin's own death and after Ragnarok, and sees Balder coming back from the world of the dead. Did it have something to do with that?

16 THOR'S JOURNEY TO UTGARD

The great story of Thor's journey to Utgard is, with the death of Balder, the best known of the Norse myths. This is partly because it is so rich in comic situation and confrontation made all the more powerful by the undertow of magic and terror, and partly because it brought out the very best in Snorri Sturluson. He lavished great care on this myth in his *Prose Edda*, telling it at much greater length than any other; and his version is the unique source.

Like 'The Lay of Thrym' (*Myth 14*), the primary function of this myth was surely to entertain. Just as the former pokes fun at Thor's virility, the latter pokes fun at his massive strength. Thor may be the most physically powerful of the gods but, faced with magic, he appears lumbering and ineffectual. He is not at all at home in the hall of illusion. Yet although Thor is entirely upstaged by Utgard-Loki, he never becomes merely laughable – after all, he makes three dents in a hillside, causes the ebb and flow of tides in the ocean, inspires dread by hauling the Midgard Serpent out of the sea, and very soon sets off on a successful punitive expedition! Our sympathies remain with Thor because he is likeable, because he is being exploited, and because he represents the essential forces of law and order. I think that both this myth and 'The Lay of Thrym' are evidence of the widespread affection in which Thor was held throughout pre-Christian Scandinavia; he was the god who was not only respected and feared but also trusted and loved, the predictable god with whom men felt they could identify. Thor in his role as guardian of the farming freeman is further discussed in the introduction.

It is consistent with the paradoxical nature of Loki's character that, untrustworthy though he was, he should have been an especial companion of two of the three principal deities, Odin and Thor. He was, indeed, said to be Odin's foster-brother, and accompanies him and Honir on two or maybe three occasions (*Myths 8* and *26* and *Note 1*). Similarly he accompanies Thor both in this myth and in *Myths 14* and *24*. His sociability is matched only by his trickery and treachery, and in Utgard-Loki, who does not appear elsewhere in the myths, we meet Loki's counterpart amongst the giants. He is, literally, the Loki of Utgard: he deals in shape-changing as does Loki on so many occasions, and achieves his ends by deception. E. O. G. Turville-Petre has argued that Loki and Utgard-Loki were originally identical and cites Saxo Grammaticus' version of this myth, written early in the thirteenth century.

The hero Thorkillus, whose name seems to replace that of Thor, sets out from Denmark on a perilous journey to seek the monster Utgardilocus in the hope of treasure. The repulsive giant was laden hand and foot with enormous chains. Utgardilocus appears to be Loki, expelled from Asgarð into Utgarð, in the form which he took after he caused the murder of Balder. He was bound with fetters, and thus he will remain until the Ragnarök.

Utgard is the citadel of the giants. Snorri says that in order to reach it, Thor and his companions have to cross the sea; this contradicts his own description of the Norse cosmology in the creation myth, where he says that Midgard and Jotunheim were adjacent, and that the sea lay beyond them (see Introduction, p. xxi).

The myth is very straightforward and needs little further glossing. When Thor sees Skrymir for the first time, he fastens on the belt of strength given to him by the giantess Grid. This anticipates *Myth 24*. The properties of Mjollnir are discussed in *Note 10*. Parallels to the episode in which Thor resurrects his goats have been found in a number of Indo-European mythologies and bodies of folklore. In Aleksandr Afanas'ev's great collection of Russian tales, for instance, there is a folktale, 'The Wondrous Wonder', in which the bones of a goose are stacked up and the goose is magically brought back to life.

17 THE LAY OF HYMIR

A struggle to the death between a sky god, guardian of men, and an appalling monster, hostile to men, is a commonplace of Indo-European mythology. In Norse myth the protagonists are Thor and Jormungand, the Midgard Serpent. They engage (the Serpent in the shape of a large grey cat) when Thor visits Utgard-Loki's court, meet again in this myth, and finally destroy one another at Ragnarok.

The story of Thor's fishing expedition with Hymir was clearly a favourite, for no less than four very early accounts survive. It was described in the ninth century by Bragi in his *Ragnarsdrapa* and in three tenth-century sources, *Husdrapa* by Ulf Uggason and poems by Gamli and Eysteinn Valdason. The best known and most detailed accounts occur, however, in the *Hymiskvitha* which was probably composed in the first part of the eleventh century and forms part of the *Elder Edda*, and in Snorri Sturluson's *Prose Edda*. The myth was certainly known in England because a stone slab from Gosforth Church in Cumberland and the top of the Gosforth Cross, both carved in about 900 AD, show Thor fishing with an ox's head and fighting the Midgard Serpent respectively.

With some regret, I have laid aside Snorri's delightfully colourful and laconic version in favour of the earlier *Hymiskvitha*, but as a prime example of Snorri's approach to the myths and of his prose style, print it here in Jean I. Young's translation:

One doesn't have to be an authority to know that Thór made amends for the expedition which has just been described [Thór's visit to the court of Útgarð-Loki]; he did not stay long at home before he got ready for a journey in such haste that he took with him neither chariot nor goats nor companions. He went out of Ásgarð disguised as a youth and came in the evening to a giant called Hymir. Thór stayed there that night, and at daybreak Hymir got up and dressed and prepared to go sea-fishing in a rowing-boat. Thór sprang up and was soon ready and asking Hymir to let him go rowing with him. Hymir said that he would not be much help, as he was such a scrap of a young fellow: 'You'll catch cold if I sit as long and as far out to sea as I usually do.' Thór, however, said he would be able to row a long way out from the shore all the same, and that it wasn't certain that he would be the first to demand to be rowed back; and he got so angry with the giant that he was ready incontinently to set the hammer ringing on his head. He controlled himself, however, as he was intending to try his strength in another place. He asked Hymir what they were to take as bait, but Hymir told him to get his own. Then Thór turned away to where he saw a herd of oxen belonging to Hymir and taking the biggest ox, which was called Skybellower, he struck off its head and went down to the sea with it. By then Hymir had launched his boat. Thór went on board and sitting down in the stern took two oars and rowed. Hymir thought they made rapid progress from his rowing.

Hymir rowed bow and the rowing went on apace until Hymir said that now he had come to those banks where he was accustomed to sit and catch flat fish, but Thór said he wanted to row much farther out and they had another bout of fast rowing. Then Hymir said that they had come so far out that it would be dangerous to sit there on account of the Miðgarð Serpent. Thór, however, declared his intention of rowing for a bit yet, and did so, and Hymir was not at all pleased at that.

When Thór shipped his oars, he made ready a very strong line and the hook was just as big and firm; baiting the hook with the ox-head he flung it overboard. It sank to the bottom, and it's a fact that, on this occasion, Thór made as great a fool of the Miðgarð Serpent as Útgarð-Loki had of Thór when he was trying to lift the serpent up with his arm. The Miðgarð Serpent snapped at the ox-head, but the hook stuck fast in the roof of its mouth and, when it realized that, it jerked away so hard that both Thór's fists knocked against the gunwale. Then Thór grew angry and, exerting [all] his divine strength, dug in his heels so hard that both legs went through the boat and he was digging his heels in on the sea bottom. He drew the serpent up on board, and it must be said that no one has seen anything to be afraid of who didn't see how Thór fixed the serpent with his eye and how the serpent glared back, belching poison.

We are told that the giant Hymir lost colour then, and turned pale with fear when he saw the serpent and the sea tumbling in and out of the vessel too. The very moment Thór gripped his hammer and raised it aloft, the giant fumbled for his bait-knife and cut Thór's line off at the gunwale, and the serpent sank back into the sea. Thór flung his hammer after it and people say that this struck its head off in the waves; but I think the truth is that the Miðgarð Serpent is still alive and is lying in the ocean. Thór clenched his fist and gave Hymir a box on the ear so that he fell overboard head first, but he himself waded ashore.

Whereas Snorri says that Thor visited Hymir to take revenge for his humiliation at Utgard-Loki's hands, *Hymiskvitha* tells us that the journey was made in order to secure a cauldron large enough to brew ale for all the gods. This cauldron crops up again in the *Lokasenna* (*Note 30*) which directly follows this myth in the *Codex Regius*, the earliest manuscript of the *Elder Edda*.

Opinions differ as to whether Tyr who accompanies Thor in his journey is the same Tyr who put his hand into the mouth of the wolf Fenrir (*Myth 7*). The former is described as Hymir's son; the latter was the son of Odin. There is too much internal evidence to the contrary to accept the suggestion of one critic that Tyr was the son of Odin and of Hymir's daughter and, as there are many internal contradictions in the myths, I have accepted the likelihood that the Tyr of this myth and one-handed Tyr are the same god.

It is possible to argue that Thor leaves his goats very readily with the farmer Egil because he has done so before. That is to say, Egil may well be the unnamed father of Thor's servants Thialfi and Roskva, who feature in 'Thor's Journey to Utgard' (*Myth 16*). With reference to the same myth, *Hymiskvitha* attributes the laming of one of Thor's goats to Loki whereas in the later *Prose Edda* it is Thialfi who splits a thigh bone with his knife so as to get at the marrow. Thor only abducted Thialfi and Roskva as his servants because of Thialfi's misdemeanour, so it seems clear that Snorri was drawing on some other lost source.

I have appropriated from Snorri's version the resonant name of Hymir's ox, *Himinhrjotr*, meaning 'Heaven Bellower' or 'Heaven Springer'. Its association with the sky – Thor's element – makes it appropriate to this myth and too good to lose.

18 HYNDLA'S POEM

The unique source for this myth is the poem *Hyndluljoth*. Although this poem comprises part of the *Elder Edda*, it does not feature in either the *Codex Regius* or the *Arnamagnaean Codex* but survives only in the *Flateyjarbok* (Book of the Flat Island) which was compiled in about 1400. Most critics agree that although this historico-genealogical poem contains much older elements, it was probably composed no earlier than the twelfth century.

I have omitted that part of the poem known as the *Shorter Voluspa*

(Song of the Sybil); this pale imitation of the much greater *Voluspa* has nothing at all to do with the dialogue between Freyja and Hyndla and its introduction into *Hynduljoth* can only be a copyist's mistake.

This myth displays Freyja as goddess of fertility (the promiscuity with which Hyndla taunts her is echoed elsewhere and in plain view in *Myth 13*), goddess of war (Hildisvini, the name of her boar – actually Ottar in disguise – literally means 'battle-boar') and goddess of witchcraft (raising flames around the giantess). There is evidence of the worship of Freyja in the passage in which the goddess describes how Ottar had raised an altar to her, and smeared it with blood; it would certainly have needed fire of tremendous heat to turn rock to glass!

The matter of lineage is invariably of immense importance to any leader in a tribal society (think of the litanies in the Old Testament) and it was customary for a pagan North-West European king to claim divine descent. The early pages of the *Anglo-Saxon Chronicle*, for example, contain genealogies of kings who traced their line back to Bældæg (Balder) and Woden (Odin).

There is no way of establishing in what relationship Ottar and Angantyr, the contenders in this myth, stood to each other; but the very fact that they were prepared to stake their entire inheritance on the outcome speaks for itself. The poet saw the situation as an opportunity to allude to a very large number of semi-mythical figures who appear either in the heroic poems of the *Elder Edda* or in Saxo Grammaticus or in the sagas. The original audience would have found the myth very much richer and more allusive than we do because so many of the names must have suggested stories now forgotten. In connecting Ottar to Sigurd and the Volsungs, the giantess is putting Ottar in a virtually unassailable position in his wager with Angantyr, since Sigurd was the greatest of all Germanic heroes and could claim divine descent.

Tacitus, Procopius and other classical writers describe special Germanic warrior communities dedicated to a war god and effectively a law unto themselves; the Berserks, twelve of whom are named by Hyndla, were the Viking successors of such communities, and had a stronghold at Jomsburg. Protected by Odin, they worked themselves into a wild frenzy before battle and fought in animal skins (berserk means 'bear shirt'). In the *Ynglinga Saga*, Snorri wrote that the Berserks in their fury

> rushed forwards without armour, were as mad as dogs or wolves, bit their shields, and were as strong as bears or wild bulls; they killed people at a blow, and neither fire nor iron injured them.

The Berserks are celebrated in heroic poems and sagas (*Egil's Saga* contains an especially memorable passage about Berserk frenzy), and their very existence must have helped to sustain belief in Odin.

Finally, Heidrun, with whom Hyndla compares the shameless Freyja, is the nanny goat who roams near Valhalla. She feeds off the twigs of Yggdrasill and provides a never-ending supply of mead for the Einherjar feasting in Odin's hall.

19 THOR'S DUEL WITH HRUNGNIR

This myth derives from the same sources as 'The Theft of Idun's Apples' (*Note 8*). Snorri Sturluson drew primarily on six and a half stanzas in the early tenth-century 'shield' poem *Haustlong*; but he used other sources, now lost, for details of the duel, the horse race and drinking bout with which the myth begins, and Groa's loss of memory with which the myth ends. That the myth was widely known in the tenth century is made clear by kennings in other scaldic poems: Thor, for instance, is called 'Hrungnir's skull-splitter' and, most interestingly, Hrungnir's shield is elaborately referred to as 'the leaf of the feet of the thief of Thrud'. Thrud was Thor's daughter, and this allusion clearly points to an early version of the myth in which Hrungnir had carried off or raped Thrud; in which case Thor originally had, so to speak, personal as well as professional reasons for disposing of Hrungnir.

Like all scaldic poems, *Haustlong* is allusive and elliptical; no satisfactory translation is possible from a literary viewpoint. The most memorable passage describes Thor's ride to meet Hrungnir: the god's chariot makes the moon's way quake; the firmament flashes with lightning; hail lashes the land; forelands spring fissures. Although we know that Thor was the god of thunder, it has never been conclusively established *how* he caused thunder. It has been argued that Thor's hammer, Mjollnir, represents either lightning or the thunderbolt, and there is some etymological evidence to support this, but the passage in *Haustlong* paraphrased above implies a belief at least as early as the first years of the tenth century that thunder was caused by the noise of Thor's chariot as he rode across the sky. There is etymological backing for this line of thought too! The Old Norse word *reið* means both 'thunder' and 'cart' or 'chariot'.

There has been much speculation as to the meaning of the double duel between Thor and Hrungnir, Thialfi and Mist Calf. In *Mythes et Dieux des Germains*, Georges Dumézil wrote:

The man of clay defeated in a lesser duel should without doubt be taken literally, and indirectly explains the giant of stone killed by Thor himself: a cumbersome target, immobile, 'defence' defeated without difficulty by agility, by the 'lightning' offensive of the god. Is Thialfi Thor's 'pupil' here, in other words is his duel against a dummy presented so that it simply duplicates the duel of his master, as every ritual imitates the myth which justifies it? Maybe: in which case we would have a story on two levels, Thialfi's initiation into warfare reproducing in a realistic and down to earth way – a bit absurd too ... Thor's almost cosmic initiation into single combat.

Dumézil goes on to compare Thor's victory with parallels in Indian mythology. That the duel cannot have been mere fancy on the part of some inventive poet is put beyond question; one wishes only that more were known about the nature of the 'initiation guerrière', the initiation into warfare (and more specifically into duelling or single combat) which Dumézil believes to be remembered in the central episode of the myth.

What is the meaning of the collision between Mjollnir and the whetstone, and why were fragments left in Thor's head? In the course of describing the building of a temple to Thor, the unknown author of *Eyrbyggja Saga* wrote: 'Just inside the door stood the high-seat pillars with the so-called holy nails fixed in them, and beyond that point the whole building was considered to be a sanctuary.'

H. R. Ellis Davidson has pointed to a possible connexion between such nails and a heathen Lapp practice of driving a metal nail into the head of a wooden image of their thunder god, and kindling fire from it. Were the nails in Thor's pillars used for the same purpose? If so, she argues

The strange fact of the whetstone being left in Thor's head might be explained by the Lapp practice of using the head of the thunder god as a source of fire. The whetstone of the giant, encountering the iron hammer of the god, would be equivalent to the kindling of fire with flint and steel, and this in turn represented the flash of lightning.

The seeress Groa appears again in *Myth 23*. The episode in which Thor describes how he hurled her husband Aurvandil's toe into the sky seems like a fragment of the creation myth caught up and used in a new context. The same is true of the occasion on which either Odin (according to Snorri) or Thor (according to *Harbardsljoth*) flung the giant Thiazi's eyes into the sky and made stars of them. There is evidence in both Old Norse and Anglo-Saxon poetry to support Snorri's comment that one constellation, in his day, was actually called Aurvandil's Toe. Which star was it? The corroborating literary evidence also points to a particularly bright star (the morning star?) but more than that, alas, we cannot say.

Snorri identifies Hrungnir as the strongest of all Thor's adversaries: he is massive, stone-hard, brazen and lustful: like two other giants (*Myths 3* and *14*) he wants Freyja, and he wants Sif too. Although Thor still has his visit to the giant Geirrod ahead of him (*Myth 24*), the war between the gods and giants comes to a climax with this duel. The giants themselves are immensely concerned about its outcome; and with Hrungnir's disintegration and death, one feels that their serious hopes of killing Thor and storming Asgard die too.

In the last phase of the cycle, the gods' greatest concern is not with the giants but with the enemy within.

20 ODIN AND BILLING'S DAUGHTER

Although *Havamal* (Words of the High One) consists primarily of a large group of proverbs and aphoristic advice on social conduct (*Myth and Note 25*) attributed to Odin, it also includes an account of how Odin won the runes and enumerates their properties (*Myth 4*), the myth of how Odin secured the divine mead (*Myth 6*), and a brief passionate account of Odin's frustrated love for Billing's daughter (stanzas 96–102). There is no other source for this myth, and no other mention of Billing or his faithless daughter.

The myth is preceded by a loosely-knit group of stanzas (81–95) commenting on love, trust and fickleness. The different verse forms used in these stanzas make it clear that they were not composed by one man; rather, they were assembled, perhaps by the compiler of *Havamal*, and the myth of Odin and Billing's daughter seems to have been introduced as an illustration of woman's untrustworthiness. It seemed appropriate, therefore, to draw selectively on these stanzas, some of which are fine short poems in their own right, by way of a lead-in to this short myth.

Of the myth itself there is little to say. Odin made love to many goddesses and human women, and boasted about it (*Myth 22*), and one cannot resist having some regard for Billing's daughter – the one female known to have withstood and indeed snubbed his advances. For all his indignation, the arrogance and caprice with which he is paid out are the very qualities that Odin himself displays elsewhere.

21 GYLFI AND GEFION

Snorri Sturluson twice told the story of Gylfi and Gefion, once at the very beginning of the *Prose Edda* and once in the later *Ynglinga Saga* which comprises part of *Heimskringla*. The two versions differ considerably and I have thought it in keeping with the character of this book to follow Snorri as mythologist rather than as historian, and therefore to work from the *Prose Edda*.

Let me, however, summarise the alternative version. In the *Ynglinga Saga* (Chapter V), Snorri describes Odin as King of Asaland in Asia. Because of his powers of foresight, he knows that his descendants will live 'in the northern part of the world'. He makes his way through Russia to North Germany, establishes his sons as rulers there, and settles on an island called Odinsö in Fyen. Odin then dispatches Gefion further north in search of new land. King Gylfi gives her ground and her motive in dragging the land out of Sweden appears to be to add to Odin's realm, although Odin himself subsequently moves on to the present-day Sigtuna in Uppsalafjord. An additional difference between the two versions is that in *Heimskringla* Gefion has to travel to Jotunheim to bear four sons to a giant and then transforms them into oxen, whereas in the *Prose Edda* her sons have already been born and are, so to speak, at the ready. Snorri rounds off both versions by quoting a verse from the ninth-century *Ragnarsdrapa* by Bragi the Old which describes the reeking sweat of the oxen and Gefion's laughter as she steals Gylfi's land to make Denmark larger.

Gefion is a fertility goddess, especially connected with the plough. Her name derives from the verb *gefa*, to give. Snorri says that she was a virgin and that virgins went to her when they died; on the other hand, in *Lokasenna* Loki accuses Gefion of selling her body for a necklace while Odin says that, like himself, she knows the future. In her fertility and foresight, Gefion seems to combine something of the qualities of Freyja and Frigg.

In *Heimskringla*, Snorri says that Gefion married the god king Skjold or Scyld, son of Odin, and lived at Leire in Denmark where it was known that she had a sanctuary. This is the same Scyld to whom the *Beowulf* poet alludes at the beginning of that poem; he was one of the traditional founders of the Danish dynasty and gives his name to the Danes who are referred to as Scyldings throughout that poem.

The myth of Gefion's great feat of ploughing round Zealand clearly lies behind the widespread North West European ritual of ploughing a token strip of land at the beginning of spring, before the fields were sown, to ensure fertility. This practice is also remembered in an eighth-century Anglo-Saxon charm for the fertility of the land that contains the words 'Erce, Erce, Erce, eorþan modor [earth mother]' and ends:

> *Then let the plough be driven forth and the first*
> *furrow made. Then say:*
>
> *Hail to thee, Earth, mother of men!*
> *Be fruitful in God's embrace,*
> *Filled with food for the use of men.*

Rituals such as this did not die out with the Norse gods. In that astounding storehouse, *Teutonic Mythology*, Jacob Grimm quoted a song embodying Odin's name formerly used in harvest festivals in Schaumburg, and also wrote that in Lower Saxony 'It is usual to leave a clump of standing corn in a field to Woden for his horse.' Indeed, it would be surprising if a few farmers did not still have their own superstitions, superstitions that echo the invocations and placations of their ancestors.

Gylfi is not only Gefion's victim but the peg on which Snorri hangs the first part of his *Prose Edda*, the 'Gylfaginning' (Deluding of Gylfi). A wise king with a taste for greater wisdom, he journeys to Asgard disguised as an old man to discover whether the deities are their own source of strength or whether they in turn worship greater deities. The Aesir foresee his arrival and set three figures – High One, Just as High and Third – whose high seats in the hall are one above the other, to answer his questions. Gylfi learns many stories about the activities of the gods and about the nine worlds from their creation until Ragnarok. And High One finally tells him, 'And now, if you have anything more to ask, I can't think how you can manage it, for I've never heard anyone tell more of the story of the world. Make what use of it you can!'

Were these strange figures speaking for the gods? How far did they believe in their own stories? Were they taking Gylfi for a ride? Snorri does not elaborate. Perhaps their stance, sometimes reverent, sometimes matter of fact, sometimes humorous, was not so very different from his own. They were, at all events, his mouthpiece – the highly effective literary device he used to describe the half-forgotten and largely discredited mythology of their forebears to Christian Icelanders in the thirteenth century.

22 THE LAY OF HARBARD

The unique source for this myth is the eddaic poem *Harbardsljoth*. It appears complete in the *Codex Regius* and missing the first twenty stanzas in the *Arnamagnaean Codex*, and is thought to date from the eleventh century. It is one of two flyting poems (see *Note 30*) in the *Elder Edda*; the other is *Lokasenna*.

Harbard or 'Grey-beard' is, of course, Odin in disguise, though Thor fails to recognise him. (The name Harbard appears in the long list of Odin's names in *Grimnismal – Myth 12*.) Although there is vestigial interest in whether Thor will prevail on the ferryman to take him across the sound, the main interest of this myth lies not in the narrative but in the way in which the protagonists reveal – through their boasts and taunts – their very different natures. They may be father and son, but their interests overlap only in the matter of women.

It is entirely in character that Thor should at once declare his identity and that Odin should assume a mask. Thor is direct, commonsensical and earthy; Odin is subtle, a deceiver, and arrogant. Odin's boasts relate to his prowess with women, his magical powers and his pleasure in stirring up strife and 'setting princes at one another's throats'. These are three familiar aspects of his character and recur in many of the myths. We know nothing of Odin's allusions to his five years on the island of Algron or to how he caused war in Valland (Land of Slaughter). Nor is it possible to elaborate on what Odin means when he says that he joined a host that massed on the frontiers of Asgard. Was there a tradition that he once allied himself with forces hostile to the Aesir? Or is he referring to the war with the Vanir? Or is he simply dissembling so that Thor will not guess his identity? Odin's suggestion that he should give Thor a little finger-ring and Thor's furious rejoinder are also difficult to understand. Maybe the ferryman is insulting Thor by suggesting that the god should enter his service; or maybe some stanzas from *Harbardsljoth* are missing at this point.

Thor's boasts all relate to his role as guardian of gods and men. He alludes to his duel with Hrungnir (*Myth 19*) and to how he killed the giant Thiazi (*Myth 8*). In saying that Thor threw Thiazi's eyes into the sky where they became stars (*Myth 9*), *Harbardsljoth* differs from the *Prose Edda* where Snorri Sturluson ascribes this act to Odin. Nothing further is known about Thor's boulder battle with the giant Svarang's sons on the banks of the Iving – the river that divided Asgard and Jotunheim – or about his slaughter of the fearsome brides of the Berserks. Odin's taunt that Thor hid in a glove refers, of course, to an amusing episode in 'Thor's Journey to Utgard' (*Myth 16*); in the only surviving version of that myth, however, the giant is not called Fjalar but Skrymir. Thor effectively sums up his own outstanding characteristic in saying that had he not slaughtered giant women, 'there would be a terrible throng of giants; and there would be no men in Midgard'.

Odin and Thor are shown to be not only dissimilar in character but to protect different strata of society. At the beginning of the myth, Odin accuses Thor of looking like a beggarman (see also *Myth 27*) and later emphasises that it is only the thralls (he is exaggerating, in fact it is the whole peasant community) who pass into his safekeeping whereas the nobly born – slain kings, princes and warriors – are in the care of Odin. This matter is further discussed in the introduction.

So malicious, insinuating Harbard holds the ford and Thor stumps away with foreboding in his heart and a curse in his ears. There is little doubt, though, that the hearts of the great majority of Norsemen would have gone with him.

23 THE BALLAD OF SVIPDAG

Although the *Svipdagsmal* comprises part of the *Elder Edda*, it survives only in manuscripts dating from the seventeenth century. It actually consists of two poems, *Grougaldr* (Groa's Charm) and *Fjolsvinnsmal* (The Ballad of Fjolsvid) which plainly tell the first and second half of one story and have therefore been united by most editors. The romantic spirit and verse style of these poems suggest that they were composed later than the other poems in the *Elder Edda*, perhaps in the thirteenth or fourteenth century.

The *volva* or seeress, alive and dead, was a common phenomenon in medieval North Western Europe. A number of sagas describe ceremonies associated with these shamanistic figures, while in the *Elder Edda* three poems, *Voluspa*, *Baldrs Draumar* and *Svipdagsmal*, revolve around the rousing of a *volva* from her burial mound to impart knowledge to gods or give protection to men. Svipdag's seeress mother is generally taken to be the same Groa who features in the myth of Thor's duel with Hrungnir (*Myth 19*). It is she who begins to work the whetstone loose that is lodged in Thor's head, only to be fatally distracted and forget her charms.

The formulaic opening to Svipdag's questions in his long exchange with Fjolsvid is a familiar convention, and has parallels in a number of other myths, including *Alvissmal*, *Harbardsljoth* and *Vafthrudnismal*. Fjolsvid's replies constitute a vicious circle: to get past the hounds, they must be fed the wings of the cock Vidofnir; the only weapon that can kill the cock is the sword Laevateinn which is watched over by the giantess Sinmora; and she will only part with the sword if she is presented with the tail feather of Vidofnir! What Fjolsvid is saying is that there is no entry to the hall except for the chosen man.

The identity of Fjolsvid and Menglad is puzzling. Fjolsvid (Wide Wisdom) is one of the names by which Odin calls himself in *Grimnismal*, and Fjolsvid claims to have made the hall Gastropnir from the limbs of a dead giant – a labour reminiscent of the way Odin and his brothers created the world from the body of Ymir (*Myth 1*). Odin's two wolves, moreover, are called Geri and Freki (both meaning 'greedy one'), while the two hounds in this myth are Gif and Geri.

While Fjolsvid has inherited some of the characteristics of Odin, Menglad appears to be a cross between Freyja and Frigg who, as suggested in the introduction, represent two aspects of the Earth Mother. Menglad means 'Necklace-Glad', and it has been established that the necklace was the principal ornament of the Mother Goddess in Indo-European cultures; it will be remembered that Freyja acquired the Necklace of the Brisings (*Myth 13*). As for Frigg, all the goddesses were subservient to her as Odin's wife and some are described by Snorri as her maidservants. It must be pertinent that Menglad sits on Lyfjaberg, the Hill of Healing, surrounded by servants who succour those who 'make offerings on the high altars', and that the name of one of her servants is Eir, goddess of healing. We can, in the end, only say that the characters of Fjolsvid and Menglad have plainly been influenced by Odin, Freyja and Frigg, but that they remain magical rather than divine figures, and that the proceedings appropriately take place not in Asgard but in Jotunheim.

Svipdagsmal refers to a great number of characters, some of whom – such as Loki, Surt and Urd – appear in other myths. The cock Vidofni may be identical with one of the two cocks Fjalar (All Knower) and Gullinkambi (Golden Comb) who crow to the giants and the gods before Ragnarok (cf. *Voluspa* vv. 42 and 43). Finally this poem, with its description of the fruit of Yggdrasill that is cooked and eaten by women in labour, is one of several in the *Elder Edda* that supports the widespread belief that the World Tree was the source of new life.

24 THOR AND GEIRROD

Geirrod was one of the most formidable of Thor's giant adversaries and the myth of their encounter was evidently a popular one. Four versions of it survive.

In 'Skaldskaparmal' in the *Prose Edda*, Snorri Sturluson not only offered his own account of Thor's visit to Geirrod's hall but also included an alternative version in the shape of an extremely intricate, late tenth-century scaldic lay by Eilif Guthrunarson, *Thorsdrapa*. Saxo Grammaticus tells the story in Book VIII of his *Gesta Danorum* and it is also the subject of *Thorsteins Thattr* which comprises part of a late fifteenth-century Icelandic manuscript; these latter two versions have Christian settings and Thor's place is taken by Thurkillus and Thorstein, a follower of King Olaf Tryggvason, respectively.

Saxo is thought to give a reliable picture of the myths as they were known in the thirteenth century, and makes it clear that his version of this myth derived from Icelandic oral tradition. My retellings, though, accept that the gods *are* gods, not cunning men, and certainly not Christians! I have therefore elected to follow Snorri and *Thorsdrapa*.

There are, however, significant divergences between these two versions. Only Snorri supplies an account of Loki's journey to Geirrod's hall (and this is the only myth in which Frigg, rather than Freyja, is described as the owner of a falcon skin); and Snorri has Loki as Thor's companion whereas in the earlier *Thorsdrapa* Thialfi accompanies Thor. In *Thorsdrapa* Thor takes his hammer with him; in Snorri's version he does not. In *Thorsdrapa* Loki refers to green fields round the giant's hall; in Snorri's version he does not. It seems obvious enough that Snorri had other sources available to him, and combined those with *Thorsdrapa*. I have modelled my retelling on Snorri, who supplies more detail than Eilif Guthrunarson, but have taken elements from *Thorsdrapa* that do not work against it.

Although these divergent sources present some problems, the myth needs little elaboration. Thor's victory is a triumph for physical strength over guile (the treachery of Loki in persuading him to visit Geirrod, and the schemes of Geirrod and his two luckless daughters). Even so, Thor would not have been able to overcome the giant brood without the help of Grid, one of several giantesses associated with the gods and so, by inference, with order rather than chaos. Grid was one of Odin's mistresses and the mother of Vidar, strongest of all the gods but Thor, and one of the survivors of Ragnarok.

Peter Redgrove and Penelope Shuttle, authors of *The Wise Wound*, (Victor Gollancz, London, 1977), think that Geirrod's daughter Gjalp was 'very likely a shamaness, who would prophesy at her menstrual flow'. Concerning the menstrual river that Thor has to cross, they wrote to me: 'Possibly the great archetype is the Egyptian yearly spring flood which comes down from the African hills, and is laden with red mud. The likeness of this to the sign of human fertility, the menstrual flow, did not escape the Egyptians, of course. Interestingly the hippopotamus, the Egyptian water-horse, one of the old forms of the genetrix, was known, rather like Gjalp, as "Roarer" (the shaman's howl).

Here the river of blood is a river of fertility; but it can equally be the river of death, as in the [Scottish] Lyke-Wake dirge. One meets this river in Chinese myth and legend, I think; the hero has to cross it on a rainbow or sword-bridge, and if he falls he is carried away with all the other souls.'

The rowan or mountain ash that Thor seizes to save himself from drowning in the river Vimur is a tree held to have protective qualities (especially against witches) in many countries. So, for instance, it figures in the ballad of 'The Laidly Worm of Spindleston Heughs', and Katharine Briggs has noted that it was once customary for a rowan tree to be planted outside every house and cottage in the Highlands. After describing how Thor climbed out of the river Vimur, Snorri comments, 'This is why we say the rowan is Thor's salvation.'

25 THE LAY OF LODDFAFNIR

At the heart of the miscellany *Havamal*, or 'Words of the High One', lie the proverbs and advice on social conduct attributed to Odin, a moral code memorable not only for its ideals but for its witty and invariably terse expression.

Some of this advice (*Loddfafnismal*: stanzas 111–38) is addressed to one Loddfafnir, a man who, as the poem tells, found his way to the Well of Urd and Odin's hall and repeats to men what the High One told him there. These stanzas form the basis of my retelling. Versions of the very similar and more substantial set of proverbs and rules of conduct that make up the first eighty stanzas of *Havamal* can be found in *The Poetic Edda* translated by Henry Adams Bellows (The American–Scandinavian Foundation, New York, 1923), *The Elder Edda: A Selection* translated by Paul B. Taylor and W. H. Auden (Faber and Faber, London, 1969), and *Poems of the Vikings* translated by Patricia Terry (Bobbs-Merrill, Indianapolis and New York, 1976).

The very first two injunctions to Loddfafnir represent the spectrum covered by *Havamal*. At one end, medieval superstition about witches is given full measure; at the other, a shrewd piece of advice about the suspicion engendered by people who are up and about while others are asleep is combined with an earthy joke. But the need to cultivate friends and shun enemies, the need to make proper provision when travelling in a hostile environment and to treat other travellers with respect, the need for a combination of generosity and thrift, and the need to do that good which is its own reward: these are the values that are celebrated above others in the aphoristic stanzas of *Loddfafnismal*.

Only two points call for further comment. The hides, pelts and guts with which the shrivelled skins of the old people are compared would have been a familiar sight in an Icelandic house. First they were dried, then used for bedding, clothing, storage and other purposes. Secondly, the list of charms in the penultimate paragraph looks like an interpolation, although it is true that earlier in the poem Loddfafnir is enjoined to find a friend who knows 'charms for healing'. Maybe the scribe who copied *Havamal* into the *Codex Regius* was momentarily bemused by the poem's endless formulaic repetition and simply wrote 'Listen, Lodd-fafnir, and listen carefully!' once too often by mistake! I have followed Bellows (see above) in lifting the last stanza of *Havamal* and placing it at the end of my retelling, for it appears to refer back to the opening words and then rounds off matters in the accepted manner.

26 OTTER'S RANSOM

The myth of Otter's ransom is told by Snorri Sturluson in the *Prose Edda*; it is the subject of the first few stanzas and prose interpolations of *Reginsmal*, a thirteenth-century eddaic poem in the *Codex Regius*; and it constitutes Chapter XIV of the late thirteenth-century *Volsunga Saga*. In outline these versions are similar and I have taken Snorri's account, which is the most detailed, as the basis for my retelling, but appropriated a number of details from the other two versions.

In both *Reginsmal* and the *Volsunga Saga*, the myth is put into the mouth of Regin, Hreidmar's son, and all three accounts go on to relate this myth to the legend of Sigurd, the greatest of the Germanic heroes. Fafnir kills his father to secure Andvari's gold, refuses to share it with Regin, turns himself into a dragon and takes the gold to a lair on Gnita Heath; Regin becomes the smith at the court of King Hjalprek in Jutland, adopts Sigurd the son of Volsung and Hjordis, and incites Sigurd to kill Fafnir. These accounts (and subsequent eddaic poems, *Fafnismal* and *Sigrifumal*) then tell how Sigurd killed the dragon Fafnir and won both his gold and wisdom, understood the speech of birds and, learning of Regin's intention to kill him for the gold, killed Regin first; they recount how Sigurd rode off with the treasure and found a fully armed woman asleep on a mountain . . . Brynhild? Sigrdrifa? A human? A Valkyrie? Here, and in the subsequent history of Sigurd the Volsung, the versions diverge.

Sigurd was a King Arthur of the Northern world, a figure with a possible historical origin who became the magnet for many unrelated stories. He is the central figure of the *Volsunga Saga* and (with the name of Siegfried) of the thirteenth-century German epic *Das Nibelungenlied* and, of course, the hero of Richard Wagner's supreme operatic cycle, *Der Ring der Nibelungen*. After translating the *Volsunga Saga*, Eiríkr Magnússon and William Morris wrote: 'This is the Great Story of the North, which should be to all our race what the Tale of Troy was to the Greeks – to all our race first, and afterwards, when the change of the world has made our race nothing more than a name of what has been – a story too – then should it be to those that come after us no less than the Tale of Troy has been to us.'

Without going into the complex problems relating to the origin, development and spread of the Sigurd legend, it should be said the legend revolves around the Rhine and the land occupied by the Franks, and that it was not Scandinavian but continental German in origin. It is quite possible that Sigurd was originally not a human but a god, but the shape in which he appears in all the Scandinavian sources (Snorri, Saxo, the sagas, and no less than a third of the eddaic poems) is that of the human or superhuman hero, sometimes credited with divine descent. I have therefore thought it inappropriate to include the story of Sigurd himself in this volume of myths, although the legend does contain mythical elements – the fated gold hoard first wrested by Loki from Andvari, and the Valkyrie called either Brynhild or Sigrdrifa.

There is no way of knowing at what date the Sigurd legend reached Scandinavia, or why it was connected with the Otter myth. But we do know that cursed gold was a commonplace of the Germanic world (another example occurs in the Anglo-Saxon *Beowulf*) and a Scandinavian poet already familiar with the myth of Otter's ransom may have heard the magnificent Frankish legend of Sigurd, with its hoard of fated gold, and decided to preface it with the myth in order to make the hoard seem grander still by giving it a divine origin. At any rate, it is generally agreed that the connexion of legend and myth must be relatively late.

Several points in the myth need brief comment. It is not clear why Odin, Loki and Honir are particular friends, although Odin and Loki are said to have been foster-brothers (*Myth 30*). This is the second or third occasion on which they are seen together (see *Note 1* and *Myth 8*).

I am aware that in following *Reginsmal* and the *Volsunga Saga* by having Loki borrow from Ran a net – the net she used to snare and draw drowning humans – I have anticipated Snorri's account of how Loki devised the first net in the world (*Myth 31*) in his desperate attempt to escape the vengeance of the gods.

Snorri is alone in attributing to Andvari's ring the power of self-renewal. In this respect, it resembles the ring Draupnir (*Myth 9*) made by the dwarfs Brokk and Eitri for Odin.

27 THE LAY OF ALVIS

The twelfth-century eddaic poem *Alvissmal* is the unique source for this myth. Although the mythological framework is not without interest, the poem is primarily a recital of colourful kennings, the most striking feature of scaldic poetry (see Introduction, p. xxxiii). In this respect, *Alvissmal* is a very useful supplement to the short chapters at the end of Snorri Sturluson's 'Skaldskaparmal' (an explanation and illustration of scaldic diction in which, incidentally, Snorri twice refers to *Alvissmal*) which list synonyms for scalds, men, women, the head, the heart, the arm, speech, understanding and expression.

As a number of myths make clear, dwarfs and giants were repositories of knowledge and magic songs and on occasion revealed their wisdom to the gods. (Alvis's apparent stupidity in failing to recognise Thor owes to the fact that Thor is often described as looking more rustic than divine!) In this myth, the dwarf does not actually meet Thor's stipulation that he should tell him the names of various objects 'in each and every world' but Thor does not seem bothered by the fact that although Alvis represents gods, men and giants in all thirteen answers, the elves occur only eleven times, the Vanir (also called 'the most holy gods') nine times and the dwarfs seven times. The poet was more interested in demonstrating an aspect of poetic technique than in satisfying the technical demands of the story, and Thor was interested only in detaining Alvis until sunrise!

Because they lived in caves, or underground, the dwarfs and giants also had in common a mortal terror of sunlight; it turned them into stone. Alvis is bitterly ironical in saying that the dwarfs call the sun 'Dvalin's Delight', for Dvalin was a dwarf and must have come to the same end suffered by Alvis himself.

It is apparent from the first that Thor has not the least intention of honouring a promise apparently made in his absence, and allowing the dwarf to take his daughter Thrud away. Like 'Thor's Journey to Utgard' (*Myth 16*) and 'The Mead of Poetry' (*Myth 6*), this myth illustrates how sheer force of mind or body can still be undermined by magic or by trickery; and like 'The Building of Asgard's Wall' (*Myth 3*), it shows that the gods, even Thor, were as ready to resort to cunning as anyone else.

28 BALDER'S DREAMS

It is clear that Balder's dreams are the beginning of the end. His dreams presage his death; and Balder's death reveals Loki as no longer equivocal but truly evil, and cruelly exposes the ultimate limitations and mortality of the gods. The gods may capture and punish Loki but they cannot retrieve Balder from Hel. The beautiful passive god who embodies the qualities of mercy and love is lost to them. The established order of the nine worlds has started to crumble and the movement towards Ragnarok has begun.

The story of Odin's descent to Hel is told only in *Baldrs Draumar*, a short eddaic poem in the *Arnamagnaean Codex*. Although the manuscript dates from the fourteenth century, the poem was probably composed early in the tenth century, and it has been argued that *Baldrs Draumar*, *Voluspa* and *Thrymskvitha* were all the work of one poet. There is in any case such a striking similarity between the description of Balder's death (in each case revealed to Odin by a *volva* or seeress) in *Baldrs Draumar* and *Voluspa* that one poem evidently influenced the other. In describing Balder's lineaments and qualities, I have made use of Snorri Sturluson's character sketch in the *Prose Edda*. Balder is one of the most enigmatic of the gods and I have discussed the conflicting descriptions of him and his death in *Note 29*.

Who is the seeress whom Odin calls 'no seeress'? One cannot but notice that, like Loki, she has spawned three monsters, and remember that Loki is not only responsible for Balder's death but, according to Snorri and *Lokasenna*, clearly associated with that part of the Balder myth relating to Hel. To say that the seeress and Loki are one and the same would plainly be an over-simplification; to deny any connexion between the two would plainly be wrong.

The goddess Rind does not appear in any other myth. Her role is simply to conceive Vali, Odin's son, who will avenge death with death as the Norse heroic code dictated.

The identity of the maidens mourning and tossing scarves into the sky has never been explained satisfactorily. The most attractive suggestion is that they are the waves, daughters of the sea god Aegir, and that in their frenzy they will throw the sails of ships sky high.

29 THE DEATH OF BALDER

The great myth of the death of Balder is probably the most widely known and certainly one of the most discussed in the entire cycle. Snorri Sturluson and Saxo Grammaticus offer widely differing versions, reflecting the conflicting traditions they drew upon, and there are a number of references to Balder's death in the eddaic poems.

Snorri Sturluson's account of the death of Balder in 'Gylfaginning' in the *Prose Edda* is a very fine piece of storytelling, rapid yet measured, dignified and finally tragic. One source for his version is a few lines of *Voluspa*; another is *Husdrapa* – but the lengthy description of Balder's death in that poem used by Snorri is now lost and all that survives is a list of those gods and goddesses who attended the cremation.

Snorri must have been familiar with other sources, too, for his accounts both of Balder's death and Hermod's ride to Hel are very full. One would have expected him to be familiar with the eddaic poem, *Baldrs Draumar* (*Myth 28*), but if he was, he made no use of it. Snorri doubtless knew what he was doing and in describing Odin's journey to Hel to discover the meaning of Balder's dream, that poem may well represent another and conflicting tradition for it is highly improbable that the myth of Balder's dream and death would have involved two divine descents to the underworld.

Saxo Grammaticus wrote his *Gesta Danorum* in about 1215. He presents the gods as strong and cunning humans – for whom he has a profound contempt – who have simply tricked men into believing that they are divine. In E. O. G. Turville-Petre's condensation, his version of the Balder story reads as follows:

Höð was the son of Hodbrodd, a King of Sweden, and brother of Athisl (ON *Aðils*, OE *Eadgils*). After the death of his father Höð was brought up by Gevar in Norway. He was early distinguished for his skill in sports, and especially on the harp. By the power of his music he could turn men's minds and, with it, he quickened love in the heart of Nanna, the daughter of Gevar.

Nanna was beautiful, and when Baldr saw her bathing, he was inflamed with lust, and resolved to kill his rival Höð.

One day when Höð was hunting, he lost his way in a fog, and came to a hut in which he found some forest maidens. They declared that it was chiefly they who decided the fortunes of war, and that they took part unseen in battle. They told Höð of the intentions of Baldr, but warned him not to attack, hateful though Baldr was, since he was a demigod. The house and the maids vanished, and Höð was left alone on an open field.

When Höð returned to his foster-father, Gevar, he sued for the hand of Nanna, but Gevar dare not give her for fear of Baldr. Instead he told Höð of a sword, capable of killing Baldr, and of an arm-ring, which would bring wealth to its owner. These treasures were in the hands of Miming, a satyr dwelling in a distant, frozen region.

Höð set off on the long journey and, by a ruse, he got the satyr in his power and seized the treasures from him.

Some adventures followed, which have little to do with the main theme. For a second time Höð went to the far north and, while he was away, Baldr came and demanded Nanna from Gevar. The decision was left to the girl, and she subtly refused Baldr on the grounds that he was a god, and their natures would be incompatible.

Enraged by Baldr's insolence, Höð and his allies joined battle with him, evidently in Denmark. Óðinn and all the gods fought on the side of Baldr, and Thór was in the forefront, striking with his club. Victory would have gone to the gods, had not Höð struck off the head of Thór's club. Then all the gods took to an ignoble flight, and Höð was free to marry Nanna. He took her to Sweden, where the people honoured him, while Baldr was held up to ridicule.

Soon afterwards, fortunes changed and Baldr won a victory over Höð in Denmark. His victory did Baldr little good, for now he began to be troubled by nightly visions of Nanna. His health declined, and he grew so weak that he had to be carried in a chariot.

For a time, the fortunes of war alternated, until Baldr won another victory over Höð, who left the field as a fugitive. Wandering alone through forests of Sweden, he came upon the same maidens whom he had met before. This time they told him that he would overcome his enemy if only he would taste of the magic food which sustained the strength of Baldr. Again the two parties joined battle and, after great slaughter on both sides, they retired for the night.

At the dead of night, Höð spied three maidens carrying the magical food. He pursued them to their dwelling and, making out that he was a minstrel, entertained them with his music. They were preparing the food of Baldr with the venom of three serpents. In spite of textual difficulties, it seems that Höð induced them to let him taste it, and they gave him a girdle of victory.

On his way back, Höð met his old enemy, and pierced him with his sword. Baldr fell to the ground mortally wounded, but was able to renew the battle next day, carried on a litter. On the following night he had a vision, or a dream, in which the goddess Proserpine promised her embraces. After three days Baldr was dead, and after a royal funeral, his body was laid in a barrow.

Óðinn now plotted revenge. He sought the help of a Lappish wizard Rostiophus (ON *Hrosspjófr*?), who told him that the avenger must be born to him by Rinda (ON *Rindr*) daughter of the King of the Ruthenians (Russians). Óðinn, assuming various disguises, took service with that King. The maid rejected his advances, until disguised as a woman, Óðinn became her servant and raped her.

Bous, the son of Rinda and Óðinn, met Höð in battle and slew him, while receiving a mortal wound himself.

The stories presented by Saxo and Snorri are by no means as contradictory as they may appear at first reading. H. R. Ellis Davidson has listed the points of agreement:

Balder has a prophetic dream or dreams foretelling his death; Balder is warmly supported by Odin and the gods; supernatural powers both help and oppose him; he is slain by Hoder; the slaying is done by a special weapon, because in general Balder is invulnerable to weapons; Odin receives a terrible set-back from Balder's death; another of Odin's sons, born after Balder dies, is destined to avenge him; a journey to the land of the dead forms part of the tale.

This makes an impressive list, but the differences between the versions are no less fundamental: in Saxo, Hod and Balder are not related; Hod is shown as virtuous while Balder is lustful, insistent and war-like; Nanna marries Hod, not Balder; the death of Balder is caused by Hod without any assistance from Loki; the instrument of his death is not a mistletoe dart but a sword. Was Snorri or Saxo nearer to the original form of the myth as it was known in Scandinavia?

In brief, it is now generally agreed that Saxo was drawing on Danish and east Scandinavian material whereas Snorri was working from Icelandic sources; it is also thought that although Saxo's version embodies a number of medieval motifs, it contains elements no less ancient than those in Snorri's retelling. I cannot here determine the relative authenticity of the two versions in detail, but let me single out a few important points of comparison.

The story of two brothers, sons of a king, one of whom unintentionally kills the other, was well known through contemporary North West Europe. In the eighth-century *Beowulf*, a moving digression tells of King Hrethel's grief at the death of Herebeald, killed by a stray arrow shot by his brother Hæthcyn. I have translated it:

> *Thus the old king, Hrethel, is agonised*
> *to see his son, so young, swing*
> *from the gallows. He sings a dirge, a song*
> *dark with sorrow, while his son hangs,*
> *raven's carrion, and he cannot help him*
> *in any way, wise and old as he is.*
> *He wakes each dawn to the ache*
> *of his son's death; he has no desire*
> *for a second son, to be his heir*
> *in the stronghold, now that his firstborn*
> *has finished his days and deeds on earth.*
> *Grieving, he wanders through his son's dwelling,*
> *sees the wine-hall now deserted, joyless,*
> *home of the winds; the riders, the warriors,*
> *sleep in their graves. No longer is the harp*
> *plucked, no longer is there happiness in that place.*

> *Then Hrethel takes to his bed, and intones*
> *dirges for his dead son, Herebeald;*
> *his house and his lands seem empty now,*
> *and far too large. Thus the lord of the Geats*
> *endured in his heart the ebb and flow*
> *of sorrow for his firstborn; but he could not*
> *avenge that feud on the slayer – his own son;*
> *although Hrethel had no love for Hæthcyn,*
> *he could no more readily requite death*
> *with death.*

The names Herebeald and Hæthcyn, and Balder and Hod, are markedly similar. It has been well argued that the *Beowulf* digression is an early version of the Balder story, and it is reasonable to suppose that Snorri was following an ancient tradition in making Hod and Balder brothers.

Much scholarly attention has been devoted to the character of Balder. Snorri's image of a passive suffering god is so beautifully wrought as to be ineradicable. It is clear that this image has its origin in the fertility gods of the near east, Tammuz, Attis, Adonis, Baal and Orpheus. E. O. G. Turville-Petre writes: 'Gods of this kind often died in youth and violently. In some societies their death was publicly lamented at festivals held in autumn, as if the participants would weep them from the Underworld. Their return, sometimes celebrated in spring, was the occasion of jubilation.' Snorri's picture of Balder was probably influenced, too, by the story of Christ. I am not the first person to have noticed the correspondence between Balder being wept out of Hel and the following passage in the Anglo-Saxon poem, *The Dream of the Rood*:

> *Shadows swept across the land,*
> *Dark shapes under the low-flying clouds. All creation wept,*
> *Wailed for the death of the King; Christ was on the Cross.*

For all this, scholars believe that Saxo's portrait of Balder goes back to equally early tradition, and that Balder may originally have been a warrior, a divine hero. The mention of the gallows – a ritual hanging, a sacrifice to the gods – at the beginning of the *Beowulf* passage is cited in support of this. It is also very much to the point that Balder's name appears in a number of Old Norse kennings for warrior. Hod's name, too, seems at odds with Snorri's picture of him; it means warlike. There is no way, in the end, of establishing whether Snorri or Saxo is nearer the original Balder.

It is generally supposed that Saxo was rationalising in saying that

Balder was killed by a sword, and that the mistletoe shaft represents an older tradition. That the mistletoe was considered throughout pre-Christian Europe as the most holy of all plants is well known and has been amply demonstrated by J. G. Frazer in *The Golden Bough*:

> From time immemorial the mistletoe has been the object of superstitious veneration in Europe. It was worshipped by the Druids, as we learn from a famous passage of Pliny. After enumerating the different kinds of mistletoe, he proceeds: 'In treating of this subject, the admiration in which the mistletoe is held throughout Gaul ought not to pass unnoticed. The Druids, for so they call their wizards, esteem nothing more sacred than the mistletoe and that tree on which it grows, provided only that the tree is an oak.'

Frazer's closely argued view (in his chapter 'Balder and the Mistletoe') that 'Balder is neither more nor less than a personification of the mistletoe-bearing oak' seems over elaborate but nonetheless establishes an early association between the god and the plant. Since, however, the mistletoe is not native to Iceland, and was perhaps quite unknown there, it may never have occurred to anyone that it is too fragile a plant to use as a weapon; and it may have been just this that persuaded Saxo to turn it into a sword!

In writing my retelling, I have followed Snorri Sturluson's version both in the interests of consistency and because it seems contrary to the spirit of this book to follow a writer who not only euhemerised but openly despised the old gods. In describing Balder's funeral, I have supplemented Snorri's account by drawing sparingly both on contemporary records (the description of Scyld Scefing's ship burial and Beowulf's own cremation in *Beowulf*, and Ibn Fadlan's account of a tenth-century Rus ship burial on the Volga) and on recent archaeological discoveries of ship burials in North West Europe. I have introduced the names of the Valkyries (see also *Myth 12*); there are conflicting lists of their names and I have drawn on *Grimnismal* (Stanza 36). A brief description of the Berserks will be found in *Note 18*, and a discussion of the use of Mjollnir for hallowing or consecration in *Note 10*. I have taken the idea that Odin whispered in the ear of Balder before he was cremated from the end of *Vafthrudnismal*; what he whispered is the last and unanswerable question that Odin put to the giant Vafthrudnir (*Myth 15*).

Hel and her abode are described in some detail by Snorri Sturluson elsewhere in 'Gylfaginning'. I have drawn on this description in portraying Hermod in Eljudnir. Before Hermod leaves the underworld, Nanna gives him a ring for Fulla. She is named by Snorri as one of the goddesses of high rank but appears only to have been one of Frigg's handmaidens, the carrier of Frigg's casket. Her name means 'filler' and her long hair indicates she must originally have been a fertility goddess.

Snorri masters his raw material and, like the great psychologist he was, plays off opposites: love and hate, innocence and guile, passivity and action. He embraces not only Asgard and Niflheim but all creation. One would like to believe without reservation in his emotionally satisfying portrait of a slain god (who, as he soon goes on to show, will rise again at domesday) and, of course, at one level it is possible to do so. But like all artists and historians, Snorri rationalised and filtered. This one myth emphasises how much lies in the shadows, half known or unknown, behind him and Saxo, the sagamen, the scaldic and eddaic poets.

30 LOKI'S FLYTING

The unique source for this myth is *Lokasenna*, a poem in the *Codex Regius* of the *Elder Edda*. It follows *Hymiskvitha* (*Myth* and *Note 17*) and a prose introduction to *Lokasenna* links the two myths: Aegir's feast is represented as a direct result of the gaining of the cauldron. But while the poem is generally thought to have been composed at the end of the tenth or beginning of the eleventh century, the prose notes accompanying it were probably the work of the scribe who compiled the *Codex Regius* in about 1170 – a man interested not so much in derivation and piecing together early beliefs as in establishing the continuity of his material and explaining cause and effect, to his audience.

The linking of *Lokasenna* and *Hymiskvitha* does not materially affect the shape of the myth, but the prose note at the end of the poem certainly does. After Loki has hurled his final insult at his host Aegir, a short passage reads:

> And after that, Loki hid in Franang's Fall, disguised as a salmon, and the gods caught him there. He was bound with the gut of his brother Vali but his son Narvi was turned into a wolf. Skadi brought a poisonous snake and hung it over him so that the poison dripped on to Loki's face. Loki's wife, Sigyn, sat beside him and caught the poison in a bowl, but when the bowl was full she carried it away and the poison, meanwhile, dripped on to Loki. Then he wrestled so fiercely that the entire world shook. And that is what we now call an earthquake.

This event is also described in greater detail, and with some variation, by Snorri Sturluson in the *Prose Edda* (*Myth 31*). The most important distinction between the two accounts is that Loki's punishment is seen in *Lokasenna* as the direct result of his venomous outburst, whereas Snorri says that Loki was punished for causing Balder's death and then preventing his return from Hel. Since it is everywhere clear that Snorri knew a great deal more about the early form of the myths than the compiler of the *Elder Edda*, it seemed proper to lop off the end of Lokasenna and treat Loki's punishment as a separate episode, explicitly connected to Balder's death. (So far as the order is concerned, it is true that it would be emotionally satisfying if Loki's punishment followed immediately after the Balder myth; however, there are references in *Lokasenna* to Balder's death and I did not want to add to the number of chronological inconsistencies in the cycle.)

Lokasenna is one of two flyting (a word that derives from the Old English *flitan*, to strive or dispute) poems in the *Elder Edda*; the other is *Harbardsljoth* (*Myth 22*). Wrangling was a literary convention for which the Norsemen displayed a predilection both in poetry and saga. But, although the poet pours abuse on the heads of the gods and goddesses he may well have still believed in them; there is certainly no evidence in the poem that the poet was a Christian. It is difficult to believe, though, that such a poem could have been composed at a time when these deities were still widely revered in Scandinavia.

Lokasenna reveals a considerable amount of information about the gods. Some of it can be substantiated from other sources. We know from Snorri, for instance, that Loki was indeed responsible, as he claims, for Balder's death; we know from the *Ynglinga Saga* that Njord had children by his sister; we know from *Skirnismal* that Freyr rewarded Skirnir with his sword and from both Snorri and *Harbardsljoth* how Thor killed Hrungnir. There is, in other words, little reason to doubt that the author of *Lokasenna* knew what he was talking about and that what cannot be substantiated nevertheless accurately represents early beliefs and traditions about the gods. Some of the more important elements in the poem, such as the relationship of the Aesir and the Vanir, are discussed in the introduction.

Lokasenna is a myth ironic in its revelation that the gods are not only glorious but also as flawed as the other inhabitants of the nine worlds; a myth tragic in its revelation that the gods cannot rise above Loki's invective but are dragged down to his level, countering his charges and slurs with accusations and threats of their own.

As for Loki, his transition from trickster to demon is complete. In the myth of the death of Balder, he embodied evil; in this myth, he infects every god with whom he comes into contact and so, by implication, every one of us. The scene is set for his capture and punishment.

31 THE BINDING OF LOKI

The powerful image of Loki lying in chains, awaiting Ragnarok, may put one in mind of the myth of Prometheus – the Titan who stole fire from heaven and was chained by Zeus to Mount Caucasus, where an eagle tore at his liver each day and each night his liver was renewed. It is agreed that these and other myths of chained monsters (some of them responsible for earthquakes) must be related in some way yet to be established, and E. O. G. Turville-Petre has further suggested that 'this chapter in Loki's history was derived from Christian legend, according to which Antichrist lies bound in Hell, and will break loose before the Day of Judgement. Just as Balder, in his innocence, was predisposed to the influences of Christ, so Loki was predisposed to those of Satan.'

Interestingly enough, the image of Sigyn holding the bowl over the bound Loki (together with a panel showing Thor hauling up the World Serpent while out fishing with Hymir) is depicted on the remains of an Anglo-Saxon stone cross built into the wall of Gosforth Church in Cumberland. At a time when new Christian and old pagan beliefs were both in men's minds, representatives of good and evil must to some extent have been interchangeable.

I have followed the outline of the myth as it is told by Snorri Sturluson in the *Prose Edda*, but the story is also related much more briefly in the prose appendage to *Lokasenna* (translated in *Note 30*). The only important variant is that whereas Snorri says Vali was turned into a wolf and tore apart his brother Narvi, *Lokasenna* says that Loki 'was bound with the gut of his son Vali but his son Narvi was turned into a wolf'. We hear plenty about Loki's three appalling children by the giantess Angrboda – Fenrir, Jormungand and Hel – but his two sons by his wife Sigyn, Vali 'and Nari or Narvi', as Snorri carefully says, are mentioned only here. This Vali should not be confused with Odin's son Vali expressly conceived by Rind to avenge Balder's death by killing Hod.

The story of Loki's punishment, which is also mentioned in *Voluspa* and, indirectly, in *Baldrs Draumar*, does not add to our knowledge of Loki's character. Rather, it is remarkable for embodying three folk traditions. First, Snorri attributes the making of the original fishing net to Loki. In this context, it is surprising to meet Kvasir once more, since Snorri himself describes how he was killed by the dwarfs Fjalar and Galar (*Myth 6*), and how his blood was mixed with honey and became the mead of poetry. The second tradition is also piscatory: it has to do with the shape of the salmon. Thor clutches at it and only just manages to hold on to it. Snorri says: '. . . he slipped through Thor's hand until

Thor secured him by the tail, and that is why the salmon tapers towards its tail'.

The third tradition is, unforgettably, that whenever Loki shudders as the snake's venom drips on to him, he causes an earthquake. The bound Loki is still a force to be reckoned with. His evil is too great to be entirely contained and he remains capable of inflicting sudden death and wreaking havoc amongst the houses of men.

32 RAGNAROK

A deep awareness of fate and life's transience pervades many of the myths and endows the actions of gods and men with tragic dignity. It is not inappropriate, therefore, that the most powerful and, in the end, the most moving verses in the whole body of eddaic poetry should describe Ragnarok, the fate of the gods. These verses constitute the second part of *Voluspa*, composed in about 1000 AD, in which Odin raises a seeress or *volva* from the dead who tells him of the world's creation and impending destruction.

As with his account of the creation, Snorri Sturluson's account of Ragnarok in the *Prose Edda* is drawn primarily from *Voluspa*. But here too he draws on other sources known (*Vafthrudnismal*) and forgotten, and possibly adds something of his own. His is very much the fullest version and I have taken it as the basis for my retelling but have introduced a number of details from *Voluspa* that Snorri did not choose to perpetuate.

End and beginning – death and rebirth – lie at the very heart of every religion. Ragnarok begins with a terrible winter, *Fimbulvetr*, that lasts three years; after this, two humans hide within Hoddmimir's Wood, another name for Yggdrasill. In discussing the creation myth (*Note 1*) I pointed to parallels with Iranian mythology and these occur again here. An Iranian myth describes a terrible winter which will put an end to life on earth, with the exception of a few men, women and animals who will escape by hiding in a shelter built by the bisexual Yama.

The nearest parallel to the loosing of the monsters and the great fight at Vigrid appears to be in Celtic mythology. Both mythologies also shared the belief that although the structure of the world itself could not be finally destroyed, and life in it would not become totally extinct, fire and water would one day bring an end to the present life cycle on earth. But here, as with Fimbulvetr, there is no way of proving whether the parallels arise from a shared origin or from later influence. It is of course quite possible that they are a result of both.

The Indo-European parallels are not confined to myth. The great Danish anthropologist, A. Olrik demonstrated that many of the elements in *Voluspa* recur widely in folklore. The bound giant who breaks his fetters, the swallowed sun and the ship built of the nails of corpses are all widely known folk motifs and the idea that dead men's nails can be put to evil use also turns up in Iranian myth. Some of the scenes from *Voluspa* are also depicted on the Gosforth Cross (*Notes 17* and *31*) which was carved by a Viking in the north of England in about 900 AD. There is, therefore, a good deal of scattered evidence that the ideas about Ragnarok expressed in *Voluspa* were common coin in the Viking world and that the poet was furthering long established heathen traditions.

A great deal has been written about the likely influence of Christian concepts of Domesday on the *Voluspa* poet. Maybe he was aware of the Christian fear that the world would end either in 1000 or 1033; and maybe he knew his gospels and had read Christ's words in Mark XIII, v. 8 and vv. 24–5:

> For nation shall rise against nation, and kingdom against kingdom; and there shall be earthquakes in divers places, and there shall be famines and troubles: these are the beginning of sorrows.

and vv. 24–5:

> But in those days, after that tribulation, the sun shall be darkened, and the moon shall not give her light,
> And the stars of heaven shall fall, and the powers that are in heaven shall be shaken.

But this does not necessarily mean that the poet slavishly imitated them. As H. R. Ellis Davidson has most sensibly pointed out:

> It must be admitted too that the falling of the stars and the darkening of the moon could well come into a poet's head, even if he had not studied apocryphal literature or the writings of the early church ... I would discount much of what has been written deriving the material of *Voluspa* from Christian sources...

Although it has often been suggested that the *Voluspa* poet's description of Ragnarok is actually based on the Christian concept of the Last Judgement, the weight of evidence (mythological and folkloric parallels and natural combustion in the poet's mind) is against it.

It might be more fruitful to explore how far the distinctive nature of Iceland is reflected in the account of Ragnarok. I suggested that it influenced the poet's description of the creation (*Note 1*) and here the influence seems equally marked and possibly more specific. It has been interestingly argued that the stages of *Voluspa* correspond to the stages of a volcanic eruption; but whether this is the case or not, terrible cold and intolerable fire, leading to melting ice and rapidly rising water levels, are experiences with which Icelanders have always been familiar. The Sons of Muspell may derive from a late ninth-century Bavarian poem in which the word *muspelle* means 'fire that will burn the world', but in visualising the world's ultimate destruction, medieval Icelanders were bound to think in terms of the dire actualities – fire and flood – that daily confronted them. And so the cycle is complete: the same elements that created life end it.

The *Voluspa* poet, so faithfully followed by Snorri Sturluson, lived at a time when belief in the Norse pantheon was giving way to Christianity. The climate was right for the composition of a poem about the death of the old gods and one man at least felt the tension and the loss, and rose superlatively to the challenge. But if the *Voluspa* poet was a fatalist and typical of his time in seeing only a glimmer of hope for the living, he was also a visionary. He describes in detail, as no other surviving poet does, the emergence of a new world, a time beyond our time, purged of all evil, new, clean, ready to begin again. In so doing, he was doubtless transmitting received wisdom, for the beliefs he expresses certainly existed in pre-Christian Scandinavia, but he gives that wisdom new tongue. He faces all the terrors that there are on earth; and having done so, he has won the position to speak with authority of a green heaven and to express our universal longing for rebirth.

GLOSSARY

The glossary contains the principal characters, places and props in the myths. Old Norse names have been simplified by omitting the final *r* (except in the case of Freyr, whose name is too well-known to need alteration) and by changing ð to *d* and þ to *th*. In a very few and relatively insignificant instances, I have used and therefore listed a name only in translation.

AEGIR God of the sea. His wife is Ran and their hall is under the waves by the island of Hlesey.

AESIR The race of gods who inhabit Asgard. Originally a group of warrior gods, led by Odin.

AFI (Grandfather) Ancestor of the race of peasants.

AGNAR Elder son of Hraudung, King of the Goths. Favoured by Frigg but disinherited by his younger brother Geirrod (Myth 12).

AGNAR Son of Geirrod, King of the Goths (and named after his disinherited uncle). Offered sustenance to Odin (Myth 12).

AI (Great Grandfather) Ancestor of the race of serfs.

ALFHEIM (Elf World) The part of Asgard inhabited by the light elves.

ALGRON (All Green) Island where Harbard (alias Odin) stayed for five years (Myth 22).

ALSVID (All Swift) One of the horses that pulls the sun along its course.

ALVIS (All Knowing) Wise dwarf outwitted by Thor and turned into stone (Myth 27).

AMMA (Grandmother) Ancestor of the race of peasants.

ANDVARI Dwarf who owned a treasure hoard, and cursed it when it was extracted from him by Loki to pay the ransom for Otter's death (Myth 26).

ANGRBODA (Distress-bringer) Giantess who was the mistress of Loki and mother of Fenrir, Jormungand and Hel.

ARVAK (Early Waker) One of the horses that pulls the sun along its course.

ASGARD World of the gods.

ASK (Ash Tree) Name of the first man created by the sons of Bor from a fallen tree (Myth 1).

AUDUMLA Cow created out of ice in the void Ginnungagap. She gave suck to Ymir, the first being, and then licked ice blocks into the shape of Buri, forefather of the gods (Myth 1).

AURGELMIR Alternative name for Ymir, the first frost giant.

AURVANDIL Husband of the seeress Groa. Thor made a star from his frozen toe by throwing it into the sky (Myth 19).

BALDER Son of Odin and Frigg. Beautiful, wise and gentle. He was killed by Hod and is to return after Ragnarok.

BAUGI Giant, brother of Suttung, who employs Odin, disguised as Bolverk, on his journey to Jotunheim to secure the mead of poetry (Myth 6).

BERGELMIR Only giant to escape the flood caused by dead Ymir's blood (Myth 1).

BERSERKS (Bear Shirts) Human warriors who went into a frenzy before battle and fought wearing animal skins. It was believed that Odin gave them special protection.

BESTLA Giantess. Wife of Bor and mother of Odin, Vili and Ve.

BEYLA Maidservant of Freyr. Wife of Byggvir.

BIFROST Flaming three-strand rainbow bridge between Asgard and Midgard.

BILLING'S DAUGHTER Human who successfully resisted Odin's advances and snubbed him into the bargain (Myth 20).

BILSKIRNIR Thor's hall in Asgard.

BODN (Vessel) One of the jars containing the mead of poetry brewed from Kvasir's blood.

BOLVERK (Evil-doer) The name adopted by Odin on his journey into Jotunheim to win the mead of poetry (Myth 6).

BOR Son of Buri, and father of Odin, Vili and Ve.

BRAGI Son of Odin. God of poetry and eloquence and husband of Idun.

BREIDABLIK (Broad Splendour) Balder's hall in Asgard.

BRISINGS' NECKLACE Incomparable necklace, or possibly belt, secured by Freyja from four dwarfs (Myth 13).

BROKK Dwarf who, with his brother Eitri, fashioned three such gifts for the gods that he won a wager with Loki (Myth 10).

BURI Ancestor of the gods licked from the ice by the cow Audumla.

BYGGVIR Manservant of Freyr. Husband of Beyla.

DAY Son of Night and Delling. He rides round the world on his horse Skinfaxi.

DRAUPNIR (Dropper) Odin's gold ring that produces eight rings of equal weight on every ninth night.

DURIN Second-in-command of the dwarfs.

DVALIN Dwarf who was turned to stone by the sun. The dwarfs ironically called the sun 'Dvalin's delight'.

EARTH (*Jorð*) Daughter of Night and Annar.

EARTH (*Jorð*) Goddess. Mother of Thor by Odin. (Also referred to as Fjorgyn.)

EDDA (Great-grandmother) Ancestor of the race of serfs.

EINHERJAR (Heroes) Dead warriors in Valhalla who fight by day and feast at night, awaiting Ragnarok, the end of the world.

EIR Goddess of healing. Possibly also one of Menglad's handmaidens.

EITRI Dwarf. Brother of Brokk. He was a master-smith who fashioned three great gifts for the gods (Myth 10).

ELDIR (Man of Fire) One of Aegir's servants.

ELIVAGAR (Stormy Waves) Eleven rivers that flow from the spring Hvergelmir in Niflheim.

ELJUDNIR Hel's hall in Niflheim.

ELLI (Old Age) Old woman who wrestled with Thor in the court of Utgard-Loki (Myth 16).

EMBLA (Elm Tree) Name of the first woman created by the sons of Bor from a fallen tree (Myth 1).

FAFNIR Son of the farmer-magician Hreidmar and brother of Otter (Myth 26).

FARBAUTI (Cruel Striker) Giant who was Loki's father.

FATHIR (Father) Ancestor of the nobly born.

FENRIR Wolf, son of Loki, who is bound by the gods and will remain so until Ragnarok, the end of the world.

FENSALIR (Water Halls) Frigg's hall in Asgard.

FIMAFENG (Swift Handler) One of Aegir's servants.

FIMBULVETR The terrible winter, three years in duration, that will precede Ragnarok.

FJALAR Dwarf. Brother of Galar and, with him, murderer of the wise Kvasir from whose blood they make the mead of poetry (Myth 6).

FJALAR Cock that will crow to warn the giants when Ragnarok, the end of the world, is at hand.

FJOLSVID Giant with some of Odin's characteristics. Warder of the hall in Jotunheim in which Menglad lives.

FJORGYN Mother of Thor by Odin and probably an earth goddess. (Also referred to as Jorð or Earth)

FOLKVANG (Field of Folk) That part of Asgard in which Freyja's hall is situated.

FORSETI Son of Balder and Nanna. The god of justice.

FRANANG'S FALLS Waterfall in Midgard in which Loki disguised as a salmon is caught by the gods (Myth 31).

FREYJA Daughter of Njord. Foremost of the female Vanir or fertility goddesses.

FREYR Son of Njord. Foremost of the Vanir fertility gods.

FRIGG Odin's wife and first amongst the goddesses. Mother of Balder.

FULLA Goddess. Servant of Frigg.

GAGNRAD Name taken by Odin when he visits the giant Vafthrudnir in disguise (Myth 15).

GALAR Dwarf. Brother of Fjalar and, with him, murderer of the wise Kvasir from whose blood they make the mead of poetry (Myth 6).

GANGLATI (Tardy) Manservant of the monster Hel.

GANGLOT (Tardy) Maidservant of the monster Hel.

GARM Hound chained in Gnipahellir, the cave at the entrance to Niflheim. He will break loose at Ragnarok and kill, and be killed by, the war god Tyr.

GEFION (Giver) A fertility goddess especially connected with the plough who tricked the King of Sweden out of a tract of his kingdom – the modern Zealand (Myth 21).

GEIRROD Giant who tried to kill Thor (Myth 24).

GEIRROD King of the Goths. Favoured by Odin, he later tortures him unwittingly and dies tripping over his own sword (Myth 12).

GERD (Field) Frost giantess whose beauty ravished Freyr. He finally married her (Myth 11).

GILLING Giant. He and his wife are murdered by the dwarfs Fjalar and Galar. They are avenged by their son Suttung (Myth 6).

GIMLI Hall which will be inhabited by the ruling gods in the world after Ragnarok.

GINNUNGAGAP (Seeming Emptiness) Void that existed between Muspell and Niflheim before the creation.

GJALL (Ringing Horn) Horn of the god Heimdall which can be heard throughout the nine worlds.

GJALP (Howler) Daughter of the giant Geirrod who tried to drown Thor in a torrent of menstrual blood and, later, to crush him against roof rafters (Myth 24).

GLADSHEIM (Place of Joy) Sanctuary of the gods on the plain of Ida in which Odin and the principal gods had high seats.

GLEIPNIR Magic fetter made by the dwarfs and used by the gods to bind the wolf Fenrir.

GLITNIR Hall of Forseti (son of Balder) in Asgard. Made of silver and gold.

GNIPAHELLIR (Cliff Cave) Cave in front of the entrance to Niflheim where the hound Garm is chained.

GREIP (Grasper) Daughter of the giant Geirrod and sister of Gjalp.

GRID Giantess who was a mistress of Odin and assisted Thor by lending him her magic gloves, girdle and staff with which to defend himself against the giant Geirrod (Myth 24).

GRIMNIR (The Hooded One) Name assumed by Odin in disguise when he visits the hall of his foster son Geirrod, King of the Goths (Myth 12).

GROA Seeress who tried to remove whetstone fragments from Thor's head (Myth 19). Wife of Aurvandil and mother of Svipdag.

GULLINBURSTI (Golden-bristled) Golden boar made by two dwarfs for Loki to give to the god Freyr.

GULLINKAMBI (Golden Comb) Cock that wakes the Einherjar in Valhalla and will crow to warn the gods when Ragnarok is at hand.

GULLFAXI (Gold Mane) The giant Hrungnir's horse on which he lost a race against Odin and his eight-legged steed Sleipnir (Myth 19).

GULLVEIG One of the Vanir (also called Heid) who is burned three times by the Aesir. She is probably the goddess Freyja.

GUNGNIR Odin's magic spear, forged by the dwarfs called the sons of Ivaldi.

GUNNLOD Daughter of the giant Suttung and guardian of the mead of poetry. Odin seduced her and won the mead (Myth 6).

GYLFI King of Sweden who is tricked by the goddess Gefion (Myth 21).

GYMIR Frost Giant. Father of the giantess Gerd who marries Freyr.

HARBARD (Grey-beard) Ferryman who wrangles with Thor. He is in fact Odin in disguise (Myth 22).

HATI Wolf who pursues the moon and will swallow it before Ragnarok. Snorri calls him Hati Hrodvitnisson.

HEID See under GULLVEIG.

HEIDRUN Goat that supplies unending mead for the Einherjar in Valhalla.

HEIMDALL God who was the son of nine mothers. Owner of the horn Gjall and watchman of the gods. He is often identified with Rig who created the three races of man (Myth 5).

HEL Daughter of Loki. A monster, half alive and half dead who rules the realm of the dead which is also called Hel.

HEL Realm of the dead, in Niflheim, presided over by the monster Hel.

HERMOD Son of Odin who rode to Hel to try to bring back his brother Balder (Myth 29).

HILDISVINI (Battle-Boar) Freyja's human lover Ottar in disguise who learns his lineage from the giantess Hyndla (Myth 13).

HIMINBJORG (Rocks of Heaven) Hall of the god Heimdall in Asgard.

HIMINHRJOT (Heaven Bellower or Heaven Springer) Ox belonging to the giant Hymir. His head is used as fishing bait by Thor (Myth 17).

HLESEY (Island of Hler) Island near which the gods Hler (Aegir) and Ran lived in their hall under the sea. It is usually taken to be the modern Läsö, in the Kattegat.

HLIDSKJALF (Hill-opening or Rock-opening) Odin's high seat in Valaskjalf from which he could survey all that happened in the nine worlds.

HNITBJORG The giant Suttung's mountain stronghold where he hid the mead of poetry (Myth 6).

HOD Blind god who unwittingly killed his own brother Balder (Myth 29). He will return after Ragnarok.

HODDMIMIR'S WOOD (*Hoddmimisholt*) Another name for the World Tree, Yggdrasill.

HONIR Long-legged god known for indecisiveness sent by the Aesir to the Vanir to seal their truce (Myth 2). He will survive Ragnarok.

HRAESVELG (Corpse Eater) Giant disguised as eagle who causes the wind.

HREIDMAR Farmer and magician. Father of Otter, Fafnir and Regin who acquired a ransom with a curse on it from Odin, Honir and Loki (Myth 26).

HRIMFAXI (Frost-maned) Night's horse.

HRODVITNIR Another name for the wolf Fenrir.

HRUNGNIR Strongest of the giants. He lost a horse race with Odin and was subsequently killed in a duel with Thor (Myth 19).

HUGI (Thought) Young giant who outstripped Thor's human servant Thialfi in a rūnning race and was, in fact, the embodiment of Utgard-Loki's thought (Myth 16).

HUGINN (Thought) One of Odin's ravens. The other is Muninn.

HVERGELMIR Spring in Niflheim under one root of Yggdrasill. The eleven rivers called the Elivigar spring from it.

HYMIR Giant. His massive cauldron required by the gods for the brewing of ale was wrested from him by Thor who subsequently killed him (Myth 17).

HYNDLA (She-dog) Giantess who discloses the lineage of Freyja's human lover Ottar (Myth 18).

HYRROKIN Giantess who drags Balder's burial boat, Ringhorn, down to the sea (Myth 29).

IDAVOLL (Field of Deeds) Central plain in Asgard, site of Gladsheim and Vingolf, the halls where the principal gods and goddesses met in council.

IDUN Goddess married to Bragi, the god of poetry. The golden apples of youth are in her keeping.

IVALDI Two dwarfs called the 'sons of Ivaldi' make three great treasures for the gods.

IVING River that divides Asgard from Jotunheim. It never freezes.

JARL (Earl or Nobly-born) The god Heimdall claimed him as his son and taught him the runes and their meaning (Myth 5).

JARNSAXA (Iron Cutlass) Giantess who was mistress of Thor and mother of Magni.

JORMUNGAND Serpent, offspring of Loki and Angrboda. He encircles Midgard and bites on his own tail. Also called the 'Midgard Serpent'.

JOTUNHEIM Realm of the giants.

KARL (Churl) Ancestor of the race of peasants.

KON (King) Son of Jarl whom the god Heimdall claimed as his son. He learned the runes and could understand the speech of birds.

KVASIR An ambiguous figure described both as one of the Vanir (Myth 2) and as a wise man created from the spittle of the gods (Myth 6). Murdered by two dwarfs (Myth 6), the mead of poetry was brewed from his blood.

LAERAD Another name for the World Tree, Yggdrasill.

LAUFEY Giantess. Mother of Loki.

LIF (Life) Man who will hide in Yggdrasill, survive Ragnarok, and father children to repeople the earth.

LIFTHRASIR (Eager for life) Woman who will hide in Yggdrasill, survive Ragnarok, and mother children to repeople the earth.

LIT Dwarf cremated with Balder and Nanna.

LODDFAFNIR Human who found his way to the Well of Urd and Odin's hall and there learned wisdom from the gods (Myth 25).

LOFN Goddess who smiled on illicit unions.

LOGI (Flames) Fire in the form of a giant who beat Loki in an eating match at the court of Utgard-Loki (Myth 16).

LOKI Attractive, ambivalent, mischief-making god (the son of two giants). Often called the Sly One, the Trickster, the Shape Changer, the Sky Traveller. He grows progressively more evil, causes the death of Balder, and is bound until the coming of Ragnarok, the end of the world.

LYFJABERG (Hill of Healing) The mountain next to Menglad's hall in Jotunheim.

LYNGVI Island on Lake Amsvartnir where the wolf Fenrir was bound.

LYR (Heat-holding) Menglad's hall in Jotunheim.

MAGNI (Might) Son of Thor and the giantess Jarnsaxa (Iron Cutlass). He and his brother Modi will inherit the hammer Mjollnir after Ragnarok.

MENGLAD (Necklace Glad) Woman sought and won by Svipdag (Myth 23) and son of the seeress Groa. She has much in common with Freyja.

MIDGARD (Middle World) The world of men.

MIMIR Wise god sent by the Aesir to the Vanir to seal their truce, and killed by them. Odin preserved his head and set it by the Well of Mimir (Myth 2).

MIMIR'S WELL Well of wisdom under the root of Yggdrasill in Jotunheim, protected by the head of Mimir.

MIST CALF (*Mokkurkalfi*) Giant made of clay, nine leagues tall. An ineffectual companion for the giant Hrungnir in his duel against Thor (Myth 19).

MJOLLNIR Thor's hammer, made by the dwarfs Brokk and Eitri. Symbol of destruction, fertility and resurrection.

MODGUD Maiden who guards bridge over the River Gjoll in Jotunheim.

MODI (Wrath) Son of Thor. He and his brother Magni will inherit the hammer Mjollnir after Ragnarok.

MODSOGNIR Commander of the dwarfs.

MOON (*Mani*) Son of Mundilfari. He drives the moon on its course and determines its waxing and waning.

MOTHIR (Mother) Ancestor of the nobly born.

MUNDILFARI (Turner) Human father of Moon and Sun.

MUNINN (Memory) One of Odin's two ravens. The other is Huginn.

MUSPELL Realm of fire in the south, guarded by the giant Surt. The fusion of its heat with Niflheim's ice led to the creation.

MUSPELL, SONS OF Fire giants who will fight under the giant Surt at Ragnarok.

NAGLFAR Ship made of dead men's nails that will carry the giants to the last battle at Ragnarok.

NANNA Balder's wife. Daughter of Nep.

NARVI Giant. Father of Night.

NARVI Loki's son by his wife Sigyn. He was killed by his own brother Vali and Loki was bound with his entrails (Myth 31). Also known as Nari.

NASTROND (Shore of Corpses) Place in Hel where hall for evil-doers is sited and where the dragon Nidhogg gnaws corpses.

NIDHOGG (Corpse Tearer) Dragon that gnaws at the roots of Yggdrasill in Niflheim and chews corpses.

NIFLHEIM A realm of freezing mist and darkness under one root of Yggdrasill. Hel lies within it.

NIGHT Daughter of Narvi. Mother of Day. She rides her horse Hrimfaxi round the world.

NJORD One of the Vanir or fertility gods and father of Freyr and Freyja. He married Skadi. Associated with the wind and sea.

NOATUN (Shipyard or Harbour) Hall of the god Njord in Asgard.

NORNS The three goddesses of destiny, Urd (Fate), Skuld (Being) and Verdandi (Necessity).

OD Freyja's lost husband. She weeps for him endlessly but he never returns.

ODIN Father of Thor and first and foremost of the Aesir. God of Poetry, Battle and Death. He has many names amongst which are Allfather, the Terrible One, One-eyed, Father of Battle.

ODRORIR (Heart Stirrer) Cauldron containing the mead of poetry brewed from the blood of the wise Kvasir.

OKOLNIR (Not Cold) Place in the world to come after Ragnarok where the ground will always be warm. Site of the hall Brimir.

OTTAR Freyja's human lover. He is disguised as a boar, Hildisvini (Myth 18). One of his ancestors was the German folk hero Sigurd.

OTTER Son of the farmer-magician Hreidmar. He was killed by Loki, and Odin, Honir and Loki paid a ransom of red gold to his father as compensation.

RAGNAROK (Destruction of the Powers). The apocalyptic final battle between the gods and the giants, involving all creation, in which virtually all life is destroyed and the nine worlds are submerged.

RAN Wife of Aegir, god of the sea. She dragged drowning men down with a net.

RATATOSK (Swift Teeth) Squirrel that runs up and down Yggdrasill carrying insults between the eagle that lives on the topmost branches and the dragon Nidhogg that lives at its foot.

REGIN Son of the farmer-magician Hreidmar and brother of Otter and Fafnir.

RIG (King) The name assumed by the god Heimdall when he created the three races of men.

RIND Goddess. Mistress of Odin. Their son was Vali.

RINGHORN Balder's boat in which he and his wife Nanna were cremated.

ROSKVA Farmer's daughter and sister of Thialfi who becomes servant of Thor. She accompanied Thor on his great expedition to Utgard (Myth 16).

SAGA Goddess who drinks daily with Odin in her hall, Sokkvabekk, in Asgard.

SESSRUMNIR (Rich in Seats) Freyja's hall in Asgard.

SIF Thor's wife whose golden hair was cut off by Loki. The dwarfs spun a skein to replace it.

SIGYN Loki's faithful wife.

SINDRI Hall in the world to come after Ragnarok with a roof of red gold.

SJOFN Goddess who inspired human passion.

SKADI Daughter of the giant Thiazi. At one time married to the Vanir Njord. Associated with skiing and hunting.

SKIDBLADNIR (Wooden-bladed) Collapsible ship. One of the three precious objects made by the sons of the dwarf Ivaldi for Freyr.

SKINFAXI (Shining-maned) Day's horse.

SKIRNIR (Shining) Freyr's messenger who won the giantess Gerd for him (Myth 11).

SKOLL Wolf that pursues the sun and will swallow it before Ragnarok.

SKRYMIR (Big Bloke) Extra large giant (in fact Utgard-Loki in disguise) encountered by Thor and his companions on their journey to Utgard.

SKULD (Future) One of the three Norns who decides the fates of men.

SLEIPNIR Odin's eight-legged horse. He was sired by the stallion Svadilfari and borne by Loki.

SNÖR Ancestress of the race of peasants.

SOKKVABEKK (Sinking Floor) Saga's hall in Asgard.

SON (Blood) One of the jars containing the mead of poetry brewed from Kvasir's blood.

SUN (*Sol*) Daughter of Mundilfari. She drives the sun on its course.

SURT (Black) The giant who has guarded Muspell (the realm of fire) since before the creation. He will set fire to the world at Ragnarok.

SUTTUNG Giant. Son of the giant Gilling. For some time custodian of the mead of poetry.

SVADILFARI Stallion that assists the giant mason to build the walls of Asgard (Myth 3). Father of Sleipnir, Odin's eight-legged horse.

SVARTALFHEIM Land of the dark elves.

SVIPDAG (Swift Day) Human son of the seeress Groa. He seeks and wins Menglad (Myth 23).

SYN Goddess. Invoked by defendants at trials.

TANNGNOST (Tooth Grinder) One of the goats that pulls Thor's chariot. The other is Tanngrisni.

TANNGRISNI (Gat-Tooth) One of the goats that pulls Thor's chariot. The other is Tanngnost.

THIALFI Farmer's son who becomes Thor's servant. Immensely fleet of foot but outstripped by Hugi ('Thought') in a running race at the court of Utgard-Loki (Myth 16).

THIAZI Giant. He stole the goddess Idun and the golden apples in her keeping but Loki retrieved them and Thiazi was killed by the gods (Myth 8).

THIR (Drudge) Human wife of Thrall.

THOKK Giantess, probably Loki in disguise, who prevented Balder's return from Hel (Myth 29).

THOR Son of Odin and Earth (Fjorgyn), and husband of Sif. Second in the hierarchy of the gods and their guardian. God of the sky and thunder and so of fertility but equally associated with maintenance of law and order in Midgard. The most common of his many names are Thunder God and Charioteer.

THRALL Human. Son of Ai and Edda. Husband of Thir.

THRUD (Might) Daughter of Thor, promised by the gods to the dwarf Alvis (Myth 27).

THRUDHEIM (Place of Might) Thor's realm in Asgard, sometimes called 'Thrudvang'. Site of his hall Bilskirnir.

THRYM Giant, described as King of the frost giants. He stole Thor's hammer and paid for it with his life (Myth 14).

THRYMHEIM (Place of Din) The giant Thiazi's stronghold in the mountains. It passed to his daughter Skadi whose husband the god Njord refused to live there (Myth 9).

TYR God of war. Son of Odin (or possibly the giant Hymir). The bravest of the gods who sacrificed one hand so that the wolf Fenrir could be bound (Myth 7).

ULL (Glory or Brilliance) God. Particularly associated with archery and skiing.

URD (Fate) One of the three Norns or goddesses of destiny. The Well of Urd, which they guard, lies under the root of Yggdrasill in Asgard. The gods held a daily assembly there.

UTGARD Stronghold within Jotunheim, ruled by the giant king Utgard-Loki.

UTGARD-LOKI Ruler of Utgard and a master of illusion who outwits Thor and his companions (Myth 16).

VAFTHRUDNIR (Mighty in Riddles) Wise giant who was tricked by Odin in a test of knowledge and paid with his life (Myth 15).

VALI Son of Loki and his wife Sigyn. The gods turned him into a wolf and he killed his own brother Nari or Narvi (Myth 31).

VALI Son of Odin and his giant mistress Rind expressly conceived to take vengeance for his half-brother Balder's death.

VALASKJALF (Shelf of the slain) Odin's hall in Asgard.

VALHALLA (Hall of the Slain) Immense hall, presided over by Odin, where the Einherjar (dead warriors) fought, feasted, and awaited Ragnarok, the final destruction.

VALKYRIES (Choosers of the Slain) Beautiful young women who chose men doomed to die in battle and brought them back to Valhalla.

VANAHEIM Realm of the Vanir or fertility gods, situated in Asgard.

VANIR The race of fertility gods who were subsequently integrated with the Aesir.

VAR (Oath) Goddess who hears marriage oaths and punishes those who do not keep them.

VE Son of Bor and brother of Odin and Vili.

VERDANDI (Present) One of the three Norns (goddesses of destiny) who decide the fates of men.

VIDAR Son of Odin and the giantess Grid who will avenge Odin's death and survive Ragnarok.

VIGRID (Battle Shaker) Plain in Asgard described variously as '120 leagues in every direction', and as a hundred miles square, on which the final battle between gods and men, giants and monsters will take place.

VILI Son of Bor and brother of Odin and Ve.

VIMUR Torrent augmented by the giantess Gjalp's menstrual blood.

VINGOLF Hall in Asgard in which the goddesses had their high seats.

VON (Expectation) River consisting of the wolf Fenrir's slaver.

VOR Goddess from whom nothing could be hidden.

YDALIR (Yew Dales) Hall of the god Ull in Asgard.

YGGDRASILL (The Terrible One's Horse) The World Tree, an ash that linked and sheltered all the worlds.

YMIR The first giant, formed from fire and ice. The world was shaped out of his body.

Bibliography

(Revised 2011)

The bibliography is restricted to books in English except for a few books of paramount interest that have not been translated into English and, of course, the sources listed in Section 1. Not all entries listed were consulted in the course of writing this book.

1. Sources

EDDA, THE ELDER OR POETIC

Die Lieder des Codex Regius nebst Verwandten Denkmälern, I–II. Edited by G. Neckel. Heidelberg, 1936. Fourth edition revised by H. Kuhn, 1962.
Havamal (The Words of the High One). Edited by David A. H. Evans. Viking Society for Northern Research Text Series 7. London, 1986.

EDDA, THE PROSE OR YOUNGER (SNORRI STURLUSON)

Edda Snorra Sturlusonar. Edited by Finnur Jónsson. Copenhagen, 1926.

GESTA DANORUM (SAXO GRAMMATICUS)

Kilderne til Sakses Oldhistorie, I–II. Edited by A. Olrik. Copenhagen, 1892–4.
Saxo Grammaticus: Gesta Danorum. Edited by A. Holder. Strasbourg, 1886.
Saxo Grammaticus: Gesta Danorum. Edited by J. Olrik and H. Raeder. Copenhagen, 1931.

HEIMSKRINGLA (SNORRI STURLUSON)

Heimskringla, I–III. Edited by Bjarni Aðalbjarnarson. Reykjavik, 1946–51.

SCALDIC POETRY

Corpus Poeticum Boreale, The Poetry of the Old Northern Tongue from the Earliest Times to the Thirteenth Century. Edited by Guðbrandur Vigfússon and F. York Powell. Oxford, 1883. Texts of scaldic poetry with translations into English.
Den Norsk-isländska Skaldedigtningen, I–II. Edited by E. A. Kock. Lund, 1946–9.
Den norsk-isländske Skjaldedigtning, A I–II B I–II. Edited by Finnur Jónsson. Copenhagen, 1908–15. This is the most complete collection of scaldic texts and contains translations into Danish.

Readers eager to learn Old Norse are advised to buy *A New Introduction to Old Norse – I. Grammar* by Michael Barnes (London, 2008) and *II. Reader* by Anthony Faulkes (London, 2001; fourth edition, 2007), and to secure *A Concise Dictionary of Old Icelandic* by Geir T. Zoëga (Toronto, Buffalo and London, 2004).

2. *Sources in Translation*

EDDA, THE ELDER OR POETIC

The Elder Edda. A Selection. Translated by Paul B. Taylor and W. H. Auden. Introduction by Peter H. Salus. London, 1969.

The Elder or Poetic Edda. Part I – The Mythological Poems. Translated by Olive Bray. London, 1908.

Poems of the Vikings. The Elder Edda. Translated by Patricia Terry with an Introduction by Charles W. Dunn. Indianapolis and New York, 1976.

The Poetic Edda. Translated by Henry Adams Bellows. New York, 1923.

The Poetic Edda. Translated by Lee M. Hollander. Second edition, Austin, Texas, 1962.

The Poetic Edda. Translated and introduced by Carolyne Larrington. Oxford, 1996.

EDDA, THE PROSE OR YOUNGER (SNORRI STURLUSON)

The Prose or Younger Edda. Translated by George Webbe Dasent. Stockholm, 1842.

Prose Edda. Translated by Lee M. Hollander. Austin, Texas, 1929.

Prose Edda. Translated by Arthur Gilchrist Brodeur. New York, 1916.

The Prose Edda. Selected and translated by Jean I. Young. Introduced by Sigurður Nordal. Cambridge, 1954. Reissued, Berkeley, Los Angeles and London, 1971.

Snorri Sturluson: Edda. Translated by Andrew Faulkes. London, 1987.

The Prose Edda. Translated by Jesse L. Bycock. London and New York, 2005.

GESTA DANORUM (SAXO GRAMMATICUS)

The First Nine Books of the Danish History of Saxo Grammaticus. Translated by Oliver Elton. London, 1894.

Saxo Grammaticus. History of the Danes. Books I–IX. Translated by Peter Fisher and with a Commentary by Hilda Ellis Davidson. Two volumes, Woodbridge, 1979–80.

HEIMSKRINGLA (SNORRI STURLUSON)

Heimskringla. Part One. Translated by Samuel Laing. Revised and with an Introduction and Notes by Jacqueline Simpson. Everyman's Library. London and New York, 1964.

Heimskringla. Part Two. Translated by Samuel Laing. Revised with an Introduction and Notes by Peter Foote. Everyman's Library. London and New York, 1961.

Stories of the Kings of Norway. Translated by Eiríkr Magnússon and William Morris. Four volumes. London, 1893–1905.

Heimskringla, or The Lives of the Norse Kings. By Snorri Sturluson. Edited by Erling Monsen and translated with the assistance of A. S. Smith. New York, 1990.

SCALDIC POETRY

The Skalds. A Selection of their Poems, with Introduction and Notes translated by Lee M. Hollander. New York, 1945. Paperback, Michigan, 1968.

Scaldic Poetry. By E. O. G. Turville-Petre. Oxford and New York, 1976.

Corpus Poeticum Boreale. (See listing under Sources: Vigfússon, G., and Powell, F. York.)

3. *Retellings of the Myths and Heroic Legends*

BOULT, KATHERINE, *Asgard and the Norse Heroes*. London, 1914. This book was written for children.

BYCOCK, JESSE L., *The Saga of the Volsungs: The Norse Epic of Sigurd the Dragon-Slayer.* London, 2004.

COLUM, PADRAIC, *The Children of Odin.* London, 1922.

CROSSLEY-HOLLAND, KEVIN (editor), *The Faber Book of Northern Legends,* London, 1977.

—— *The Norse Myths.* London and New York, 1980. Reissued by Penguin Books as *The Penguin Book of Norse Myths: Gods of the Vikings.* London, 1993.

GREEN, ROGER LANCELYN, *Myths of the Norsemen.* (First published as *The Saga of Asgard,* 1960.) Harmondsworth and Baltimore, 1970. This book was written for children.

GUERBER, H. A., *Myths of the Norsemen.* London, 1908.

HOBHOUSE, ROSA, *Norse Legends.* London, 1930.

HOSFORD, DOROTHY, *Thunder of the Gods.* New York, 1950, and London, 1964. This book was written for children.

KEARY, ANNIE, *The Heroes of Asgard and the Giants of Jötunheim.* London, 1857.

MABIE, HAMILTON WRIGHT, *Norse Stories.* London, 1902.

MORRIS, WILLIAM, *The Story of Sigurd the Volsung and the Fall of the Niblungs.* London, 1877.

PICARD, BARBARA LEONIE, *German Hero-Sagas and Folk Tales.* London and New York, 1958. This book was written for children.

—— *Tales of the Norse Gods and Heroes.* London and New York, 1953. This book was written for children.

THOMAS, EDWARD, *Norse Tales.* Oxford, 1912.

WILMOT-BUXTON, E. M., *Told by the Northmen.* London, 1908.

4. Related Contemporary Literature

The Anglo-Saxon Chronicle. Translated by Dorothy Whitelock. Revised edition, London, 1961.

The Anglo-Saxon Chronicles. Edited and translated by Michael Swanton. London, 2000.

The Anglo-Saxon Chronicle. Translated and edited by G. N. Garmonsway. London, 1990.

Anglo-Saxon and Norse Poems. Translated by N. Kershaw. London, 1922.

Anglo-Saxon Poetry. Translated by R. K. Gordon. Everyman's Library, London and New York, 1926.

The Battle of Maldon and Other Old English Poems. Translated by Kevin Crossley-Holland and edited by Bruce Mitchell. London and New York, 1965.

Beowulf. Translated by Kevin Crossley-Holland and introduced by Bruce Mitchell. London and New York, 1968. Reissued, Cambridge, 1977.

Eaters of Dead: The Manuscript of Ibn Fadlan. Translated by Michael Crichton. New York, 1976.

Egil's Saga. Translated by Hermann Pálsson and Paul Edwards. Harmondsworth and Baltimore, 1976.

Eirik the Red and Other Icelandic Sagas. Selected and translated with an Introduction by Gwyn Jones. World's Classics, London and New York, 1961.

Eyrbyggja Saga. Translated by Hermann Pálsson and Paul Edwards. The New Saga Library. Edinburgh, Toronto and Buffalo, 1973.

The Heroic Legends of Denmark. By Axel Olrik. Translated and revised by L. M. Hollander. New York, 1919.

Hrafkel's Saga. Adapted and retold by Barbara Schiller. New York, 1972.

Hrolf Gautrekson. A Viking Romance. Translated by Hermann Pálsson and Paul Edwards. New Saga Library. Edinburgh, 1972. Toronto and Buffalo, 1973.

Illustrations of Northern Antiquities. Translated by Henry Weber, R. Jamieson and W. S. (Walter Scott). Edinburgh, 1814.

King Harald's Saga. Translated by Magnus Magnusson and Hermann Pálsson. Harmondsworth and Baltimore, 1966.

Landnamabok (The Book of Settlements). Translated by Hermann Pálsson and Paul Edwards. Volume I in the University of Manitoba Icelandic Studies. Manitoba, 1972.

Laxdaela Saga. Translated by Magnus Magnusson and Hermann Pálsson. Harmondsworth and Baltimore, 1969.

Das Nibelungenlied – Song of the Nibelungs. Translated by Burton Raffel. New Haven and London, 2000.

The Nibelungenlied. Translated and with an Introduction by Cyril Edwards. Oxford and New York, 2010.

The Nibelungenlied. Translated by A. T. Hatto. Harmondsworth and Baltimore, 1965.

Njal's Saga. Translated by Magnus Magnusson and Hermann Pálsson. Harmondsworth and Baltimore, 1960.

The Norse Discoverers of America: The Wineland Sagas. Translated by G. M. Gathorne-Hardy. London, 1921.

The Northmen Talk. Translated by Jacqueline Simpson. London, 1965.

The Saga Library. Translated by William Morris and Eiríkr Magnússon. Six Volumes. London, 1891–1905.

Stories and Ballads of the Far Past. Translated by N. Kershaw. London, 1921.

The Story of Gisli the Outlaw. Translated by George Webbe Dasent. Edinburgh, 1866.

The Vinland Sagas. Translated by Magnus Magnusson and Hermann Pálsson. Harmondsworth and Baltimore, 1965.

Volsunga Saga. This appears in Volume VII of the *Collected Works* of William Morris. Twenty-four volumes. London, 1910–15.

Voyages to Vinland. Translated by Einar Haugen. New York, 1942.

Note: many more of the Icelandic sagas are mercifully now available in the Penguin Classics series.

5. Myth and Religion

BRANSTON, BRIAN, *Gods of the North*. London, 1955. Reissued 1980.

—— *The Lost Gods of England*. London, 1957. Reissued 1974.

CAMPBELL, JOSEPH, *The Masks of God*. Four volumes. London, 1973.

CHADWICK, H. M., *The Cult of Othin*. London, 1899.

CRAIGIE, W. A., *The Religion of Ancient Scandinavia*. London, 1906.

DAVIDSON, H. R. ELLIS, *Gods and Myths of Northern Europe*. Harmondsworth and Baltimore, 1964. Reissued as *Gods and Myths of the Viking Age*. London, 1980.

—— *The Lost Beliefs of Northern Europe*. London and New York, 1993.

—— *Myths and Symbols in Pagan Europe: Early Scandinavian and Celtic Religions*. Manchester, 1988.

—— *Roles of the Northern Goddesses*. London, 1998.

—— *Scandinavian Mythology*. London, 1969.

DU BOIS, THOMAS A., *Nordic Religions in the Viking Age*. Philadelphia, 1999.

DUMÉZIL, GEORGES, *Mythes et Dieux des Germains*. Paris, 1939. Translated by John Lindow et al. as *Gods of the Ancient Northmen*. Berkeley, 1973.

ELIADE, MIRCEA, *Images and Symbols: Studies in Religious Symbolism*. Translated by Philip Mairet. London, 1961.

—— *Myth and Reality*. World Perspectives, London, 1964.

—— *Patterns in Comparative Religion*. London, 1958.

FRAZER, J. G., *The Golden Bough: A Study in Magic and Religion*. Abridged edition. London, 1922. Paperback, London, 1957.

GRIMAL, PIERRE (editor), *Larousse World Mythology*. Feltham, Middlesex and New York, 1965.

GRIMM, J., *Deutsche Mythologie*. Berlin, 1875–8. Translated into English by J. S. Stallybrass under the title of *Teutonic Mythology*. Four volumes. London, 1882–8.

GUIRAND, FELIX (editor), *New Larousse Encyclopaedia of Mythology*. Introduced by Robert Graves. Feltham, Middlesex, 1963.

LEVI-STRAUSS, CLAUDE, *The Raw and the Cooked: Introduction to a Science of Mythology*. Translated by John and Doreen Weightman. London and New York, 1970.

LINDOW, JOHN, *Scandinavian Mythology: An Annotated Bibliography*. New York and London, 1998.

—— *Norse Mythology: A Guide to the Gods, Heroes, Rituals and Beliefs*. Oxford, 2001.

MACCULLOCH, J. A., *The Celtic and Scandinavian Religions*. London, 1948.

—— *Mythology of All the Races*. Thirteen Volumes, Volume II, London, 1930.

MUNCH, PETER ANDREAS, *Norse Mythology*. In the revision of Magnus Olsen. Translated by Sigurd Bernhard Hustvedt. New York, 1927.

O'DONOGHUE, HEATHER, *From Asgard to Valhalla: The Remarkable History of the Norse Myths*. London, 2007.

ORCHARD, ANDY, *Dictionary of Old Norse Myth and Legend*. London, 1997.

PAGE, R. I., *Norse Myths*. London, 1990.

PHILLPOTTS, BERTHA S., *Edda and Saga*. London, 1931.

SIMEK, RUDOLF, *Dictionary of Northern Mythology*. Translated by Angela Hall. New edition (Garland Folklore Bibliographies, 13). Woodbridge and Rochester, 1993.

TURVILLE-PETRE, E. O. G., *Myth and Religion of the North*. London, 1964.

6. History, Archaeology and Literary Criticism

ARBMAN, HOLGER, *The Vikings*. Translated by Alan Binns. London, 1961.

AUDEN, W. H., 'The World of the Sagas' in *Secondary Worlds: The T. S. Eliot Memorial Lectures*. London and Boston, 1968.

BAILEY, RICHARD N., *Viking Age Sculpture in Northern England*. London, 1980.

BRØNDSTED, JOHANNES, *The Vikings*. Translated by Kalle Skov. Harmondsworth and Baltimore, 1965.

CARLYLE, THOMAS, *On Heroes, Hero-Worship and the Heroic in History*. London, 1840.

CHAMBERS, R. W., *Beowulf: An Introduction to the Study of the Poem*. With a supplement by C. L. Wrenn. Cambridge, 1959.

EINARSON, STEFÁN, *A History of Icelandic Literature*. New York, 1957.

ELLIOTT, R. W. V., *Runes*. Manchester, 1959. Corrected edition, 1963.

FELL, CHRISTINE, *Women in Anglo-Saxon England*. London, 1984.

FERGUSON, ROBERT, *The Hammer and the Cross: A New History of the Vikings*. London and New York, 2009.

FOOTE, P. G., and WILSON, D. M., *The Viking Achievement*. London, 1970. Revised with a supplement, 1980.

GILCHRIST, CHERRY, *The Soul of Russia: Magical Traditions in an Enchanted Landscape*. Edinburgh, 2008.

GILLESPIE, G. T., *A Catalogue of Persons Named in Germanic Heroic Literature*. Oxford, 1973.

GRAHAM-CAMPBELL, JAMES, AND KIDD, DAFYDD, *The Vikings*. London, 1980.

HALLBERG, PETER, *Old Icelandic Poetry – Eddaic Lay and Skaldic Verse*. Translated by Paul Schach and Sonja Lindgrenson. Lincoln, Nebraska and London, 1975.

HAYWOOD, JOHN, *Encyclopedia of the Viking Age*. London, 2000.

—— *The Penguin Historical Atlas of the Vikings*. Harmondsworth, 1995.

HODGKIN, R. H., *A History of the Anglo-Saxons*. Two volumes. Third edition. London and New York, 1952.

HOLMAN, KATHERINE, *Historical Dictionary of the Vikings*. Maryland, 2003.

JESCH, JUDITH, *Women in the Viking Age*. Woodbridge, 1991.

JONES, GWYN, *A History of the Vikings*. Revised edition. Oxford and New York, 1984. Paperback, London, 1973.

JONES, PRUDENCE, and PENNICK, NIGEL, *A History of Pagan Europe*. London, 1995.

KENDRICK, T. D., *A History of the Vikings*. London, 1930.

KER, W. P., *Epic and Romance*. Essays on Medieval Literature. London, 1897. Reissued, New York and London, 1957.

—— *The Dark Ages*. London, 1904. Reissued, London, 1955.

KNUT, HELLE (editor), *The Cambridge History of Scandinavia, Vol. I (Prehistory to 1520)*. Cambridge, 2003.

LOGAN, F. DONALD, *The Vikings in History*. London and New York, 1991.

MAGNUSSON, MAGNUS, *Vikings!* London, 1980.

OLRIK, AXEL, *Viking Civilisation*. London, 1930.

OLSEN, M., *Farms and Fanes of Ancient Norway*. Translated by Th. Gleditsch. Oslo, 1928.

PAGE, R. I., *Chronicles of the Vikings. Records, Memorials and Myths*. London, 1995.

POLOMÉ, EDGAR (editor), *Old Norse Literature and Mythology: A Symposium*. Toronto, 1969.

PULSIANO, PHILLIP (editor), *Medieval Scandinavia: An Encyclopedia*. New York and London, 1993.

ROESDAHL, ELSE, *Viking Age Denmark*. Translated by Susan Margeson and Kirsten Williams. London, 1982.

—— *The Vikings*. Harmondsworth, 1987.

SAWYER, P. H., *The Age of the Vikings*. London, 1962.

—— (editor), *The Oxford Illustrated History of the Vikings*. Oxford and New York, 1997.

SIMPSON, JACQUELINE, *Everyday Life in the Viking Age*. London, 1966.

—— *The Viking World*. London, 1980.

SVEINSSON, EINIE ÓL, *The Age of the Sturlungs*. Translated by Jóhann S. Hanesson. Ithaca, N.Y., 1953.

TURVILLE-PETRE, G., *The Heroic Age of Scandinavia*. London, 1951.

WILSON, DAVID M. (editor), *The Northern World: The History and Heritage of Northern Europe* AD 400–1100. London, 1980.

WRENN, C. L., *A Study of Old English Literature*. London, 1967.

7. A Personal Miscellany

Mythology and folklore are neighbours and, as I have tried to show in the notes, a number of the myths embody folk motifs. Those who wish to read or reread Scandinavian folktales for themselves have a reasonably wide choice available to them. I particularly like Jacqueline Simpson's translation of folk material collected in the nineteenth century by Jón Árnason, *Icelandic Folktales and Legends* (London, 1972); George Webbe Dasent's unsurpassed translations from the Norwegian collection of Peter C. Asbjornsen and Jorgen I. Moe, *Popular Tales from the Norse* (Edinburgh, 1859; reissued London, 1969); *Folktales of Norway*, edited by Reidar Christiansen and translated by Pat Shaw Iversen (Chicago and London, 1964); and J. Grant Cramer's versions of Svendt Grundtvig in his short *Danish Fairy Tales* (New York, 1919; reissued New York and London, 1972). Much the finest collection devoted to Sweden is *Swedish Folktales and Legends*, edited by Lone Thygesen Blecher and George Blecher (New York, 1993), while the two best selections representing all these countries are Gwyn Jones's spirited and affectionate *Scandinavian Legends and Folk-Tales* (London, 1956), and *Scandinavian Folktales*, translated and edited by Jacqueline Simpson (London, 1988). *Northern Tales: Traditional Stories of Eskimo and Indian Peoples*, selected by Howard Norman (New York, 1990), also contains motifs derived from the Norse myths.

Mythology and heroic legend are even closer neighbours, but here the interested reader will have to scratch around for adequate versions. For those heroic legends that comprise part of the *Elder Edda,* perhaps it is best to turn to the direct translations listed in Section 2. I have also listed a number of retellings in Section 3, but there is a clear need for a single volume that makes available a selection from the full range of heroic material.

Heather O'Donoghue is the author of the invaluable *Old Norse–Icelandic Literature: A Short Introduction* (Oxford, 2003). In addition to many renowned Scandinavian novelists, a number of native English-speaking writers have been drawn to Viking Scandinavia, including Cecelia Holland, Jane Smiley, Francis Berry and George Mackay Brown. The latter's wonderful poems about the Vikings in Orkney, with their 'undersong of terrible holy joy', form part of *The Collected Poems* edited by Archie Bevan and Brian Murray (London, 2005).

Since the Norse myths were written down in Iceland, it may be that some readers will want to read more about that country. The best nineteenth-century accounts are

Lord Dufferin's *Letters from High Latitudes* (1858) and William Morris's *Journal* (1871–3). In the twentieth century, *Letters from Iceland by* W. H. Auden and Louis MacNeice (London, 1937) has no rival. It is a brilliantly confident and highly idiosyncratic mixture of poems and prose, Old Norse proverbs, diary entries, advice to tourists, and 'An Anthology of Icelandic Travel', and includes W. H. Auden's celebrated long poem 'Letter to Lord Byron'. In the same spirit, Simon Armitage and Glyn Maxwell collaborated to write *Moon Country: Further Reports from Iceland* (London, 1996).

In *Letters from Iceland*, W. H. Auden writes that, 'Few English people take an interest in Iceland, but in those few the interest is passionate.' Those readers who decide to go one step further and see the island for themselves can turn to the excellent Lonely Planet and Rough Guides (by Fran Parnell and David Leffman respectively). Katharine Scherman's *Iceland – Daughter of Fire* (London, 1976) is particularly strong on the island's history, its geology, and the compelling blend of past and present that awaits the traveller.

In one of the better topographical books about Norway, *The Fellowship of Ghosts* (London, 2004), Paul Watkins describes a journey through the country's mountains, 'a world where myth and reality meet', while Peter Davison's compelling *The Idea of North* (London, 2005) pursues the concept by engaging with a remarkably wide range of literature and legend, painting, landscape art and photography. I hope that someone will do the same for music.

I could go on to write of Edward Burne-Jones's brooding portrait of Odin – an Odin become the very essence of Pre-Raphaelite sensibility; of William Morris's long and fertile preoccupation with the Norse tradition; of Wagner's superb operatic cycle *Der Ring der Nibelungen*, which is certainly the most successful of all 'recyclings' of Norse mythological material; of Eric Ravilious's fascination with northern scape and northern light in his paintings as a war artist; or I could write of J. R. R. Tolkien's epic piece of storytelling, *The Lord of the Rings* (London, 1954–5), which owes so much to that great scholar's knowledge of the language and mythology of the Norsemen. But to go further would be to cross some kind of boundary. Beyond these names, there are many, many others, working in different artistic disciplines in different countries, who have consciously or unconsciously been influenced by the Norse myths, one of the greatest of all the inheritances of the north-west European world.

INDEX

The myths, introduction and notes have been indexed, but not the glossary or the bibliography.

A figure 2 in brackets immediately after a page reference indicates that there are two separate references to the subject on that page.

Words in brackets immediately after a page reference are intended to locate the reference in a case where the subject is not named on the page indicated.

'Quoted' should be understood to mean comment or opinion in either direct or indirect speech.